DILEMMAS *of* DESIRE

DILEMMAS *of* DESIRE

Teenage Girls
Talk about
Sexuality

Deborah L. Tolman

Harvard

University

Press

Cambridge,

Massachusetts

London,

England

First Harvard University Press paperback edition, 2005

Library of Congress Cataloging-in-Publication Data
Tolman, Deborah L.
Dilemmas of desire : teenage girls talk about sexuality / Deborah L. Tolman.
  p. cm.
Includes bibliographical references and index.
ISBN 0-674-00895-2 (cloth)
ISBN 0-674-01856-7 (pbk.)
1. Teenage girls—Sexual behavior. 2. Teenage girls—Attitudes. 3. Interpersonal
relations in adolescence. I. Title.

HQ27.5 .T65 2002
306.7'0835—dc21   2002024134

For my parents, E. Laurie and Sylvia Tolman,
     for raising me to ask the question
For my husband, Luis Ubinas,
     for sustaining me as I answered it

CONTENTS

ACKNOWLEDGMENTS

In a recently rediscovered photograph taken right after I graduated from college, I am standing with one of my roommates; we are laughing at a road sign that reads "Hidden Drives." We are laughing because I had just announced that "when I grow up" I will write a book with this title. Well, it's not exactly that title but it is fairly close. And so this book has been a very long time in the making. First and foremost, I am grateful for the trust and enthusiasm of the staff in the two anonymous schools involved in this study, who opened the necessary doors to make this project happen. I am equally grateful to the girls who shared their thoughts, feelings, and experiences with me in the service of "this little research thing," as one of them called it. I also want to thank another group of adolescent girls, who participated in a subsequent two-year discussion group about adolescent sexuality and girls' sexual desire, for deepening my insights into the complexities of growing up female these days. My gratitude goes to Angela von der Lippe, former acquisitions editor at Harvard University Press, to Elizabeth Knoll for shepherding the manuscript through the Press, and to Elizabeth Hurwit for marvelous editing.

Over the years, I have benefited from the love and support of my growing family, the faith and care of loyal friends, and the intellectual stimulation and challenge of an expanding community of colleagues. Two women whom I love and admire have gently but firmly pushed me to the edge of my thinking and writing capacity for over a decade. My adviser at the Harvard Graduate School of Education, Carol Gilligan, has always believed in this book and its theme of resisting the status quo, supported this work with constant encouragement as well as funds from a senior Spencer Foundation grant, and continues to inspire me with her insight and wisdom. Michelle Fine's constant availability to talk through countless ideas that appear in this book and elsewhere, her insistence that I not "laminate" desire, her perfect solutions for structural roadblocks, and her frank calls for consistency, social justice, and real-world implications have been instrumental in shaping this book. I thank them both and continue to marvel at how lucky a girl can be.

I have been very fortunate to have had the support—emotional and otherwise—and freedom for pursuing my passions for the past seven years at the Center for Research on Women at Wellesley College. Susan Bailey, Nan Stein, Nancy Marshall, Laura Palmer Edwards, and Pam Baker Webber have each in their own way contributed to this work. My colleagues at the Gender and Sexuality Project have been my sustenance, especially Michelle Porche, Renee Spencer, and Myra Rosen-Reynoso. Their intellect, humor, and care are an endless source of energy for me. I am most especially grateful to Mary Harris, Kate Collins, and Lynn Sorsoli (who also came to the rescue to care for my children on a regular basis), as well as to Kathleen Ford from afar, for their hard work in tracking down references, dealing with formatting crises, and seeing to all the details beyond the actual writing. New directions in my ongoing research program on adolescent sexuality have influenced this book. Grants from the Ford Foundation, the Spencer Foundation, the Henry A. Murray Center at Radcliffe College, and the

National Institute of Child Health and Development supported various such projects. In particular, I want to thank Susan Newcomer at the National Institute of Child Health and Development and Sarah Costa at the Ford Foundation for their counsel and encouragement, and for really getting it.

My colleagues and friends seem to work as a collective to keep me in line while urging me to cross boundaries. I am especially grateful to Margaret Keiley, Tracy Higgins, Laura Szalacha, Elizabeth Debold, Jean Rhodes, Lisa Diamond, Alice Stone and Gary Stoloff, Connie Bauman, Janie Ward, Joanne Zaiac, Thania and Tony St. John, Helene Sanghvi York, Bambi Schieffelin, and Vita Rabinowitz. I was fortunate to be part of the Harvard Project on Women's Psychology and Girls' Development, a formative experience in my intellectual development. In particular, Lyn Mikel Brown always generously shared her extraordinary and transformative ideas with me. J. D. Kleinke reappeared just in time to offer the advice, succor, and true friendship I needed at a crucial time. And I owe an enormous debt to my dear, dear friend Kathy Goodman, whose sharp eyes and mind went right to the heart so many times, and whose passion is reflected in the pages of this book. I am deeply grateful to Syssa Felisberto for the understanding and care that she provided in keeping my household going so that I could finish.

My husband, Luis Ubinas, has, quite simply, made it possible for me to write this book. His patience, amazing mind, perspective, and unending desire to provide whatever I need are there between each line. The last twenty years together make me thirsty for more, an ongoing reminder of the importance of desire in a woman's life. My parents, E. Laurie and Sylvia Tolman, as always, inculcated and continue to believe in my persistent refusal to be a good girl. My two little boys, Maximilian and Benjamin Ubinas, give me so much every day, and gave up too much for this project. It was with them in mind that I wrote every word.

Parts of this book appeared in earlier versions in the following books and journals. I gratefully acknowledge the publishers for permission to reuse the materials. "Doing Desire: Adolescent Girls' Struggles for/with Sexuality," *Gender and Society,* 8(3) (1994): 324–342, Sage Publications; "How Being a Good Girl Can Be Bad for Girls," written with T. Higgins, in N. B. Maglin and D. Perry, eds., *Bad Girls/Good Girls: Women, Sex, and Power in the Nineties,* pp. 205–225, Rutgers University Press, 1996; "Adolescent Girls' Sexuality: Debunking the Myth of the Urban Girl," in B. Leadbeater and N. Way, eds., *Urban Girls: Resisting Stereotypes, Creating Identities,* pp. 255–271, New York University Press, 1996; "Dimensions of Desire: Bridging Qualitative and Quantitative Methods," written with L. Szalacha, *Psychology of Women Quarterly,* 24(4) (1999): 365–376, originally Cambridge University Press, with permission of Blackwell Publishers.

> Once more there is a question which gives
> me no peace: "Is it right? Is it right that I
> should have yielded so soon, that I am so
> ardent, just as ardent and eager as Peter
> himself? May I, a girl, let myself go to this
> extent?"
>
> —Anne Frank, *The Diary of
> Anne Frank: The Critical Edition*

On a May morning when the warmth of the sun seemed to be finally winning out over the last chilly breeze of a New England winter, I met Inez, a seventeen-year-old Latina junior in a public high school, who agreed to participate in my study of adolescent girls' sexual desire. Sitting in an out-of-the-way, sun-filled corner of a seldom-used corridor, I listen to Inez's voice as she speaks about her experiences of her sexuality. Our heads bend down around the quiet whirling of my tape recorder, shielding us both from intrusions and from being overheard. In the hour and a half that we talk, Inez seems to find it easy to respond to my questions. Her stories are detailed, punctuated with reflections on what she thought and how she felt. One of the first stories she chooses to tell me is about the first time she had sexual intercourse, with a boy with whom she was "in love":

> The first time I ever had sex, it was something that I least expected it. I didn't actually go to his house and expect something to happen, because it, he was kissing me, and I felt like I wasn't

there, it was like my body just went limp. It was like, I had went out with him for a year, and I was like, I was like wow, and um, he was just kissing me, and I was like, and then all of a sudden like, just, like my body just went limp, and then everything just happened. To me, I feel like I didn't notice anything.

There are several ways to hear Inez's story. Developmental psychologists might explain it as evidence of her immaturity, because it demonstrates that she has not yet constructed a sexual self. Since Inez never says directly that she wanted to have sex, some might think that this story reflects an experience of victimization and coercion. Yet Inez offers this experience as one of sexual pleasure, which to her means the pleasure of "being wanted" and "show-[ing] him that I loved him more, in a physical way." And so another way to think about Inez's story is as a condoned version: The main theme, that sex "just happened," is an explanation girls frequently offer for how they come to have sex. Having sex "just happen" is one of the few acceptable ways available to adolescent girls for making sense of and describing their sexual experiences; and, given the power of such stories to shape our experiences of our bodies, it may tell us what their sexual experiences actually are like. In a world where "good," nice, and normal girls do not have sexual feelings of their own, it is one of the few decent stories that a girl can tell. That is, "it just happened" is a story about desire (Plummer, 1995).

"It just happened," then, can also be understood as a cover story. It is a story about the necessity for girls to cover their desire. It is also a story that covers over active choice, agency, and responsibility, which serves to "disappear" desire, in the telling and in the living. But "it just happened" is much more than a story told by yet another girl to describe her individual experience. Focusing on Inez's individually unfolding sexual development leaves out the fact that girls' sexuality does not develop in a vacuum. It leaves out the ways in which girls are under systematic pressure not to feel, know, or act on their sexual desire. It covers up both our consistent refusal to offer girls any guidance for acknowledging, negotiating, and integrating their own sexual desire and the consequences of our refusal: sexual intercourse—most often unprotected, that "just happens" to girls. "It just happened" is undoubtedly one of a multitude of stories that a girl can tell about any single experience. Its veracity is not on the line; the wisdom of telling and living this story about female adolescent sexuality is. I suggest that "it just happened" is an unsafe and unhealthy story for girls.

How do we define healthy sexuality and healthy adolescent development? The classic *Handbook of Adolescent Development* states that "within the context of other developmental goals, one is supposed to become a self-motivated sexual actor" (Miller & Simon, 1980, p. 383). We so rarely think of sexuality in positive or healthy terms that doing so requires a shift in mindset. In 2001 the U.S. surgeon general, David Satcher, urged just such a shift when he released *A Call to Action to Promote Sexual Health and Responsible Sexual Behavior*. In his introductory letter, Satcher wrote, "it is necessary to appreciate what sexual health is, that it is connected with both physical and mental health, and that it is important throughout the entire life span, not just the reproductive years." This position echoes the statement released several years before by the National Commission on Adolescent Sexual Health, endorsed by thirty-seven professional associations, including the American Medical Association and the American Psychological Association. The Religious Institute on Sexual Morality, Justice, and Healing, a network of over two thousand religious leaders from over twenty-five denominations, in its 2001 declaration recognizes "sexuality as central to our humanity and as integral to our spirituality." Sexuality is so often thought of only in negative terms, so frequently clustered with problem behaviors such as smoking and drinking, in our minds as well as in research, that it is easy to forget that while we are not supposed to become smokers or drinkers in adolescence, we are supposed to develop a mature sense of ourselves as sexual beings by the time we have reached adulthood. Without a clear or sanctioned path, developing this sense is even harder for girls, as a closer look at the words of Inez and the other girls I interviewed reveals.

VICTIMS AND VICTORS: TWO ROADS TO SEXUAL MATURITY

How far our conceptions of male and female adolescent sexuality diverge came into startling focus one night at a dinner party I attended with some friends who have teenage children. A man I had not met before began bragging about how his teenage son showed every sign of being a "ladies' man." He beamed with pride as he described his son's ability to elude the "grasp" of any single girl, how his boy was so successful at "playing the field." The father winked at another man at the table, hinting that, by the age of sixteen, his son had "gotten" plenty of sexual experience, showing all the signs of having the "raging hormones" that he appeared to believe was normal for his son. His pleasure that his son was a heartbreaker was evident.

Later in the evening, this same man spoke about his fifteen-year-old daughter. A different picture of the terrain of adolescent sexuality came to the fore. On the one hand, he was clearly proud that his daughter was considered an attractive and desirable date by her male peers; on the other, he was uncomfortable when she actually went out with them. While he understood that she wanted to have a boyfriend, which he ascribed to her desire to be like her friends, he preferred that she bring boys home rather than be out with them. He worried that "things might happen to her" that she

would "regret." His fear that she would be sexually victimized or
"taken advantage of" by boys was palpable.

Several things struck me about this conversation. It was clear
this man had two entirely different ideas about appropriate and
normal sexuality for male and female adolescents. It was also clear
he did not see how they were connected. His belief that boys are
sexual predators and his encouragement and approval of this
behavior in his own son fueled his conviction that girls, including
his daughter, need to be protected *from* boys while also being
attractive *for* boys. Unstated but eminently implicit in his formulation was the assumption that girls are the objects of boys' sexual
desire and have no desires of their own. This man's perspectives on
his son and his daughter illustrate the ways in which our beliefs
about sexuality are gendered.

As a society, we parcel sexuality out, assuming that normal boys
but not girls have "raging hormones"—and that normal girls but
not boys long for emotional connection and relationships. We
assume that adolescent boys are burgeoning sexual beings. We
believe that they are obsessed with their sexuality and expect them
not only to feel sexual desire but to be compelled to act on it, or at
the very least to make the attempt. In many circles, if a boy reaches
mid-adolescence without having shown any perceptible sexual
interest in girls, those around him may become concerned about
his masculinity and sexual orientation. In contrast, when it comes
to girls, what we still expect, and in many ways continue to en-
courage, is their yearning for love, relationships, and romance.
Acknowledgment of their sexual longings as an anticipated part of
their adolescence is virtually nonexistent. We have effectively
desexualized girls' sexuality, substituting the desire for relationship
and emotional connection for sexual feelings in their bodies.

These constructions of girls' sexuality leave out their sexual
subjectivity. By sexual subjectivity I mean a person's experience of

herself as a sexual being, who feels entitled to sexual pleasure and sexual safety, who makes active sexual choices, and who has an identity as a sexual being. Sexual desire is at the heart of sexual subjectivity. Karin Martin (1996) argues that "sexual subjectivity is a necessary component of agency and thus of self esteem. That is, one's sexuality affects her/his ability to act in the world, and to feel like she/he can will things and make them happen" (p. 10). Sexual subjectivity can and should therefore be at the heart of responsibility in sexual decision making—whether deciding not to have sexual intercourse or to have protected sexual intercourse, to have sexual experiences that have nothing to do with sexual intercourse or not to act on those feelings at all. From this perspective, it is not only unfair to deny female adolescent sexual desire but ultimately unsafe and unhealthy.

Despite the sexual revolution, this picture of the condoned social order of adolescence has not improved. Even as we enter the twenty-first century, the possibility that girls might be interested in sexuality in their own right rather than as objects of boys' desire is met with resistance and discomfort. To wit, in 1998, a film entitled *Coming Soon,* about white, middle-class, heterosexual adolescent girls who seek to have sexual experiences on their own terms, was shown only at film festivals (where "teenage girls came back for a second screening"), because no distributor would pick it up. The filmmaker, Colette Burson, fully aware of the subversive quality of her film, commented, "When I showed the script to male directors, they'd say, 'I love it, but let's make it less about the girl-sex thing . . .' Meanwhile, every teen movie you see is all about boys' getting lucky" (Schillinger, 1999, p. 15). As early as middle school (Tolman et al., 2002) or even the waning moments of elementary school (Thorne, 1993), girls and boys are relentlessly exposed to a set of rules, principles, and roles that are mapped out for the production of "normal" heterosexual adolescent relationships and sexual behavior, in which gender is the most salient factor. Teenage girls continue to be denied entitlement to their own sexuality, and girls who do defy the irrepressible double standard continue to do so at their own risk.

Despite the incessant flow of sexual images and relationship advice, girls do not get many positive messages about their sexuality. They are barraged with an ever more confusing and contradictory set of guidelines for how they should manage their developing sexuality: don't be a prude but don't be a slut; have (or fake) orgasms to ensure that your boyfriend is not made to feel inadequate, if you want to keep him. Ultimately, though subtly, the media continue to represent the belief that adolescent girls should be sexy for boys and not have their *own* sexual desires. Although Monica Lewinsky's sexual assertiveness may not have been as shocking to her peers (Kamen, 2000) as it was to adults (Fineman et al., 1998), their reaction to it was similar: to label her "an unrepentant little slut" (as at smileandactnice.com) and to criticize and satirize her appearance (as on *Saturday Night Live* regularly). As one young woman writing on missclick, a popular web site for adolescent girls, observed: "She could win the Nobel Peace Prize, and they'd make cigar jokes as she accepted her award."

Teen magazines, movies, and television contribute to the pervasive paradox: They offer advice on how to provide pleasure to boys juxtaposed with stories of sexual violation and harassment (Brumberg, 1997; Ussher, 1997; Carpenter, 1998). Madonna powerfully models female sexual freedom; yet, despite their admiration and even awe at her willingness to defy social norms, few teenage girls feel that they themselves—ordinary girls, not gorgeous celebrities—could "get away with it" without a besmirched reputation (Kitzinger, 1995, p. 193). Music directed at adolescent girls continues to mix the message. At the same time Christina Aguilera sings about "what a girl wants, what a girl needs," she presents herself as a sex symbol, consciously turning her body into a commodity, an object of admiration and desire for others, obscuring how or even whether her own desires figure in her willingness to do "whatever keeps me in your arms." In her memoir *Promiscuities* (1997) Naomi Wolf observed that even today "girls must speak in a world where they are expected to be sexually available but not sexually in charge of themselves" (p. 136; see also Orenstein, 1994). And so the conundrum: while *sexualized images* of adolescent girls are omnipresent, *their* sexual feelings are rarely if ever portrayed.

We remain disturbed when forced to face the possibility that girls, too, might be engaged in a process of sexual maturation that involves more than developing breasts and getting their periods. According to current estimates, 65 percent of girls have had sex by the age of eighteen;[1] in 1995, 49 percent of girls aged fifteen to nineteen had had sexual intercourse at least once (Abma & Sonenstein, 2001). However, it is not simply girls' sexual activity per se that troubles us, since we believe that, for various reasons, girls "give in" to boys' supposedly relentless demands for sex or that they are intractably bad. It is evidence of their sexual *desire* that is more often than not met with shock, a diagnosis of pathology, and impassioned calls for the imposition of social controls. A distressed mother of a teenage boy wrote to Ann Landers to complain about teenage girls who had telephoned and left a flirtatious message that unmistakably conveyed their interest in him. The column provoked twenty thousand responses, causing Ms. Landers to comment, "If I'm hearing about it from so many places, then I worry about what's going on out there . . . What this says to me is that a good many young girls really are out of control" (Yoffe, Marszalek, & Selix, 1991). Girls who step out of the bounds of appropriate, controlled female sexuality instigate what has been called a moral panic (Foucault, 1980; Petchesky, 1984; Nathanson, 1991; Jenkins, 2001), a kind of societal nervous breakdown. Consider whether Ann Landers would have published or, more to the point, even received a letter from a concerned mother of an adolescent girl complaining that her daughter had received this telephone call. Such behavior on the part of boys might be considered rude or even harassing, but what are the chances that such a letter would get this kind of response? While girls may have more degrees of sexual freedom now than in past generations, sexual girls continue to make and get into trouble (Kamen, 2000). If we not only accept but in fact expect healthy adolescent boys to have strong sexual feelings they need to learn how to deal with, why don't we expect the same of girls?

It is significant that such resistance is identifiable not only at the dinner table and in the media but also in developmental psychology. When I searched the literature to find out what psychologists knew about adolescent girls' sexual desire, I found that no one had asked about it. In the many hundreds of studies that have been done to determine what predicts adolescent girls' sexual behavior, only a handful had identified girls' sexual desire as a potential factor.[2] We tend to conflate adolescent sexuality with risky behavior, to define "sex" only in terms of sexual intercourse without distinguishing its various component parts, such as sexual feelings and desire, and the different types of behavior that express those feelings. This tendency, an artifact of public policy and funded research geared toward avoiding the risks of sexuality, leads us to single out girls as the receptacle of our concerns. Our fear about girls' sexual behavior thus conceptualized has understandable roots, since it is still girls who suffer overwhelmingly the physical, social, psychological, and material consequences of unprotected intercourse.

This fear offers a partial explanation for the intensity with which we deny girls' sexual desire. If girls do not really have sexual feelings to explore, then they are necessarily at some level being exploited. And this fear has generated a virtual cottage industry of research that amounts to a relentless surveillance of female (but not male) adolescent sexual behavior. We maintain careful records of whether girls are using contraception—and now, in the age of AIDS, whether they are successful in asking their partners to use condoms—and how many partners they have had. We have also begun determining how old their partners are and what their abuse history is (newly identified risk factors for bad outcomes of sexual encounters). There is rising alarm about adolescent oral sex (read "fellatio"), with hysterical demands to know who the troubled girls are who engage in this behavior and how often, paradoxically coupled with the refusal of adults to give consent for their children to report this information so that we would actually know. We chart and follow the pregnancy rate, with inordinate attention to the shifting differentials between girls of different races and ethnicities. There are hundreds of studies in which predictors of "good" and "bad" outcomes of girls' "sexual decision making" are identified.

It is not difficult to argue that there are palpable dangers associated with adolescent girls' sexual behavior. For young women, the dangers of pregnancy and early parenting lurk in the shadows of sexual activity. If using no contraceptives, fifteen- to nineteen-year-old girls have a 90 percent chance of becoming pregnant (Harlap, Kost, & Forest, 1991); at any given time three-quarters of adolescent girls who have had sex are at risk of unintended pregnancy (Kahn, Brindis, & Glei, 1999). Each year one in five sexually active adolescent girls becomes pregnant (Alan Guttmacher Institute, 1999). Although pregnancy rates in the United States are declining, they still rank the highest of any in developed countries (Singh & Darroch, 1999). Adolescents are one of the fastest growing groups at risk for contracting HIV (DiClemente, Hansen, & Ponton, 1996), and adolescent girls may have a higher risk of contracting sexually transmitted diseases than do adult females (Alan Guttmacher Institute, 1998).

Additionally, statistics indicate that sexual violence is prevalent in the lives of all female adolescents. Sexual harassment is pervasive in junior high and high schools: 83 percent of girls report having been sexually harassed in school (American Association of University Women, 2001), and girls are significantly more likely than boys to report being negatively affected by harassment (Bochenek & Brown, 2001). Recent research suggests that one out of five female adolescents has experienced dating or sexual violence during their high school years (Silverman et al., 2001). Half of all rape victims are under the age of eighteen.[3] Of girls age sixteen and younger who have had sexual intercourse, 24 percent had involuntary or forced sex; for those fifteen and younger, the figure is 40 percent (Abma, Driscoll, & Moore, 1998; Moore, Driscoll, & Lindberg, 1998). In the most recent findings from the national Youth Risk Behavior Survey of adolescents in the ninth through twelfth grades, 12.5 percent of girls reported having been forced to have sexual intercourse (Centers for Disease Control and Prevention, 2000).

Girls have to contend not only with physical consequences but also with social fallout. The so-called Madonna-whore split is surprisingly alive and well in the public imagination and in the lives of adolescent girls; even girls who do feel entitled to their own sexuality negotiate this label. One fifteen-year-old girl writing on a teen web site, who described herself as "unashamed" about being "sexual," recognized that such behavior by a girl is still frowned upon: "I am a slut . . . to some people it's someone who sleeps around, and to others it's someone who is open about her sexuality. Either way, I guess that's me" (missclick, September 18, 2000). While some girls may fear being labeled a prude, this moniker is not about their own desire but about their refusal or failure to meet the sexual demands of boys. Though the possibility of being thought a prude may be uncomfortable for some girls (Shalit, 1999), the threat of being branded a slut still looms large for teenage girls and unmarried women (Lees, 1993; Wyatt, 1994; Tannenbaum, 1999). Some girls and young women do openly resist being placed into these categories (Carlip, 1995; Edut, 1998; Kamen, 2000), but many more girls continue to report living in constant fear of a ruined reputation, although the dynamics underpinning pressure on girls to restrain their sexuality are more subtle and variable than in earlier generations (Moore & Snyder, 1994; Kitzinger, 1995; Martin, 1996). Fear of a sullied reputation has a multiplying effect on the physical dangers of sexuality for girls, because girls who use the pill, carry condoms, or ask boys to use condoms are fair game for the label (Holland, Ramazanoglu, & Thomson, 1996; Hillier, Harrison, & Warr, 1998). And so it is not simply physical danger that sexuality poses for teenage girls. To act upon one's own sexual feelings and desire is still, for girls, to invite the risk of being known as a "bad" girl, a girl who deserves any consequences she suffers, a girl who loses her eligibility for social and legal protections against sexual harm (Tolman & Higgins, 1996). The enduring split between "good," chaste, feminine girls and "bad," sexual, aberrant girls is a crucial aspect of societal denial of female adolescent sexual desire. On the larger canvas of social hierarchies, this categorization is premised not only on girls' perceived behavior but also on assumptions about their race, ethnicity, and social class (Gibbs, 1985; Caraway, 1991; Fine, Roberts, & Weis, 2000).

These risks are real, pose significant threats to adolescent girls' health, and must be diminished. But acknowledging that we need to prevent unwanted, unintended, or undesirable pregnancies or sexually transmitted diseases, or to eliminate violence against young women or their vulnerability to ruined reputations, does not fully explain our obsessive surveillance of the sexual behavior of adolescent girls. If these risks were our deepest concerns, we would be pouring funds into effective, accessible forms of birth control and protection against diseases, providing comprehensive sexuality education, widely disseminating information on masturbation and mutual masturbation as the safest forms of sexual exploration, declaring "zero tolerance" for sexual violence or the threat of it and for homophobia. And if these risks accounted for all our concerns, we would be conducting many more studies of adolescent boys' sexuality, since boys too are vulnerable to becoming parents, getting sexually transmitted diseases, and being victims of violence.[4]

An examination of our conception of male adolescent sexual desire sheds light on this tendency to deny girls' sexuality.[5] It is, indeed, a frightening conception. We believe that desire is a demanding physical urge, instinct, or drive, embedded so deeply in the body that it gains a life of its own once ignited. It is impossible to control, absolutely necessary to satisfy (through sexual intercourse), and aggressive to the point of violence. It is the unstoppable artifact of testosterone overload. In our worst scenarios, we think of desire as a kind of selfish, exploitative monster, as a force that demands its bearer find satisfaction at the expense of or without concern for someone else. Desire is uncivilized. It is all about individual needs and has nothing to do with relationships. It is male, and it is masculine. Thus conceived, desire is not only incompatible but at odds with society's conceptions of femininity, precluding it from being part of the array of feelings and behaviors that we expect from girls who are developing in an acceptable fashion (Bartky, 1990). Given these beliefs, no wonder we think of those first stirrings of adult sexual desire in adolescence—either "healthy" boys' sexual desire or "bad" girls' sexual desire—as dangerous.

What I have just described and illustrated are *conceptions* rather than definitions of desire, and of male and female adolescent sexuality. They are social constructions—cultural beliefs or stories that provide a way for us to make meaning out of our experiences and give us the sense that these meanings constitute objective facts or reality (Gergen, 1985; Tiefer, 1987). As Richard Parker and John Gagnon (1995) have observed, this epistemological stance diverts us from understanding and researching sexuality as a set of behaviors, pushing us instead to attend to the cultural norms that produce and give meaning to sexual acts. These organizing cultural stories or "master narratives" are so compelling that most of us come not only to tell them but to live them and feel them to be the "truth" of human experience. This perspective on sexuality is not meant to reject or usurp the place of the body. Rather, researchers have noted how the "material body and its social construction are entwined in complex and contradictory ways which are extremely difficult to disentangle in practice" (Holland et al., 1994, p. 22; see also Cosgrove, 2001). Such a social constructionist perspective, then, while acknowledging a role for hormones in the vicissitudes of desire, shifts the debate about the differences in male and female sexuality from purely physiological explanations (lust) toward the importance of how we make meaning out of our bodily, emotional, and relational experiences (desire). Even research that specifically addresses hormonal fluctuations in pubertal development finds that they are but one contributing factor in adolescent sexual behavior and also that, especially for girls, societal factors outweigh or affect biological ones (Udry, Talbert, & Morris, 1986; Halpern, Udry, & Suchindran, 1997; Halpern, in press). The stories that we do—and do not—tell about normal female adolescent development reflect what Michelle Fine (1988) has called "the missing discourse of desire," marking our insistence on defining female adolescent sexuality only in terms of disease, victimization, and morality and our avoidance of girls' own feelings of sexual desire and pleasure. At the heart of the interlocking stories that organize girls' and boys' sexuality are the complementary ideas about the ferocity and omnipresence of male adolescent sexual desire and the utter absence of female adolescent sexual desire.

The obsessive quality of our focus on teenage girls' sexual behavior and vulnerability calls attention to less obvious motives for our intense anxiety about them. Recall the Spur Posse case in Lakewood, California: A group of high school boys who were discovered to be competing for how many girls they could manipulate into having sex. Although many people criticized their behavior as an example of unchecked adolescent sexuality, the boys' parents were publicly untroubled by their sons' actions. But try to substitute "girls" for "boys": Can anyone imagine a girl who coerced a boy to have sex being shrugged off or even defended and admired by her parents on national television because of her "raging hormones" or because of their belief that "girls will be girls"? Such concerns about boys are glossed over by the assumption that adolescent boys not only are sexual beings but are overwhelmed by their sexuality, and that such intense sexual desire is a *natural and normal part of male adolescence and male sexuality.*[6] A gendered perspective on adolescent sexuality offers more explanation for what is behind the urgency of resisting girls' sexual desire: Girls' *lack* of desire serves as the necessary linchpin in how adolescent sexuality is organized and managed. To the extent that we believe that adolescent sexuality is under control, it is adolescent girls whom we hold responsible, because we do not believe boys can or will be. We are left with a circuitous argument that fails to include the reality or importance of female adolescents' own sexuality: Boys will be boys ergo sexuality is dangerous for girls. Our impulse to keep girls safe by keeping them under control seems so necessary that the cost of denying them the right to live fully in their own bodies appears unavoidable. Just as impossible standards of thinness serve to curtail girls' and women's hunger for food, this seemingly justified worry about their sexuality fuels denial and demonization of female adolescent sexual desire. In essence, we let boys off the hook for a wide array of consequences *for girls* because of what we denote and perceive to be their inevitable and uncontainable sexuality, as was so blatantly conveyed by my dinner companion. In the process, we also make it hard for adolescent boys to experience a full range of emotions and connections. In the wake of these beliefs, how could we not worry about girls? Why would we want to acknowledge *their* desire?

AN INVISIBLE SYSTEM OF CONTROL

Feminist scholars have offered extensive social analysis of how controlling female sexuality is a key component of the oppression of women on which patriarchy is premised (Rich, 1983; Snitow, Stansell, & Thompson, 1983; Vance, 1984). Adrienne Rich, a feminist theorist, poet, and writer, identified the social construction of what she called *compulsory heterosexuality* as an essential means for controlling women within patriarchy. She asserted that heterosexual sexual desire—that is, women having sexual desire for men—is not a natural state but the result of specific involuntary socialization processes. As a result, social hierarchies are premised on gender and produce social constructions of proper female sexuality and appropriate gendered behavior for women. She suggested that we are all under enormous pressure to internalize and comply with these social mandates. Rich wove together seemingly discrete social phenomena that, she argued, constitute the systematic dehumanization and oppression of women through sexuality, both directly and indirectly, identifying specific processes by which women's sexuality has been and is manipulated as a way to control women. These include the objectification of women, the socialization of women to feel that male sexual "drive" amounts to a right, the idealization of heterosexual romance, ideologies of femininity

and masculinity, the denial or denigration of female sexual pleasure or agency, rape and sexual violence, pornography, sexual
harassment, and the erasure of lesbian existence from history and
culture.[7] Thus, thinking about heterosexuality as an institution
includes but is not limited to the idea of heterosexuality as a sexual
orientation, that is, as simply desiring the opposite sex.

What is most compelling about Rich's theory is that she showed
how heterosexuality is "a political institution which disempowers
women" (p. 182). She revealed this institution *as an institution* by
naming and connecting what appear to be separate features of
society, thereby identifying its invisible contours. By linking these
various features of social life, she showed how the institution of
heterosexuality functions by being nowhere in particular and at
the same time embedded in every aspect of society and social life.
And it is in being institutionalized as what is "natural" and "normal" through condoned social discourses, or ways of framing and
speaking about social life, that the "compulsory" part of heterosexuality is invisible. Rich's theory reveals how socializing girls and
women into conceptions and practices of femininity that write
their sexual desire, pleasure, and agency out of normal female
behavior contributes to the production of the institution of heterosexuality. Her theory also makes clear how the institution is
maintained or reinforced by the constant threat of violence or
other negative repercussions for refusal to comply with such
restrictive norms of normalcy and femininity; conversely, constraints on women's freedoms are imposed in the name of protection from vulnerability to male sexuality.

Evidence of the institution of heterosexuality at work can be
seen everywhere: parents telling girls to be nice (and boys not to
cry), movies in which the hero rescues the girl from certain disaster
and romance prevails (and they marry and live happily ever after),
expectations that women and only women want to have and

should care for children. Disregard for the scientific evidence that "abstinence-only-until-marriage" sex education is insufficient to meet the health needs of children (Kirby, 2001) and the current federal policy of funding only this approach, going so far as to threaten its removal if other aspects of sexuality and relationships are discussed by teachers, are good examples of the institution of heterosexuality and of its compulsory nature.

The importance of the institution of heterosexuality to our social order and organization becomes especially evident when the institution itself has been violated. In the 1999 film *Boys Don't Cry*, Hilary Swank gave a compelling, Academy Award–winning portrayal of the true story of Teena Brandon. Born a girl, she felt so intensely that she was a boy trapped in a female body that she attempted to live as a boy, and did so very convincingly. She was a boy for all intents and purposes in the eyes of those around her, including the girl with whom she fell in love. When the community discovered that this person they knew as a boy, who was having what appeared to be and felt to the girlfriend to be a "normal" heterosexual relationship, was in fact a girl, not only did they beat and rape her, but ultimately they killed her. By successfully making others experience her as a boy when her body was female, she had both unveiled and challenged the institution of heterosexuality at its heart. The result: violence of unspeakable proportions.

Rich's identification of the institution of heterosexuality offers a powerful theoretical lens through which to view adolescent sexuality. The effect of this invisible system of social control is that we all, adults and adolescents alike, construe the "problem" of girls' sexuality as an individual rather than a social one. We think about girls' sexuality only as a personal phenomenon, a personal set of decisions, choices, consequences, or even feelings; we obscure the extent to which societal norms and ambivalence offer girls a range of poor "choices," which rarely, if ever, include the reality or importance of their own sexuality. Where society is ambivalent, there is a tendency to focus on those with the least power; we are able to constrain, blame, and punish them for the anxiety they provoke in us, and the more disenfranchised the individual, the more she bears the brunt of our fears about social disorder and personal threats (Fine & Weis, 2000). In the case of adolescent girls, we distort and justify this displacement because of society's sense of entitlement, even sense of obligation, to regulate and control their sexuality.

AND NOW FOR SOMETHING COMPLETELY DIFFERENT . . .

This book is not about the usual dangers that we associate with adolescent girls' sexuality: unintended pregnancy and the risk of HIV/AIDS or other sexually transmitted infections. It is not about the "problem" of female adolescent sexual activity and its consequences. It is not even about girls' sexual decision making. I do not begin from a position that the only or even the best way to think about girls' sexuality is in terms of avoiding risks. An understanding of how and why male and female sexuality is socially constructed in the ways described above yields a counterintuitive stance that is grounded in a different set of concerns. In this book, I begin with a different assumption: Girls live and grow up in bodies that are capable of strong sexual feelings, bodies that are connected to minds and hearts that hold meanings through which they make sense of and perceive their bodies. I consider the possibility that teenage girls' sexual desire is important and life sustaining; that girls' desire provides crucial information about the relational world in which they live; that the societal obstacles to girls' and women's ability to feel and act on their own desire should come under scrutiny rather than simply be feared; that girls and women are entitled to have sexual subjectivity, rather than simply to be sexual objects.

The skewed portrait of desire that we have drawn for ourselves and propped up so effectively is a disservice to girls and women, as well as to boys and men. This set of beliefs leaves out many possibilities and experiences that could make desire more desirable. Sexual desire, in and of itself, is not dangerous, essentially masculine, or monstrous. Desire is part of our relational world, a sign and manifestation of our connection with our own bodies and connection with other people. Developing sexual subjectivity is at the heart of the adolescent developmental task of becoming a "self-motivated sexual actor" and of making responsible choices about sexual behavior. Jean Baker Miller, in *Towards a New Psychology of Women* (1976), identified sexual authenticity—that is, the ability to bring one's own real feelings of sexual desire and sexual pleasure meaningfully into intimate relationships—as a key feature of women's psychological health. From a psychological point of view, developing a strong sense of self and engaging in authentic, meaningful, and joyful intimate relationships requires an acknowledgment and acceptance of one's own bodily feelings. As William James (1890/1970) observed in psychology's earliest hour, "The world experienced . . . comes at all times with our body as its center" (pp. 21–23). That is, the body is the counterpart of the psyche in the ongoing process of composing and constructing one's sexual subjectivity. Thus, desire is one form of knowledge, gained through the body: In desiring, I know that I exist.

Making sexual desire a fundamental aspect of a girl's sense of self offers a way to think about adolescent sexuality, a revision of what developmental psychologists have long acknowledged to be a task of the adolescent period: to learn how to bring all aspects of oneself into relationships, which can lead to a sense of connection, entitlement, and empowerment that can go beyond sexuality by including sexuality. To "know" one's own body means to have knowledge about it and also the ability to feel the feelings in it, to have access to the range of physical sensations that course through one's body, providing information about the experiences—emotional as well as physical—that one is having. Feeling desire in response to another person is a route to knowing, to being, oneself through the process of relationship: "The psyche cannot cut off one kind of desire without affecting another. When sexual desire is truncated, all desire is compromised—including girls' power to love themselves and to know what they really want" (Debold, Wilson, & Malave, 1993, p. 211).

In other words, *not* feeling sexual desire may put girls in danger and "at risk." When a girl does not know what her own feelings are, when she disconnects the apprehending psychic part of herself from what is happening in her own body, she then becomes especially vulnerable to the power of others' feelings as well as to what others say she does and does not want or feel.[8] Keeping in mind this different view of female adolescent sexual desire, let us return to Inez and notice what this vantage point enables us to hear that was not audible before.

If I listen to Inez from the perspective that girls have sexual feelings and can or should act on them, I listen for her acknowledgment of her own sexual feelings, for the presence and absence of her own desire in her description of her sexual experiences. Prior to telling this story, Inez has told me that she is capable of feeling sexual desire and can describe those embodied feelings: When she gets in the "pleasure mood," she explains, her "body says yes, yes, yes." She identifies herself as Latina, and the specific qualities associated with acceptable feminine demeanor and behavior for Latina girls suffuse everything she says (Espin, 1984, 1999; Amaro, Russo, & Pares-Avila, 1987; Hurtado, 1996). In this story, I listen specifically for what Inez says about herself and her body—"I felt like I wasn't there, it was like my body just went limp . . . I feel like I didn't notice anything." Inez describes a body that is present yet not feeling; a self that is not there, that does not act but is acted upon, that does not contribute or even "notice"; a body that is "limp" rather than alive or engaged. From this perspective, Inez's story is about how *she* disappears when she has sex for the first time—literally and figuratively. Her body is silent—and consequently, (unprotected) sex "just happened." In this story, there is no hint that her own sexual desire was part of her first experience of sexual intercourse.

Inez's story illustrates how, by disallowing female sexual desire, we manufacture danger and risk by throwing a roadblock in the pathway of girls' psychosocial development, psychological health, and ability to form authentic relationships. We create an impossible situation for girls: Healthy sexuality means having sexual desire, but there is little if any safe space—physically, socially, psychologically—for these forbidden and dangerous feelings. Girls who embrace or even resist the stories we offer about female and male sexuality inevitably face dilemmas when they feel sexual desire: Do they feel and act on their desire and risk the negative, even punitive, possibly disastrous consequences, or do they deny, discount, or distract others from their desire and suffer a profound disconnection from themselves?

I am aware that considering the importance of sexual desire in girls' lives and in their psychological development is for many people not only counterintuitive but also suspect. So I want to emphasize that I am not advocating that adolescent girls engage in sexual intercourse or suggesting that early sexual intercourse or sexual activity of any sort is inevitable or good. Rather, I am advocating a shift in the whole way we think and talk about girls' sexuality, and in how we talk to and support adolescent girls— regardless of whether or not girls are having sexual intercourse. I am not offering an evaluation or judgment of girls' sexual behavior, and I am not outlining a timetable for when adolescents, girls or boys, should have sexual intercourse or any other sexual experi-ence. *I am suggesting a different conversation altogether.* By equating and confounding sexuality with sexual intercourse, we limit how all adolescents learn to conceptualize their romantic relationships and themselves as sexual beings. We also undermine our efforts to educate them and to learn more ourselves about adolescent sexual-ity through research. Sexual desire is not the same as sexual inter-course or even desire for sexual intercourse. Intercourse is one of an array of behaviors with which a person can respond to such feelings. By focusing on sexual intercourse, which is an act or a behavior, we have left out and glossed over another key aspect of sexuality and sexual development: *sexual feelings.*

With this distinction in mind, rather than designing yet another study to investigate girls' sexual activity, behavior, or attitudes, I organized my research around a new line of inquiry: When asked in a straightforward and safe way about their own sexual desire, what do adolescent girls say? In this book, I report the findings from an in-depth study of two ordinary groups of teenage girls, one from an urban public school and one from a suburban public school. I listened to Inez and twenty-nine other girls answer direct questions about their experiences of sexual desire as a means of researching not the *prevalence* of sexual desire among adolescent girls but the *phenomenology* of their sexual desire. That is, this study is not about how many girls feel how much sexual desire; it is about how two groups of girls describe their experiences of their sexual feelings. The point is not to represent all girls or provide a comprehensive or definitive taxonomy of female adolescent sexual desire. The idea of this kind of a study is to develop an understand-ing of some of the ways girls describe experiencing and dealing with their sexual feelings. It is an attempt to let girls tell other sto-ries about their sexuality besides "it just happened." These girls are the first to describe their experiences of sexual desire, what it is like for them, what it means to them, and how they negotiate their own feelings. These girls did something quite courageous; their willingness to speak about a part of their lives that is, essentially, unspeakable made it possible to crack open a closed window into adolescent girls' sexuality and take note of the initial breeze that wafted in.

Although this book focuses on the experiences of girls,[9] you will hear a range of stories, *from girls' perspectives,* about adolescent boys and their struggles with their sexuality and desire for intimacy or their sense that they are entitled to satisfy their own sexual wishes, even if it means taking psychological or physical advantage of girls. You will also hear girls speak about their wishes and fears regarding adolescent boys. I do not attempt to compare boys' and girls' experiences of sexuality or intend to condemn boys' sexual behavior, but inevitably (given our complementary beliefs about boys' and girls' sexuality) girls' stories about desire are also stories about gender relations. It is likely that what girls tell us about desire may raise new questions for boys about their experiences of their own sexuality.

Ultimately, the stories these girls tell must be understood as larger than their individual biographies; taken together, they constitute a narration of how a patriarchal society tries to keep girls and women at bay by forcing, or attempting to force, a wedge between their psyches and their bodies and how girls deal with these forces. As part of a larger tale, their stories make visible the permeability of any distinction between private experiences and public realities regarding their sexuality.

> In order to perpetuate itself, every oppres-
> sion must corrupt or distort those various
> sources of power within the culture of the
> oppressed that can provide energy for
> change. For women, this has meant sup-
> pression of the erotic as a considered source
> of power and information within our lives.
>
> —Audre Lorde, *Sister Outsider*

In recent years, mainstream research-
ers have called for more experiential studies of girls' sexuality and
acknowledged that girls' sexual desire is not only a legitimate but
a necessary area for study (Brooks-Gunn & Furstenberg, 1989;
Petersen, Leffert, & Graham, 1995). Feminist researchers have
extended how we study female adolescent sexuality by asking adolescent girls about their perspectives on and experiences with
romantic relationships and sexuality. Interestingly, these studies
demonstrate that when girls do speak about their sexuality, they do
not talk spontaneously about their own desire. That is, when girls
do tell sexual stories, their own desire is left out. For instance,
Karin Martin (1996) notes that in her study of adolescents' experiences of puberty, girls talked about relationships and not about
sexual pleasure or desire when asked to speak about their sexual
experiences. Lisa Dodson (1998) used a variety of methods—
structured interviews, more casual conversations, and group discussions led by girls—to study the experiences of black and white

poor adolescent girls, who spoke of the dangers of love, sexual pre-
dation by boys, and pervasive sexual abuse. She noted that these
girls did not seem to be aware that what they were describing was
male dominance or how rarely they spoke of sexual desire or pleasure. Do these findings mean that girls are not having experiences
of desire, or that their desire is not important in their sexual experiences or heterosexual relationships? The "missing discourse of
desire" in these studies suggests that it is unlikely that girls themselves will raise the taboo topic of sexual desire *unless specifically
asked.*

I did specifically ask and found that their own sexual feelings
posed great dilemmas for the girls I interviewed. In the first part of
this chapter, I explain the methods of my study: the sample, the
procedures for collecting and analyzing the data, and the research
principles and theory that guided these choices. In the second part,
I report how these girls speak, when asked, about their sexual
desire and the kinds of dilemmas they identify as endemic to their
own sexual feelings.

WHOM I ASKED

When I began this research the first and most obvious question
was whom to ask about the experience of female sexual desire in
adolescence. Michelle Fine and colleagues have pondered the ram-
ifications of collecting stories only from "victims" of racism and
poverty, noting that such narratives can be used to shore up stereotypes and political agendas that are harmful to individuals while
convenient for society (Fine et al., 2000). Social science literature
and research on adolescent sexuality is a case in point. The unstated assumption that certain girls—poor girls, girls of color,
urban girls—are more sexual and thus are at higher risk of negative outcomes is reproduced by the intensive study and surveillance
to which these girls are subjected. The girls whose sexuality—

whose sexual behavior and contraceptive practices—are studied are the girls whose sexuality results in *visible* problems: adolescent pregnancies and births, school dropout, the "cycle" of poverty. This stance is then justified by the knowledge that we thus produce. I had several options for dealing with this conundrum. One was to collect narratives to illustrate the complexity of girls' experiences from those whose sexuality is scrutinized and, in effect, demonized. This option could have been seen as benevolent, righting an injustice done to urban girls. Although the narratives told by the urban girls did in fact provide a window into this anticipated complexity, limiting the group under study to only these girls might have indeed invited misuse of their stories. To dismantle the deepseated popular notion that urban girls embody female adolescent sexuality and the complementary implication that suburban girls are not sexual, I made a conscious and purposeful choice to include both groups of girls in this study. Including girls from different locations allowed me to find out if girls' descriptions of their sexuality cohere within their group and also how their experiences compare with the myths and stereotypes about both urban and suburban girls' sexuality.

I was particularly interested in how girls who are or are becoming sexually active describe and experience their sexual desire, since one might expect or hope that their own sexual feelings would be a part of those experiences. Reflecting the average age of initiation of sexual intercourse (16.2 years, according to the data then available), most of the participants were juniors in high school, ranging in age from 15 to 18, with an average age of approximately 16.5.[1] The girls who participated in this study were selected at random from a complete roster of girls in the junior classes of each school—not, as one girl in the suburban school feared, because I knew something about their sexual or relationship histories. I sought to avoid hearing the stories only of girls

who volunteered and to include girls who might not have made
such an active choice to participate.[2] In the urban school, I made
an effort to include girls who represented the diversity of the student body; in the suburban school, I made an effort to include
some of the few girls of color.[3] Both the girls and their parents
received a written invitation to participate and a description of the
study;[4] all the girls under the age of 18 had to supply written
parental consent to be part of the study. I made follow-up phone
calls to the homes of girls from whom I did not hear back. About
half of the girls I approached to be in the study agreed to participate. While it is possible that there is something idiosyncratic
about this group of girls, as compared to those who did not participate, the teachers and administrators with whom I worked did not
identify any girl from the list of participants as particularly different from any other girl in their school.

Because there had been no previous study of this question, my
goal was to generate a heterogeneous group of girls from whom to
cull an initial understanding of girls' experiences of desire.[5] The
thirty girls who participated represent a range of races and ethnicities, religions, sexual abuse histories, and sexual experiences.[6] The
table labeled "Who the Girls Are" presents salient demographic
and personal history information for each girl. It is important to
point out that a multitude of factors are relevant to their experiences of desire. They had a range of sexual experiences and of
experiences with romantic relationships. They came from a variety
of family structures: those with two parents at home, one parent
at home and one on the road, divorced parents, older or younger
siblings, no siblings, step families, single mothers, single fathers,
sisters as primary caretakers. They were Protestant, Catholic, and
Jewish; some were religious, some were not. Almost a third of
these girls, when asked about something bad happening to them
regarding sex, told of some experience with sexual abuse or sexual

Name	School	Age	Race	Sexual violence reported	Sexual orientation
Alexandra	Suburban	17	White	Raped	Bisexual
Amber	Suburban	17	White	No	Heterosexual
Amy	Suburban	17	White	No	Heterosexual
Angela	Urban	16	Latina/Puerto Rican	Childhood sexual abuse[a]	Heterosexual
Barbara	Urban	16	White	Childhood sexual abuse[a]	Heterosexual
Beverly	Urban	17	Black/African American	No	Heterosexual
Cassandra	Suburban	16	White	No	Heterosexual
Charlene	Urban	17	White	No	Heterosexual
Ellen	Urban	16	Black/Caribbean	No	Heterosexual
Emily	Suburban	16	White	No	Heterosexual
Eugenia	Suburban	17	White	No	Heterosexual
Honore	Urban	18	Black/Caribbean	No	Heterosexual
Inez	Urban	17	Latina/Puerto Rican	No	Heterosexual
Jane	Suburban	16	White	No	Heterosexual
Janine	Urban	16	Black/Caribbean	No	Heterosexual
Jenny	Suburban	16	White	Raped?	Heterosexual
Jordan	Suburban	16	White	No	Heterosexual
Julia	Suburban	16	Latina/Puerto Rican	No	Heterosexual
Kim	Suburban	17	White	No	Heterosexual
Laura	Urban	18	Black/African American	Childhood sexual abuse[a]	Heterosexual
Lily	Urban	17	Latina/Colombian and White	Almost raped	Heterosexual
Liz	Suburban	17	White	Childhood sexual molestation[b]	Heterosexual
Magda	Urban	18	Black/Caribbean	No	Heterosexual
Megan	Suburban	15	White	Childhood sexual molestation[b]	Bisexual
Melissa	Urban	16	White	No	Lesbian
Nikki	Suburban	16	White	Hit by boyfriend	Heterosexual
Paulina	Urban	17	White	Attacked by a friend	Heterosexual
Rochelle	Urban	18	Black/African American	Hit by boyfriend	Heterosexual
Sophie	Suburban	16	White	No	Heterosexual
Trisha	Urban	18	White	Childhood sexual abuse[a]	Heterosexual
Zoe	Suburban	17	White	No	Heterosexual

a. "Abuse" refers to ongoing violation over significant periods of time.
b. "Molestation" refers to a single instance or several individual instances of violation.

violence; others told of crushed hopes and broken hearts.[7] This
pertinent information is incorporated into the case descriptions in
the next three chapters.

Recruitment provided ready evidence of the silence about, and
silencing of, girls' sexual desire that feminist analyses have revealed
in society at large. In phone conversations several suburban mothers expressed concern about how tapes of their daughters speaking
about sexual desire might incriminate them or ruin their chances
of success in the future; one mother consented, contingent upon
my agreement to destroy the tape at the end of the study. One
urban girl's father, a girl whom I later discovered from some of the
participants had wanted to be involved, not only refused to provide
consent but berated me for wanting to speak with his daughter
about her sexuality and accused me of being immoral.

Cultural factors also surfaced in the recruitment process. I spoke
to several Asian girls on the phone who said in hushed tones that
they were too busy to be in the study or that they simply did not
want to participate. A Chinese colleague I consulted about this
phenomenon expressed little surprise, explaining that since it is
anathema for Asian girls to recognize or acknowledge their own
sexuality, the idea of speaking to anyone, never mind a white
woman in school, was out of the question. One Indian mother kept
assuring me pleasantly that the permission form was in the mail; it
took a few weeks for me to figure out that this was her polite way of
asking me to leave her and her daughter alone.

The girls themselves knew how dangerous it could be even to
consider saying what they knew about desire: Any awareness or
acknowledgment of their own sexual desire could be associated
with being thought of as "bad." In one phone call a mother told me
her daughter not only did not want to participate but had actually
found the letter from me addressed to her mother and hidden it.

When the mother discovered what had happened, she asked her daughter why she had taken mail not addressed to her. The girl told her mother in unusually vociferous tones that she did not want to participate. At first, I accepted this refusal, but something about the strength of this girl's response bothered me. I called again, and she happened to answer the phone. She asked me why she had been chosen; she wanted to know how I "knew about" her, that is, how I had gotten wind of her bad reputation. I explained that she was selected randomly and that I knew nothing about her at all. She agreed to participate, and my interview with her was one of the most lively and complex in the study. Several girls mentioned in interviews that they would not want their teachers knowing what they were telling me about themselves, because they feared they might be thought less of by these adult women in their lives. Given the girls' vigilance about protecting themselves and their fears of judgment, I was aware that they could not easily volunteer the information I was asking them to share and had to acknowledge to them that my enterprise was not only unusual but in most cases taboo. These recruitment experiences heightened my awareness that I needed to provide evidence to these girls that I was not judging them, as well as opportunities for them to evaluate my trustworthiness.

HOW I ASKED

Prior to the interviews, I met with the girls in each school in a group, to explain my research and, I hoped, to begin a conversation with them about their own sexual pleasure and sexual desire in an explicitly public forum. Thinking that they might not feel comfortable asking or telling me things in a one-on-one interview, I figured that as a group they might feel more empowered to challenge me or ask me questions. I was especially conscious that the girls in the urban school had been the subjects of studies in which white women and men asked them about their sexual behavior— do you have sexual intercourse? how often? with whom? under what conditions?—and I wanted to let them know that this study was going to be different. Ironically, it was in the suburban school that this group approach succeeded. Almost all of the suburban participants attended. After discussing confidentiality, a concept they were familiar with from their family-life education classes and took seriously, they asked me what I meant by desire, why I was doing this study, why they in particular had been selected, what I planned to do with the information they gave me.

In contrast, the group meeting at the urban school was a complete flop. Most of the girls who agreed to be in the study said they would come to the group, but fewer than half actually came, and no one wanted to ask any questions. The girls scattered around an empty classroom, a few sitting together. It was an extremely uncomfortable situation for all. I explained what I was doing, why I was asking these questions, and how they were selected; I assured them of confidentiality and my willingness to answer any questions they wanted to ask. Two of the girls affirmed my suggestion that desire may be a part of girls' experience that is not talked about with knowing looks and bubbling laughter. After several attempts to engage them in a discussion, it was obvious that it wasn't going to happen. They all agreed to set up times for individual interviews and vanished as soon as it was reasonable to leave.

I was puzzled about this partial and silent group. Why hadn't the others shown up? Why hadn't the ones who did said anything? I decided to ask them about it in the individual interviews. One after another, the girls explained that they did not show up or that they did not speak, because they did not want to reveal themselves in front of one another. By contrast, with varying levels of comfort they revealed themselves to me in the privacy of the individual

interview, what Trisha called a "one-on-one type of conversation."
They did not trust their words, their experiences, even their questions about a study of girls' desire *in front of the other girls,* so fearful were they of saying something about themselves that could be
used against them. Trisha distinguished safe from unsafe spaces for
girls to speak about their sexuality:

> I don't feel comfortable saying it in front of them, because I just,
> I always have the feeling, you know, they're gonna, oh, guess what
> she said in there, you know, just kinda makes you feel uneasy. If I
> don't know the person, I don't talk to them, I won't say any-
> thing . . . if they were with their friends, they would have no
> problem talking about it, it was because we were all in the same
> room. We know each other, but it's just not something that they
> want everybody else to know about. Like I said before, they
> wanna keep it within their friends and nobody else is to know.

With the urban girls, the girls whom I had most wanted to "em-
power" by giving them a chance to outnumber me and thus tip the
balance of power in their favor, I learned that speaking to one
another outside the safety of intimate friendships seemed to be far
more treacherous than speaking to an unknown adult. They believed confidentiality would be maintained by the interviewer but
not by their peers. I had underestimated how dangerous talking
and knowing about desire in the presence of other girls could be.

My method of data collection was a one-on-one, semiclinical
individual interview. Rather than a strict protocol that ensures that
each girl is asked exactly the same questions in the same way, this
method utilizes clinical principles of asking a question, listening to
the answer, and then asking the next question in response to what
the girl is saying within a set protocol of key questions. A traditional survey would not have provided the opportunity to collect the rich, nuanced, complex information that the interview

relationship makes possible in order to understand a phenomenon of human experience (Reinharz, 1992).[8] In addition, survey instruments have been shown to be an ineffective means for collecting written female narratives of sexual experience (Brodkey & Fine, 1998).

Primarily, I asked girls to offer descriptions of and to tell stories, or narratives, about specific experiences they had had with their own sexuality, including their own sexual desire, pleasure, and fantasies. I asked specifically how their bodies figured in these experiences and also if they had had "bad" experiences. I chose to avoid asking the "usual" questions that girls, especially girls in the urban school, had come to expect. I was aware that when asked to speak about sexual desire, some girls would disclose experiences of sexual abuse or violence to me. Some girls who chose to tell me about childhood sexual abuse had never spoken about it before, or had spoken and found their words essentially ignored by the women in their lives. At the outset, I made arrangements to refer these girls to therapists. I made these referrals on several occasions.

Some of the most important, even "interruptive," questions I asked the girls were about their bodies; since I could not expect them to volunteer this information, I asked them to develop the story line of how their bodies were and were not involved in their experiences with their sexuality. It was clear that acknowledging their bodies was new and different for most of them, interesting and helpful for some, confusing or strange for others, and impossible or simply irrelevant for still others. Every girl I interviewed said that no adult woman had ever talked to her before about sexual desire and pleasure "like this," that is, so overtly, specifically, or in such depth. More than half of them said they had never spoken about their sexual desire and pleasure with anyone. I was aware that if I was going to ask girls to break the silence about their desire, to talk about aspects of their experience that, as they reported, no other adult had been or perhaps seemed willing to hear, I had to be prepared to respond to whatever feelings the interview raised for them—distress, joy, curiosity, fear. I had to be prepared for how the connection between me and an individual girl would shape what she did and, in a few cases, did not say to me and what I did (and did not) ask her. I wish I had been more prepared for how their words and silences would affect me.

HOW THEY DID (NOT) ANSWER

Given that there was an element of self-selection in the process (not all girls who were approached agreed to participate), I was surprised by the range of reactions I encountered in the individual interviews with these girls. Some girls reacted as I expected: enthused, even relieved, to have an opportunity to speak, puzzle about, and explore this aspect of their experience with an interested adult. A number of girls in both schools talked with me for almost two hours. One girl came to find me a few days after her interview, to thank me and tell me that "everything had changed and it was 100 percent better" with her boyfriend because of the insights she had gained into herself through our interview; I heard that he had tried to find me to thank me, too.

Yet a few of the girls expressed excitement or real interest on the phone or in a brief personal contact and then remained reticent or even silent in the interview. The threat of silence looms large in any interview. Although race and class may have been important factors (Ward & Taylor, 1992), in the sense that some of the girls of color or poor girls may have said what they believed I as a white, middle-class adult wanted to hear (Taylor, Gilligan, & Sullivan, 1995), many of the girls in the urban school enthusiastically engaged in the interview, despite or perhaps because of these differences between us (Way, 1998). Similarly, a number of girls in the suburban school may have resisted my inquiry because of the similarities between us. Some of the suburban girls refused to answer most of my questions while claiming they wanted to remain in the study; others smiled and answered politely while not really saying much. I am sure that religion and other cultural factors powerfully shaped the narratives these and other girls chose to tell or not tell me.

I encountered different forms of silence. Angela wanted to participate, yet found it difficult to do so. She said she "never really talk[s] about" sexuality and feels it is a "touchy subject." She told me enough about her experience for me to know that she did not feel desire—"I don't know about ever, but for right now"—and did not wish to discuss it. I felt it would have been cruel to continue the interview and ask her to tell me a narrative about sexual desire, as if I had not heard what she had just said. She did confide in me that she had been sexually abused on several occasions but did not want to talk about it. Throughout the book, I explore the possible impact that a girl's history of sexual abuse may have had on her experiences with sexuality and on her participation in the study.

One girl who said little had had few experiences with romantic relationships or sexuality. Jordan, an athletic white girl in the suburban school, described having fun with a friend while watching boys drive by her stoop in cars, but her sexuality did not appear to be an active part of her current life. A few girls were clearly offended by my questions and became angry; they resisted what they obviously experienced as my intrusion into their experience or "business." Amy, a white girl in the suburban school who sat stiffly and did not look me in the eye, offered one-word answers; Honore, a black girl from the Caribbean in the urban school, thought I "must be a pervert" to want to know the answers to such questions. Interestingly, despite my suggestion that we stop the interview, Honore did offer answers, though relatively brief ones,

to my questions. Another girl was obviously ambivalent: Beverly, a
slim and sharp black girl in the urban school, did talk to me, but
her responses were extraordinarily sparse. In answering my questions she never told elaborate stories, though she was quite frank
and asked me a lot of questions about sexuality. I was sure that she
experienced sexual desire. Given what I now know about the dangers girls perceive in acknowledging their desire to an adult, it is
likely that these girls did not trust me. It is possible that sexual
desire is not a part of their lived experience. It is possible that these
girls were shy, not "big talkers" in general. It is possible that talking
about their sexuality was such a new experience that the words
were simply hard to find.

HOW I LISTENED

"One of the primary ways—probably *the* primary way—human
beings make sense of their experience is by casting it in a narrative
form" (Gee, 1985, p. 11; see also Plummer, 1995). And there are
myriad approaches to making sense of the narratives these girls
told me: one could, for instance, compare girls' stories about sexuality to boys' (Moore & Rosenthal, 1993; Martin, 1996), identify
the genre of story that girls tell (Thompson, 1995), or highlight
and detail the sociological contours of girls' sexuality through
ethnographic methods (Stern, 1994). But I am aware that these
girls told *me* their narratives. As a result, the narratives necessarily
incorporate me and my questions about desire as well as what the
girls had to tell. Our brief relationship forms the context in which
these narratives were told. To learn something about the context in
which the experiences reflected in these narratives were lived, I
asked the girls specifically about how girls' sexuality has been
talked about in their families, in religious institutions, and at
school; I also asked whether they talked with their parents, peers,

boyfriends, or teachers about their own sexual feelings. Not only did this information create a backdrop for listening to them speak about their experiences, it also highlighted the paucity of safe spaces they had for exploring their questions, thoughts, fears, or hopes about their sexuality.

At the heart of my analyses of these narratives are two perspectives, individual and societal. Girls' psyches and bodies do not exist in a vacuum. A girl's personal and family history shapes her experience with desire. Her personal development, her developing sense of herself and how she feels about herself, her developing body and how she and others respond to it also come into play, as do her experiences with romantic and peer relationships. Any experiences with sexual violence or abuse, and her own response as well as that of others to such experiences, may further affect her sexual desire. The specific social contexts of a girl's life, such as her friends and the ethos of her school and her community, are likely to bear upon her sexual choices and the meanings that she makes of her behavior, thoughts, and feelings. That is, girls' experiences with their own sexual desire are highly individualistic. At the same time, girls' descriptions of the specific heterosexual relationships in which they experience their sexual feelings illustrate the different and consistent ways that the institution of heterosexuality "operates" in the lives of individual girls. My approach, then, was to embed a psychological analysis of individual girls' experiences with sexual desire within the specific context of each girl's life and also within a feminist understanding of various social constructions of female adolescent sexuality.

In analyzing these narratives, I adopted a variation of the Listening Guide, a systematic psychodynamic method for interpreting narrative data. Much like a therapist listening to a client, this method captures the multilayered meanings of what a girl says and how she says it. The method was developed originally by Lyn

Brown, Carol Gilligan, and others for listening to narratives of choice and relational conflict (Brown et al., 1989; Brown & Gilligan, 1992); it has been adapted subsequently to answer a variety of research questions about relational experiences (e.g., Brown, 1999; Tolman, 2001; Way, 2001). This method has been called a "voice-based" analysis, because its central feature is systematic attention to the voice of the person interviewed and the various "voices" or themes that compose the narratives. It was developed as an explicitly feminist method in that it enables the researcher to "bring to the surface the 'undercurrent' of female voices and visions as it filters through an androcentric culture" (Brown & Gilligan, 1990, p. 3). It also embraces the relational nature of this kind of interview and interpretive work, not seeking "objectivity" or "avoidance of bias," but acknowledging the ways that making meaning is a relational process. This analytic tool meets the challenge of listening to desire narratives; clinical methods for interpreting pregnant pauses, uncontrollable giggles, or a sudden inarticulateness are part and parcel of the analysis; the obligation to theorize these silences and nonverbal expressions is embedded in the method.[9] It also forces the interviewer to attend to his or her own responses as a source of information. In this case I had to clarify my own ideas and feelings and appreciate how they did and did not correspond to the words of various girls.

This method is distinctly different from traditional methods of coding qualitative data, in that one listens to, rather than categorizes or quantifies, the text of the interview (see On Methodology for a detailed explanation of this type of analysis). In analyzing narrative data, the researcher rarely finds "hard facts" to report, unlike with other forms of data, such as surveys or experiments—though these, in fact, have their own often unacknowledged limits in generating "hard facts" as well (Rabinowitz & Weseen, 2001). In listening, another person is always engaged in the act of making an interpretation about what he or she has heard. And so I do not simply report what these girls said; I present my interpretation, which is supported by evidence from the texts of the interviews.[10] In writing up the cases these interpretive practices yield, researchers commonly include large amounts of text from interviews, so that the reader can evaluate the interpretation presented and also consider alternative and additional interpretations.

A question often raised about any form of social science research, especially about sexuality, is how reliable the reports provided by participants really are. More specifically, how do I know that these girls did not, in essence, lie or make up their answers? This is a complex question that has received quite a bit of attention. In survey research, some standard practices include asking the same question in different ways and comparing answers to evaluate the validity of responses. In longitudinal research, some believe it is possible to evaluate what a respondent says about the same question (for example, "When did you first have intercourse?") over time. In this study, however, worrying about the extent to which these reports mirror reality misses the point; what I was trying to learn was how girls themselves make sense of their own feelings and experiences (Luttrell, 1997). The "face validity" of their stories, the extent to which they ring true, is powerful. Their frequent departure from the stock, socially acceptable "it just happened" story and the complexity of the experiences they describe lend their stories credibility.

Because it is clear from this study and from other studies of female adolescent sexuality that all girls are denied safe spaces for their own sexual feelings, my primary goal in organizing the girls' narratives was to highlight their commonality as girls coming of age in a patriarchal society. I report the results of this analysis in the next section of this chapter and in Chapters 3, 4, and 5. In addition, because of the potential differences in how the urban girls and the suburban girls narrate their experiences of sexual desire, I report in Chapter 6 on the results of several analyses that I have done to address the question of the differential experiences of the girls in these two groups.[11]

HEARING AN EROTIC VOICE

In her essay "Uses of the Erotic: The Erotic as Power," Audre Lorde (1984) described what she called the power of the erotic as "the *yes* within ourselves, our deepest cravings," and "how fully and acutely we can feel in the doing." She formulates the erotic as "the sensual—those physical, emotional, and psychic expressions of what is deepest and strongest and richest within each of us . . . the passions of love, in its deepest meanings" (p. 55). When I listened to these girls describe their sexual desire, they expressed the power, intensity, and urgency of their feelings, which resonated with Lorde's description of the erotic. This resonance led me to call how girls speak about their sexual desire an *erotic voice*. All but three of these girls could and do speak in an erotic voice—that is, do feel embodied sexual desire, can describe these feelings and, when asked, can include them in their narratives about their sexual experiences.

I was struck by the discrepancy between how adolescent girls are generally portrayed, studied, and discussed and what these girls said. The belief that girls' sexuality is focused exclusively on relationships and that their own sexual feelings are nonexistent or irrelevant did not match these girls' descriptions of desire. While some said the feeling of desire leads them into adventure and explorations of themselves, they also said that it can lead them into risky situations and thus is sometimes a warning. Sexual desire is, for these girls, a feature of being in a relationship with someone else and, in so doing, knowing themselves. These girls made a key distinction, however, between their sexual desire and their wish for a relationship. While their feelings of sexual desire most often arise in relationships, they are not the same as or a substitute for wanting a relationship.

What comes across powerfully in the narratives of the girls who said they feel sexual desire is that they experience it as having an unmistakable power and intensity. Inez knows she is feeling desire when "my body says yes yes yes yes." Lily calls feeling desire "amazing." Rochelle feels it "so, so bad . . . I wanna have sex so bad, you know"; she adds, "you just have this feeling, you just have to get rid of it." Liz explains: "I just wanted to have sex with him really badly and I just, and we just took off our bathing suits really fast [she laughs] and um, it was almost like really rushed and really quick." For Barbara it is "very strong . . . an overwhelming longing" and "a wicked [strong] urge." Paulina's heart "would really beat fast"; she is "extremely aware of every, every touch and everything." Alexandra speaks of being "incredibly attracted" to her friend. Jane calls the power of her desire "demanding" and says, "the feelings are so strong inside you that they're just like ready to burst." These direct acknowledgments of the power of sexual desire came from girls of different geography, race, and sexual orientation.

Some girls also conveyed the intensity of their desire by the strength of their voiced resistance to it; in response to her body's "yes yes yes yes," Inez explains that "my mind says no no no, you stop kissing him." Cassandra evidences the strength and the urgency of her feeling in narrating what she does not want to do, "stop": "he just like stopped all of a sudden and I was like what are you doing? 'cause I didn't want to stop at all"; she says that for her, desire is "powerful." Lily contrasts not being "in the mood to do anything . . . because I just have all my clothes on . . . because it's just too inconvenient" with the power of her desire when she feels it, "once in a while": "even though it's inconvenient for me, sometimes I just have this feeling, well I just don't care, if I have to put my pantyhose on or not," the power of her desire overriding the normally paramount concern she has for maintaining a proper appearance.

Whereas these girls spoke about feelings in their stomachs, shoulders, necks, and legs, as well as sensations all over their bodies, Megan was one of the few girls to connect her desire to her vagina. Very few girls named the sexual parts of their bodies in these interviews about their sexual desire. Megan speaks of knowing she is feeling sexual desire for boys because of what she feels in her body; as she says, "kind of just this feeling, you know? Just this feeling inside my body . . . my vagina starts to kinda like act up and it kinda like quivers and stuff, and um, like I'll get like tingles and and you can just feel your hormones [laughs] doing something weird, and you just, you get happy and you just get, you know, restimulated kind of and it's just, and oh! Oh!" and "your nerves feel good."

HEARING DILEMMAS OF DESIRE

In phenomenological research, the point is not to test hypotheses but to develop an understanding of experience. When I began this research, however, I did harbor a hypothesis. I believed that the disjuncture between my own experience of powerful, physical sexual desire as an adolescent girl and the "missing discourse" about girls' sexual desire in the literature was simply an artifact of previous studies, in which no one ever asked girls about this part of their lives. When I set out to provide girls with an opportunity to talk about their experiences of sexual desire, I imagined that I would be tapping into a secret life of girls' sexual pleasure. I thought girls would confirm my guess that they experienced sexual excitement, power, and joy in relation to their desire, even if they usually kept that dangerous information to themselves.

As girls' descriptions of their desire illustrate, they did indeed experience powerful sexual feelings. But the secret life of sexuality that I had imagined did not materialize. What I heard instead was how the social dilemma that societal constructions of female and male sexuality set up for girls, a choice between their sexual feelings or their safety, was experienced as a personal dilemma by them. Given that this dilemma is framed *as if* it were an individual rather than a social problem—if a girl has desire, she is vulnerable to personal physical, social, material, or relational consequences— it is in a way not especially surprising that girls would experience their desire and these resulting difficulties as their own personal problem. Although girls themselves did not use the word "dilemma" in narrating their experiences, they described dilemmas and private efforts to solve what they perceived to be personal problems, since talking about and thus revealing their own desire is itself taboo.

This dilemma of desire takes different forms for different girls, with certain consequences or potential bad outcomes more evident or salient to some than to others. In telling their stories of desire, and of not having desire, these girls articulated the various consequences they were aware their sexual desire could invite. Their stories illuminate how dealing with desire makes important normative adolescent developmental processes difficult. Specifically, these adolescents reveal how their experiences of desire get in the way of their relationships with peers, romantic partners, parents, and other important adults in their lives. They tell stories elaborating how their desire challenges their ability to develop identities as "good," acceptable, moral, and normal women, and how confusing it is to develop a sexual identity that leaves their sexuality out. Their desire narratives show how the girls juggle and at the same time integrate the logistics of being an adolescent and the belief systems of their religions, their cultures, and their communities, including the specific communities of their schools.

Ellen feared that her own desire could lead to risking pregnancy, a fear intensified by her perception that she must choose between her own sexuality and the material consequence of losing her chance of getting an education as a way out of poverty. Kim internalized her father's stated belief that a desiring girl is more likely to be considered at fault by others if she is raped. Jane described her guilt at having betrayed her boyfriend by kissing another boy, her confusion about her own culpability in this choice, and her fear about how her boyfriend, her mother, or her sisters would judge her if they found out. Lily acted on her desire and was thrown out of her mother's house. Nikki's stories reflected the not unlikely possibility of male violence. Emily, confused by the social mandate to appear sexy, was afraid of being used. Magda did not want her sexual feelings to prevent her from fulfilling her immigrant mother's expectations that she would be the first in her family to go to college. Megan worried that her desire would lead her to lose control of herself and make choices she might later regret. Zoe found waiting for a boy to figure out and take the initiative to satisfy her desire frustrating but the only possibility she could imagine for herself. Sophie managed to work around her perception that girls were not supposed to want or initiate sexual encounters. Julia believed that if she were to act on her desire, she would be considered "just as promiscuous" as the girls whose behavior she herself frowned upon. Melissa was highly aware that her desire for girls could lead to rejection and violence as well as constant disappointment. Barbara talked about the risk of embarrassment and frustration when her feelings were not returned or when someone considered her "perverted" because of her desires. Charlene was afraid that her desire would make her seem like a "slut."

A few girls were able to skirt, resist, or even transform such denial and demonizing of their desire in some contexts but experienced their desire as a dilemma in other situations. For instance, while Megan resisted the formulation of her desire as problematic in heterosexual relationships, her desire for girls was "blocked" by her awareness of homophobia and compulsory heterosexuality. Eugenia felt safe as a desiring girl in a long-term monogamous heterosexual relationship but worried about judging herself and being judged by friends and family as "bad" because of sexual desires that did not fit neatly into that specific configuration. Beverly related her concern about hurting a boy's feelings or having to deal with his violent reaction if she had told him that he could not please her. Virtually all of the girls spoke about how girls who act on their desire leave themselves open to getting a bad reputation, though not all of them were worried about this outcome for themselves. None of these examples is exclusive to any single girl; even the few girls who were aware of and fully rejected the sexual double standard and refused to accept the conditions that make their own sexual feelings appear to be "the problem," even the girls who articulated the positive possibilities that may result from acting on the basis of their sexual desire and talked about their sexuality in more nuanced and complex ways, could not shake the shadows of these unrelenting threats of what can happen to a desiring girl.

These remain reasonable fears, *under current gender arrangements.* Not being able to find a comfortable fit for desire in their sexual identities or their social and relational terrains made it hard or sometimes impossible for these girls to be aware of or feel, let alone accept or validate, their own sexual feelings. What came through all of their stories of desire was how their acute and astute

awareness of the dangers associated with their sexuality, the denigration of their sexual feelings, and their expectations about boys'
sexuality led most of them to consider the source of danger to be
their own sexuality. In effect, these girls described how social
processes and meanings that clearly originate outside the body end
up incorporated into its physiological demeanor and both unconscious and conscious behaviors (Grosz, cited in Fausto-Sterling,
2000, p. 23). As Lynn Philips (2000) has so succinctly put it, "we do
not simply live inside our cultures. In many ways our cultures live
inside of us" (p. 17).

Embedded in the stories about desire that these girls told was a
multitude of strategies, more and less conscious, for negotiating
the tricky terrain of their own sexual feelings. It turned out that my
question about desire was often a question the girls themselves had
already been struggling with in some form, always in silence and
isolation, outside any relationship with other girls or adult women,
sometimes consciously and sometimes not. For some, this question was like a low-grade fever, making them a little bit uncomfortable, but not really a major problem. For other girls, the question
of their desire was crucial, an important clue to their identity that
remained elusive for them (Raymond, 1994). As girls tried to sort
out their feelings on their own, the question of their sexual desire
remained both unspoken and unresolved until we began talking
about it. Sometimes the question itself had never been articulated.
Instead, they essentially lived the question.

Among this group of girls, I discerned three distinct ways of
talking about the dilemmas of desire.[12] In Chapter 3, we will listen
to girls who reported not feeling desire or being unsure, having
what I call "silent bodies" and "confused bodies." Since this analysis
assumes that having sexual feelings is to be expected, we will consider why they said that they did not feel desire. In Chapters 4 and
5, we will listen to girls in the study who did say they felt desire. We

will track how they responded to or dealt with their sexual feelings, how they understood these feelings, and in what ways these feelings informed their sexual experiences and romantic relationships. We will be listening especially to the interplay between their psyches and their bodies.

Girls who said they felt sexual desire deal with the dilemma of that desire in two ways. Chapter 4 elaborates strategies of resisting sexual desire. One such approach is for girls to shut down their feelings, to defuse and delimit their desire, that is, to disappear desire. Another approach is to be ambivalent about desire. Neither denying themselves desire nor embracing it unequivocally, these girls err on the side of danger, without completely sacrificing pleasure, living in constant fear that they are crossing into territory that leaves them completely vulnerable and without any recourse to protection. Chapter 5 covers girls who describe a sense of entitlement to their sexual desire. Some of them describe openly engaging in a micropolitics of their own desire. Yet with rare exception, these girls also identify and deal with their desire as a personal dilemma; their solution is to create safe spaces for sexual desire within their social and relational circumstances.

For over a hundred years, feminist scholars have offered extensive social analysis of the politics of women's sexuality: the powerful and persistent tension between sexual danger and sexual pleasure that, while experienced differentially by individual women, is an involuntary aspect of being a woman in a patriarchal society. Ken Plummer (1995) tells us, "Sexual stories ooze through the political stream . . . power is not a simple attribute or a capacity, but a flow of negotiations and shifting outcomes . . . *Sexual stories flow through this power. The power to tell a story, or indeed not to tell a story, under the conditions of one's own choosing, is part of the political process*" (p. 26). Before moving on to the girls' stories of desire, I want to emphasize that their personal stories serve to refract the larger societal denial of and ambivalence about female sexuality. Most girls were not conscious of this political dimension of their desire, but the ones who were embraced what they realized was their hard-won sexual subjectivity defiantly and fiercely. All of their stories reflect their difficult and, for the most part, isolated juggling of multiple and often contradictory mandates, deeply important relationships, and real and layered difficulties and worries that are part of their experiences of sexuality.

It was heartbreaking to see, on [the girls' return from having had their clitorises removed], how passive Tashi had become. No longer cheerful, or impish. Her movements, which had always been graceful, and quick with the liveliness of her personality, now became merely graceful. Slow. Studied. This was true even of her smile, which she never seemed to offer you without considering it first. That her soul had been dealt a mortal blow was plain to anyone who dared look into her eyes.

—Alice Walker, *Possessing the Secret of Joy*

Embodiment is the experiential sense of living in and through our bodies. It is premised on the ability to feel our bodily sensations, one of which is sexual desire. While the body is the site for the experience of, though not necessarily the incitement of, sexual desire, no one lives in a vacuum. Sexual desire may be in part a bodily process regulated by hormones, but being embodied—feeling and knowing the information that comes to us from the world in which we live through the sensations and reactions that occur in our bodies—is in part a social process that shapes our experience of sexual desire (Basson, 2000; Tolman, 2000; Heiman, 2001). In this sense, sexual desire is socially constructed. As Gayle Rubin (1984) has so eloquently explained, "this does not mean the biological capacities are not prerequisites for human sexuality. It does mean that human sexuality is not comprehensible in purely biological terms" (p. 276).

It was a relatively small proportion of the girls in this study who said that they had never recognized sexual feelings in themselves. If we start with the assumption that embodied sexual desire is a normative and anticipated part of adolescent development, that we live in bodies that are and need to be sentient, then an explanation is required for the absence of these feelings in girls' descriptions of their romantic and sexual relationships and experiences. Why would a girl report that she does *not* feel sexual desire, or that she may be unsure about it? Although it is possible that girls might be reluctant to relay such sensitive, even forbidden, thoughts to a stranger, an adult woman who is different from or similar to them, the complexity of the stories these girls tell strongly suggests their veracity. They truly have not felt or consciously ever recognized or acknowledged feelings in their bodies that they associate with or call sexual desire. They are dissociated from their desire.

DISEMBODIMENT AND DISCONNECTION: HALLMARKS OF FEMININITY

Dissociation—the psychoanalytic concept of a loss of knowledge, memory, or physical or emotional feelings—is an outcome, as well as a psychological red flag, of trauma (Herman, 1992). One form of dissociation is disembodiment, a disconnection or splitting off of the body and its feelings from the apprehension of the psyche. In describing how victims of sexual abuse become disembodied, Leslie Young (1992) considered how disembodiment may serve as a form of protection: "Whether by choice or blind necessity, the survivor [of sexual violation] can forget or wall off memories of traumatic events by consigning them to the body, and excluding all bodily sensations and intense affects from consciousness. But such a solution entails an enormous sacrifice, since it also makes problematic experiencing the everyday pleasures, sensations, and comforts of human embodiment" (p. 93). I would add knowledge or information to Young's litany of the sacrifices inherent in disembodiment: knowledge about relationships and the sociopolitical landscape in which one is living (Tolman & Debold, 1993). What traumatic experiences might the girls who have silent or confused bodies have experienced that could result in this kind of disembodiment or lack of clarity about their sexual feelings? Sexual abuse? While one of the girls in this group described explicit sexual abuse, the others did not; in addition, not all of the girls in the study who described sexual abuse or violation have silent or confused bodies. It is possible that the others did not recall or chose not to tell me about such experiences.[1] Another possible framework for understanding these girls' stories can be found in feminist theories about sexual violence, female adolescent development, and femininity, which are embedded in and produced by the institution of heterosexuality.

Sexual violence is now a well-documented feature of girls' and women's lives, and it can severely affect their sexuality and their relationship with their own bodies (Kaplan, 1991; Herman, 1992; Young, 1992). It is not only the experience but the constant *threat* and not always conscious *fear* of various forms of sexual violation, including sexual harassment, rape, and unwanted sexual attention, that constitute a constant, low-grade trauma for girls and women.[2] Such experiences are so frequent that they are, in some sense, everyday violations (Tolman, 2000). I was reminded recently of this ever-present sense of being vulnerable that women experience when I was showering and changing in a locker room after the gym I was in had officially closed. The entire time I was aware of the man who was cleaning the foyer (who had always been kind and polite to me), planning how I would avoid being attacked or raped and how I would defend myself if I were. My pulse rate was up, my body was tense, and I was afraid, though I had no explicit reason for being so.[3]

Other fears associated with the dangers and vulnerabilities of female sexuality under patriarchy may also be experienced in this way. For instance, the terror some girls feel about the possibility of pregnancy or the risk of contracting HIV, and the ensuing perceived and often truly ruinous consequences, could constitute such an incessant source of trauma, as could the profound worry that one's education and material existence could be in jeopardy (Fordham, 1993). These threats may affect girls in different ways, depending on their social, familial, and community circumstances. Not having access to or accurate information about reproductive choices or protection may be more of a problem for girls who live in poor communities than for girls in middle-class homes (Fine, 1988). Historically, black women have been more vulnerable to rape (Wyatt, 1997) and have had to deal with the complexities of checkered justice in their communities in its aftermath (Fine, 1984). There are cultural twists and turns in the social control of female sexuality that may intensify or highlight particular dangers and subsequent fears for individual girls (Asch & Fine, 1992; Hurtado, 1996, 1998; Espin, 1999).

Dissociation from sexual desire echoes patterns of female psychosocial development theorized and researched by feminist psychologists. This work has tracked how, at the threshold of adolescence, girls face demands to conform to norms of femininity,[4] essentially becoming socialized into their proper place as women in a patriarchal system. Taking up these norms—not being disruptive, not inciting or engaging in conflict, meeting the needs of others at the expense of their own—often creates a disparity between what girls are supposed to think, feel, and know (that girls can be anything they want; that Daddy hurt Mommy by accident) and what girls actually experience and observe (there has been no female president; when Daddy was angry, he hit Mommy so hard she got a black eye). At this moment, girls experience what Carol Gilligan and Lyn Brown called a "doubling of voice and vision" (Gilligan, 1990, p. 506; Brown, 1991). Girls are forced to make a tragic choice: to capitulate to norms of femininity and dissociate from their true thoughts and feelings or to resist this framing of who they are and the "reality" in which they live. The fear that if they continue to "know what they know," they will be inviting conflict into their relationships with peers and with those who have the authority to say what reality is (including their teachers, their mothers, and other adults in their lives) can lead girls to solve this painful discrepancy by dissociating from their authentic thoughts and feelings. To resist openly is to risk punitive social, psychological, or even physically violent repercussions for disrupting the smooth waters of relationships as they are organized within patriarchal constructions of reality.

Other feminists have considered how absolutely central the social constructions of femininity and masculinity are to our experiences of our bodies. Sandra Bartky and Susan Bordo both theorize that girls and women produce and at the same time experience femininity as a form of embodiment, making the point that girls and women "become" feminine not only in their behavior but also in their bodies, in response to particular expectations about what is appropriate, normal, and acceptable female comportment, appearance, and sexuality. Bordo claims that "the discipline and normalization of the female body, perhaps the only gender oppression that exercises itself, although to different degrees and in different forms, across age, race, class, and sexual orientation, has to be acknowledged as an amazingly durable and flexible strategy of social control" (1993b, p. 91). Because the absence of active embodied sexual desire is a hallmark of femininity, one specific developmental dilemma for girls in adolescence is the dilemma of desire. Psychologically, socialization into and internalization of norms of femininity associated with the female body create pressure for girls and women to "disconnect" from their bodies (Miller, 1976; Tolman, 1991; Tolman & Debold, 1993; Debold, 1996).

SILENT BODIES

A few of the girls in this study describe "silent bodies." Even in talking about explicitly sexual events, they show no sign of embodied sexual desire and convey no traceable erotic voice. Some of them speak specifically about an absence of embodied sexual feelings. The two narratives that follow exemplify the difference in both style and content in stories about having a silent body. Janine tells extraordinarily sparse narratives, pointing to crevices in her life into which desire threatened to find its way, while Jenny tells elaborate stories about romantic relationships and sexual experiences in which the absence of her desire is striking. The stories of these girls stand in stark contrast to the chorus of descriptions of sexual desire offered by most of the girls in this study. What Janine and Jenny do say, however, provides clues about how they have come to be dissociated from their sexual desire and what impact having a silent body has on them.

Janine: Disembodying Desires

Janine and I sit in an empty classroom. She is an extremely quiet girl who holds herself as if to appear small, with arms across her chest, so as not to be noticed. Sitting with her, I feel her fragility. Janine lives with her sisters and her father; her mother is currently living in Haiti, where Janine was born, though Janine has lived in the United States since childhood. She tells me about adolescent girls' lives in her Haitian community: "they hold you tight, you know. You never go out. You never do anything." When I ask her if she talks to her parents about sexuality, Janine tells me that her parents are "old-fashioned," meaning "they just don't want you to know . . . what could be happening to you when you're growing up. You just have to find out by yourself." In Haiti, she says, "they don't talk about this stuff." Despite or perhaps because of her silent body, Janine holds a critical perspective on this adult silence about girls' sexuality: Adults, she explains, "don't want you to get more educated, they just don't want you to know what is going on . . . if their parents don't tell them, I think that's why there's things happening to them. My opinion is, I don't think it's fair for the kids." Rather than preventing girls from developing sexually, the absence of talk about romantic relationships and sexuality sets them up for trouble, Janine thinks. She has picked up a lot of information about the potential dangers and devastating consequences of girls' sexual activity, by listening to what she is told by her elders and by witnessing these outcomes herself among her peers.

In a soft-spoken voice, Janine explains that she "never" feels sexual desire: "I don't have sexual feelings to know . . . I don't know anything about sexuality . . . I'm not curious. This is the problem, I'm not curious." Janine links desire with being "curious" and confides in me that not having curiosity about her sexuality is a "problem." In what she does say about her relationships, observations, and thoughts, explanations for why she might feel neither curiosity nor desire come to light. She feels pressure from her sisters to do well in school, which she has internalized. She is a very good student, earning mostly As and some Bs, and this identity is important to her. At the end of the interview, Janine and I have a lengthy conversation about going to college. Her sisters have warned Janine about the pitfalls awaiting her as she struggles to succeed; they tell her, "you have to protect yourself. You know, because there's a lot of dangers outside . . . to just be careful because there's a lot of violence outside, just watch out." Janine is a careful observer of her environment and can see for herself that her sisters' cautions have merit; she also values her sisters and does not want to upset them by disobeying them. To get a decent education and make something of herself, Janine puts her energies into being a "good" girl. For a young female Haitian immigrant living in poverty, that means avoiding the interpersonal and educational risks of exploring her sexuality.

It has been made clear to Janine that one of the most fearsome dangers is boys' sexuality. Having a boyfriend means exposing herself to a boy's sexual desires and the possibility of pregnancy, which would bring shame not only upon herself, she states, but also upon her family. When her sisters talk of danger, the possibility that her own sexual feelings could be a source of risk is not even mentioned; it seems to be simply assumed that her desire would not be a threat. She explains: "Why do I not have a boyfriend now is . . . I wanna take my time, and plus my sisters, they, they don't like that so, they don't like me to have a boyfriend, so and they trusting on me, so I just wanna be me, you know, I just don't wanna disappoint them." To keep them happy, she has had no boyfriends nor any sexual experiences. Having been deeply schooled in the importance of her ability to realize danger in order to avoid it, Janine has a clear vision of the problems that her sexuality might invite, and it appears that she avoids these difficulties by not "having feelings to know."

Given what she stands to lose—school, the love and respect of her sisters—it is no wonder that her body is silent. Janine says she does not think about sexuality because "I'm always busy in my school." It is hard to know if she is operating on the principle that such an exclusive focus on her education will keep her body silent and safe, or if she feels that her body's silence enables her concentration. Yet as we talk about desire, the notion that she has no desire because she is not curious comes undone; in fact, her curiosity emerges instantly. It seems that curiosity about sexuality, precursor to desire, floats not too far below the surface of her consciousness; it is also possible that the safe space of our interview created a new opportunity for her, igniting curiosity that she may not have felt previously. When I ask her what happens when girls in her school do sexual things, whether she has noticed what, if any, consequences there are when girls evidence sexuality, she laughs quietly and in the softest whisper says, "I don't know, you can tell me though." Her willingness to share what amounts to a secret and eager wish to learn about girls' sexuality and what really happens in its wake suggests that, while she is pleasing others and also staying safe, something important is missing for her.

Janine then tells an incredibly terse story about a time when she came close to having a conversation with a boy that could have been or become tinged with romance or desire; while her own desire never quite makes it into the story, it is indeed a story about desire. She tells me about how her sister chased him away, an act Janine explains as her sister "protecting me." However, she also says that her sister's vigilance in this situation made her feel "bad." While she says she wants to "take [her] time" in having a boyfriend, her story suggests that a part of her wants to find out what such relationships might be like. She seems to have no way to do so safely.

So what does Janine lose by living in a silent body? Janine describes an isolated and lonely life; she is "always by myself . . . all my friends, they always talk about boys and stuff, so they just don't talk to me no more . . . It's not that I don't like to talk about, it's just I don't have feelings to talk about." For Janine, having a silent body is associated with a rupture in her relationships with other girls, who are more engaged with their developing sexuality. I wonder what other feelings Janine may be sacrificing unintentionally in her effort to evade the dangers of desire. In spite of her silent body, she seems to struggle with a tension between herself—her curiosity, her wish for intimacy, her bashfully admitted wish to have a boyfriend—and her intense desire not to jeopardize either her relationship with her sisters or her understanding of herself as "good."

Janine speaks in a hushed voice; everything about her is subdued. I wonder if her demeanor is typical for Haitian girls, but I think of how her low energy contrasts with other Haitian girls I have interviewed. Janine is missing a certain vitality, a certain adolescent excitement, engagement, and intensity. She lacks strong feelings of passion or anger—or curiosity. Her voice recalls the adolescent girls of color Fine described in a study of poor, urban school dropouts (1986). Fine observed that many of the girls who did stay in school or were not pregnant were compliant, passive, and visibly depressed, perhaps trading in educational benefits for psychological and relational losses.

Janine's own critique of adult silence about girls' sexuality suggests that she may have misdiagnosed her "problem." Rather than having no curiosity, perhaps Janine has nowhere she can safely be conscious of and express her curiosity, not necessarily to act on or even to have sexual feelings but simply to wonder out loud, in some kind of relationship, about this part of her developing self. Without anyone to whom she can speak or who might respond to her questions and her wish to know about sexuality with answers rather than judgment or fear for her safety, Janine's curiosity appears not to exist, even to her. But Janine's puzzled observations about the absence of her curiosity, coupled with its instant appearance when the coast is cleared, indicate that these are feelings she herself is keenly missing. Curiosity that is dissociated from the self and has no relationship in which to flourish will not go away; like any dissociated knowledge, it will find an indirect, more protected way to express itself (Herman, 1992). Having no one with whom to talk nor any way to express her curiosity, to know what her own desire feels like and the various ways in which she could choose to express it or not, could ultimately put Janine at risk of having sex "just happen."

Jenny: How Being Good Can Be Bad for Girls

Jenny embodies the mainstream image of the "good" girl, both as a foil for the highly sexualized images of teen girls who are desirable but not desiring and as the contradictory fantasy of ongoing female adolescent innocence and purity despite well-defined breasts and full lips. Blonde, fair, and slim, she sits with her legs tensely crossed; she is polite and smiles at me often. Although Jenny has had a number of boyfriends during adolescence, and a number of sexual experiences, she tells me that she has never experienced feelings she calls sexual desire: "I actually really don't think I've ever like, wanted anything, like sexually that bad . . . I've never really felt that way before, so I don't know. I don't really think that there's anything that I would, I mean want." She goes on to explain, "I never had like sexual desire when I was in a relationship. Everything just sort of happened. I never really had to want it, 'cause it would always just be there." Echoing Janine, Jenny says, "I don't have any curiosity about [my sexuality]."

Jenny's descriptions of her experiences bring to life the sexual passivity that middle-class norms of femininity demand; her body is "appropriately" silent. She expresses a discomfort with and disinterest in masturbation different from most of the other girls, who explain that they usually have sexual feelings in relation to another person and so they want to respond only to that person. She confides that "I just have never really had the desire to do anything to myself . . . I don't think I would like doing it . . . if I'm with someone else, I allow them to do things to me." She is so accustomed to being the object of someone else's desire, "allow[ing] them to do things" to her, that exploring her sexuality on her own is not only a violation of femininity, it simply does not make sense.

She has told me that getting a bad reputation or getting called a slut happens "a lot" and is "awful." She has also noticed a confusing difference between boys and girls when it comes to the consequences of having sex outside a "long-term" relationship: "whenever a girl and a guy do something and people find out, it's always the girl that messed up . . . the guys like, get praise for it [she laughs] and the girl's sort of like called either a slut or just like has a bad reputation." When I ask her what she thinks about that, she says, "it's awful, I mean it's just as much the guy's fault as it is the girl's fault . . . we don't like make fun of the guys, I don't know why, it's just sort of a strange thing, it's just like the guys and girls make fun of the girls but no one makes fun of the guys." She notices also that there are few consequences for guys, even if they get someone pregnant or hurt someone's feelings, or a girl gets a reputation. When I ask her how she makes sense of this inequity, she answers, "I really don't know why it is." Like most of her peers, she herself judges other girls who have sexual experiences under the "wrong" circumstances in this negative way.

Her silent body is at the center of the tensions and vulnerabilities that organize the story she tells about the first time she had sexual intercourse, just days, it turns out, before this interview. Fresh in her mind, this experience was not what she had hoped it would be:

> We got alone together, and we started just basically fooling around and not doing many things. And then he asked me if I would have sex with him, and I said, well I didn't think I, I mean I said I wanted to wait, 'cause I didn't want to, I mean I like him, but I don't *like* him so, and I mean he sorta pushed it on me, but it wasn't like I absolutely said, "no, don't," I—it was sort of a

weird experience. I just, I sort of let it happen to me and never like really said no, I don't want to do this. I mean I said no, but I never, I mean I never stopped him from doing anything . . . I was so drunk. I don't really know what was in my mind. I mean I did think about it. I guess maybe I wanted to get it over with, I guess. You can say, 'cause all my friends basically have had sex, and I was one of the only ones who haven't. And I wanted to get it over with, although I wanted it to be special the first time . . .

I thought like, it's with a friend and it's not, I don't know but this is scary, he told me he was wearing a condom and, he wasn't, and so I was very scared [laughs], for about a week I thought I was pregnant [laughs] . . . So that's another reason I'm sort of, I was really upset too, because he lied to me and, told me, and so I don't know . . . I didn't enjoy it at all. It hurt. A lot. I don't know if you're supposed to enjoy your first time having sex . . . I don't know, I, I just, I mean I could've said no, I guess, and I could've pushed him off or whatever 'cause he, I mean, he wasn't, he's not the type of person who would like rape me or whatever. I mean, well, I don't think he's that way at all.

I was always like, well, I want to wait, and I want to be in a relationship with someone who I really like, and I want it to be a special moment and everything, and then it just sort of like happened so quickly . . . with someone who I didn't like and who I didn't want a relationship with and who didn't want a relationship with me, and it was just sort of, I don't, I don't know, I regret it . . . I wish I had just said no. I mean I could've, and I did for once but then I just let it go. And I wish that I had stood up for myself and really just like stood up and said "no, I don't want to do this. I'm not ready or I want it to be a different experience." I mean I could've told him exactly how I felt . . . I don't know why I didn't.

In this story, Jenny is unsure about how to understand her first experience with sexual intercourse. In listening to her, I too am unsure. At first, Jenny knows that she did not want to have sex with this boy, although she did not mind "fooling around." She in fact said no when the boy asked her if she would have sex with him. There is a clarity to her "no" that she substantiates with a set of compelling reasons for not wanting to have sex with this boy, including she "wanted to wait," she didn't "like him" or "want a relationship with him," and she wanted it to be "a special moment." After the fact, she continues to say that she had not wanted to have sex. She "regrets it." She "wish[es] that [she] had just said no." Given that her story is about a girl who said no, how can she or I understand what exactly happened and why?

Jenny's story reveals how social constructions of gendered sexuality and norms of femininity operated in tandem to yield this confusing experience. Just as she does not know why girls get reputations and boys don't, why she and her friends police and punish girls with the label slut and no one holds boys accountable, Jenny says she "doesn't know why" she didn't "tell him exactly how [she] felt." She gave consideration to whether her "no" had been token resistance, that is, to whether her "no" had in fact meant "yes," a way to comply with norms of femininity, another cover story for desire (Muehlenhard & Hollabaugh, 1988; Muehlenhard & Rodgers, 1998). The detailed list of reasons why she had meant "no" when she said it, and of what she had hoped her first experience would be like, lend credibility to her repeated statements that she did not want to have sex with this boy at this time. The reasons she gives for why they ended up having sex despite her saying no "for once" is that she "just let it go." Assuming responsibility, Jenny suggests that she "never stopped him from doing anything," as if saying no were not sufficient to hold him accountable for refusal to comply with her stated wishes. Her story suggests that she felt she had no right or reason to expect that he should, would, or could respond to her admittedly uncharacteristic attempt at agency on her own behalf. Her belief that girls are ultimately responsible for boys' sexual behavior stands in the way of her questioning why this boy behaved as though she had not said no; instead she tries to explain what happened in a way that would make sense of his behavior.

One of the few ways to explain his actions is to erase her "no" from the story. By the end of her story, it is as if Jenny no longer knows that she had actually said no to this boy: the definitive "I said no" becomes the uncertain "I sort of let it happen to me and never like, *really* said no, I don't want to do this," which eventually transmogrifies into "I mean I could've said no, I guess, and I could've pushed him off or whatever," and finally becomes "I wish I had just said no." Because this boy behaved as though Jenny had not said "no," in telling this story Jenny loses track of what she knows and what she said, of the reality of her experience, becoming confused not only about what she wanted but also about what she said. It is also possible that, since she was drunk, Jenny may not be sure about what she said at which point during this experience, or that she may fear that being inebriated undermined her clarity or credibility. In fact, the confusion she narrates may reflect her confusion at the time about what was happening, due at least in part to drinking. Not surprisingly, she makes no reference to the absence of her own sexual desire in her telling of this story. It is only later in the interview, in response to my direct question about whether she has experienced sexual desire, that Jenny refers back to this story and notes that she "hadn't felt desire for the person I was with."

But Jenny's own desire has never been available as a guide to her choices. Had Jenny felt entitled to her own sexual feelings and been accustomed to taking them into account in sexual situations, her lack of sexual desire in *this* situation might have provided a clear signal to her, perhaps leaving her less vulnerable to her palpable confusion. Not having sexual feelings has contributed to her having sexual intercourse she did not "want," which has made her feel sad, regretful, bad, guilty, afraid she was pregnant, and fearful of being ostracized by other girls and boys. Accustomed to being the object of someone else's sexual desire and not considering that her own sexual desire might be relevant or significant, like so many other girls, Jenny pastes over the complexity of what did in fact happen with the usual cover story—"it just sort of like happened."

Although she can tell a story of outrage at the boy's lie about using a condom when he had not, and a story of fear about the possibility of pregnancy, Jenny's invocation of the cover story "it just sort of happened" keeps another story at bay, a story of a girl whose spoken wish was not heeded, of a girl who may have been coerced or taken advantage of. Was Jenny raped? It is Jenny herself who brings the word "rape" into her story: "I mean I could've said no, I guess, and I could've pushed him off or whatever 'cause he, I mean, he's not the type of person who would like rape me, or whatever. I mean, well, I don't think he's that way at all." She may indeed, at some level, associate this experience with rape. This word signifies something about how it felt for her, and what it sounded like to me: a time when what she said was not respected, taken into account, or perhaps even heard; a time of violation, when the practice of sexual passivity made her vulnerable to another person's desires. Although she stopped saying no eventually, this sexual experience, like all of her other sexual experiences, was not related to any feeling of "yes" on Jenny's part—not in her mind and not in her body. For Jenny, a dilemma arises in the absence of her desire. Since rape is predicated on a woman not wanting a sexual experience, if Jenny never has feelings of want or desire, how can she know if she has been raped?

CONFUSED BODIES

Another group of girls describe "confused bodies" in that they are not clear about whether they have felt sexual desire. Two different examples of girls who have confused bodies follow. In the first, Laura is confused about how to interpret physical feelings that she can describe but cannot decide whether to call sexual. In the other, Kim simply does not know if she has felt sexual desire; her stories are a portrait of dissociation in action. Not only do these girls illuminate how distressing a lack of clarity about one's own feelings can be, their stories map how insidiously social constructions of male and female sexuality generate both the experience and the reality of sexual vulnerability, which leaves little room for girls' sexual desire.

Laura: One Story of Sexual Abuse

Sitting with Laura, I sense her intelligence. Laura is a tall and unassuming girl who attends the urban school. Neat, tight braids surround her alert brown eyes. She speaks with a measured and cautious voice, telling a complicated story about sexual desire, harm, betrayal, and confusion. For Laura, talk about sexuality is all about danger. Her grandmother and mother admonish her to "just think about school" and "[don't] say much else." In school, Laura observes that "there's a lot of rumors about people goin' around . . . No one knows if it's true or not, only you know." She says she "doesn't really talk to anyone in school" in case "people go around talkin' about you and sayin' that you do all this other stuff. And you know you don't or you know you do. It's gonna, you know, make you feel bad either way." For her to speak, she has to ascertain that she has found a safe space. From Laura's descriptions of how she does and does not talk about sexuality, it seems that such safe spaces are few and far between. Thus, our interview offers a potential and unusual opportunity to talk about her sexuality, which Laura seems to find difficult but also clearly wants to do.

Laura is trying to figure out if she experiences sexual desire. When I ask her if she has felt something she calls sexual desire, Laura pauses for a moment, watching me, perhaps wary or puzzled and says, "I don't think I would know." To clarify my understanding of her experience and to convey my genuine wish to listen to what she has to say, I ask her again if she has experienced such a feeling, and she hedges: "you could say that. I don't know. I didn't really know what it was at the time, so I wasn't, you know, that sure. Since like no one really discussed these kinds of things, you know, I didn't really know if it was or not." Laura links her confusion about her feelings to never feeling able to talk with anyone about them. Like Jenny, Laura talks about sex that seems to leave her body out, that "sometimes . . . just happens. It's not something that you really think about, when we was in the room together, it just happened, I don't know why I did it, just, I did it. Well, I was touchin' him, it was just somethin' that happened. It's not like I had thought about it ahead of time, like I wanna do this." Women frequently use the passive voice to talk about things they have done that are not socially acceptable, so Laura's use of it here may or may not tell me whether she had sexual feelings.

But she can talk about having such feelings, if vaguely, when asked to do so explicitly. Laura tells me about a time that she had feelings for a boy in her school: "There was this guy I used to like, well I still kinda like him. I liked him a lot, you know." In his presence, she says, she has "felt like I wanted to do somethin,'" though she does not say what it is she might want to do. She adds, "I knew that was somethin' I would have wanted to do if it, you know, came down to that situation with him, you know . . . So I guess you could say that was a desire or need or whatever." Her vague description, her unconvincing "guess" about the feeling being a "desire" or "need" (or "whatever"), knowing that she "would have wanted to do it" in "that situation," leaves me confused. What is "that situation"? What is the "somethin'" she "would have wanted to do"? Is it reaching out to hold his hand or touch his shoulder? Is it kissing? Is it sexual intercourse? Perhaps she does not have the words to describe desire. Perhaps keeping it all vague absolves her from feeling responsible or culpable. Or perhaps Laura is testing me, making sure I am listening but not judging, trying to decide if I can be trusted. As a black girl, she may be suspicious of a white woman asking her such questions.

As the interview progresses, she talks more, and more openly, about her feelings, and contours of genuine confusion emerge. We try to piece together what her feelings have been, puzzling over what she has and has not felt in her body, and what the feelings she can identify might be about. A helpful starting place is to compare her feelings for this boy with how she feels around other boys. It seems easier for her to talk about how she responds to boys for whom she knows distinctly she does not have any special feelings: "it wasn't like, you know, like the other guys I was like yeah . . . it was just like, I acted around them like I acted around anybody else . . . I would act the usual way . . . I blew them off."

She says that her body feels "different" around this boy. She attributes this feeling in her body as evidence that she "likes" this boy, and she interprets an ebb and flow of the feeling as an indicator of whether she likes him; it disappeared when she "stopped liking him. But sometimes, I see him, and then the feeling comes back, so I know I like him still, even if it's only a little bit." This embodied feeling provides Laura with information about her emotional feelings. The question of whether or not this feeling is sexual desire is still unclear. To try to diagnose it together, I ask her to describe it in detail:

D: What did it feel like? How did you feel, around this guy?

L: I don't know, jumpy I guess.

D: Yeah?

L: I just felt jumpy.

D: Did it feel good?

L: Yeah, you could say that yeah. It felt strange, I know that.

D: Were you surprised?

L: Yeah, because I, I didn't feel that way before. I mean, jumpy around guys, you know. I feel comfortable around certain guys, but I mean, I didn't feel jumpy when I was around, you know, other guys, it was just like, I acted around them like I acted around anybody else. It's not like they were, you know, different, it was like he was different. It's like, I was all jumpy and stuff, like I was takin' drugs or something [laughs], I was all hyper and stuff, I guess. I guess you could say it was a sexual feeling, you feel it all over.

In answering questions about how her body feels, Laura gets a little more specific: She feels "hyper," "jumpy," like she "was takin' drugs or something." She "guess[es]" that this feeling was sexual. While she is describing some kind of arousal, there is no indication that it has a sexual quality. It is just as possible that she is describing an experience of anxiety. When I ask whether Laura's "jumpy" feelings feel good to her, she describes them as "strange." Her body is sending her signals that are confusing—she is physically aroused in the presence of this boy, and this bodily feeling occurs in conjunction with a sense of "want" in relation to him. But this experience has an unpleasant quality about it. Later she calls the feeling "an unwanted visitor."

What is at stake for Laura in having clarity about her desire? Laura's confusion about whether or not these feelings are sexual desire stands in counterpoint to, and may be explained by, having been sexually abused as a child. Her story is not only about sexual violation but also about women not hearing her or responding to her—a story about betrayed relationships. Laura tells me that when she was seven years old, a neighborhood teenage boy "did unspeakable things to me." She says that, despite threats from him, she "eventually did tell someone, but nothin' ever happened to him, I mean, he went on with his life like nothin' happened. I don't think that's right." When I asked her if she'd ever talked to a counselor about it, she said that the "therapy I had didn't really help. She just wanted to know what happened, and I was supposed to see another therapist, but my mother never took me, I don't know why." In fact, her mother acted as if this violation had never happened:

> She talks to me about him like I care, you know, because it was her friend's son, it was her best friend's son, that's what made it even worse, so it's like, I don't know, it's like they can't accept the fact . . . she doesn't talk about it anymore, she clammed up about it. And we went to visit her [friend] in [another state], and like my mother acted like nothin' happened, I mean, it's not like he ever apologized for anything or nothin' like that, so why does he get to walk off free?

As Laura tells me what happened, she gets increasingly angry. Not only does Laura's mother not talk to her about sexuality, she "acted like nothin' happened" when something "horrible" did happen, and she did not respond to Laura's need to talk about a frightening violation or have it resolved by either adult woman confronting the boy. Laura understands that this boy was not held responsible for his actions; she is angry not only at his lack of apology or acknowledgment that he had done something that required his apology, but also at his "getting to walk off free." Laura's adolescent sexuality may be tainted by the possibility that she experienced pleasure in this exploitative situation; therefore pleasure may be confusing or painful, a difficult experience she may wish to avoid, from which she may dissociate (Kaplan, 1991; Young, 1992). A connection between pleasure and violation may also limit Laura's psychic motivation to clarify the messages that her body is sending her.

I tell her I notice it still bothers her a lot and ask her if it affects the rest of her life now; she replies, "I don't know. Like if I wanna do something, like with that guy, you know, it might stop me. I don't know." Laura considers making an uncertain connection between this sexual violation and her lack of clarity about her own sexual desire. The framing of girls' sexuality into simplistic and dualistic good and bad categories, which suggests that the desire-less girl is normal and safe, does not give her any guidance for making sense of what happened to her when she was seven or of what does and does not happen in her body now. How can she feel unequivocal desire in a relational terrain that is full of possible pitfalls?

Kim: The Sorrows of Silence

Sitting with Kim, I find the room still and simultaneously thick with tension. Her interview is like a puzzle, cut into seemingly dis-crete and mismatched pieces that fit together in an unlikely way to tell a larger story about how it is that she is "not sure" if she has experienced sexual desire: "I probably wouldn't be able to [tell you about a time I did] . . . No, I don't think I'll be able to remember. I don't think I'll be able to come up with something." Not "be[ing] able to remember" may mean that she has never had such feelings and so has nothing to remember or, conversely, it could mean that she has and cannot remember them. In considering how she might know if she was feeling desire, Kim responds thoughtfully, halt-ingly—the average length of the pauses in her answer is eight seconds (take a moment to feel how long an eight-second pause is!): "Um, I don't know if I'd be able to, because I have, um [pause], well there's um [pause], well I suppose your heart would beat faster, but that's just another reaction. There's um [pause], I'm not sure how it would feel." While "not sure," she does connect feeling desire to her body—"I suppose your heart would beat faster." It is as if she has a hypothesis rather than a recollection of sexual feelings she has actually experienced.

Despite her hesitations, Kim provides a lot of information indirectly, in how she says some things and reacts to others. As the interview progresses and she responds consistently to my questions about her experiences of sexual desire in the same way—"I don't know," "I'm not sure," "maybe if you asked something more specific," "can you ask the question again?"—despite her serene facial expression, her body becomes more and more agitated. Perhaps she is uncomfortable talking with an adult about sexuality. Nevertheless, she gives my questions a lot of thought. As we talk, Kim seems to be coming to a realization about what she does not know, and cannot say, about her own experience. She is visibly distressed when she interprets her own answers: "well, I certainly don't know what I'm thinking. I guess I don't know what I really want." When we sit together during her many long pauses, I can tell that Kim is struggling to bring her own thoughts and feelings into her conscious awareness and to tell me about them, trying to overcome a "blanking in [her] head," to not "block it from [her] head or something." She wants help, a second opinion, asking me several times, "What do you think?" when she finds she is not sure or cannot answer my question.

There are clues to her lack of clarity about her desire sprinkled throughout the interview. Kim's tendency to dissociate from her thoughts and feelings becomes a pattern as the interview progresses. It is evident in her difficulty "spitting out" the words, in disjunctures between her comportment and her words or between her facial expressions and her body language. She explains that she has gone out with a few different boys; she says that she "hasn't really enjoyed having boyfriends" and that "sometimes when kissing or something, it seems like they're not really, it doesn't matter who they'd be kissing, just because, it's more pleasure for themselves, and it doesn't really matter who it would be . . . and it kind of bothers me sometimes." Whether as cause or effect, Kim links "not enjoying" sexual experiences with feeling that she is being treated as the object of someone else's desire for the purpose of his own satisfaction, as if who she is does not matter.

Talking about another experience with a boy she was dating, she describes an absence of agency on her part that further suggests a dissociative state:

> My first boyfriend, I was fourteen, and I really liked him an awful lot, and he was really nice, and I remember being upset after we were going out for awhile, after he was feeling up my shirt, and I was upset about that afterwards, because I just wasn't ready for that, at the time he was eighteen, I was upset just because I didn't want to feel hurt . . . I guess I didn't really mind that much at the time, but then afterwards, I just was upset that it had happened.

Like Laura, she gives the impression that she in essence blanked out during the experience and came only to discover she had had an experience for which she wasn't "ready." When I ask her if that wasn't what she wanted to do at the time, she pauses. "I guess I didn't really mind, I don't know [long pause]; I have a bad sexual history." When I ask her if anything bad has happened to her regarding sex or the sexual parts of her body, she replies, "I don't think so." It is possible that Kim has experienced some kind of sexual abuse she does not recall or does not want to disclose, but there are indications of other kinds of "bad" encounters she has had that may also explain her confusion.

Just when I begin to think that Kim does not in fact experience sexual desire, she tells me that she masturbates. She is one of only three girls in this study who say they have ever masturbated. She realizes that "it's not really discussed that much, at all." She tells me that "it's not fulfilling or anything." As happens throughout our conversation, Kim's ability to talk about her experience seems to unravel as she speaks:

> It's not that I would feel guilty, 'cause I know that's not, I mean, everyone does, but I just feel that if that's physically so, afterwards, it feels fine when I did it, but then afterwards [long pause] I don't know, maybe it's pleasurable during, but then afterwards it feels, I don't know, I guess I just don't feel good afterwards, not mentally, I wouldn't that often, it's kind of really uncomfortable for me to talk about that, but I'm not sure why it is . . . I mean it's nothing new, and you've heard it all before, but the topic isn't very accepted or whatever, you know? It's just not very comfortable, because, I mean people, it's been considered like criticized, or whatever, oh but Ann Landers always says that everyone does it, but it's still like considered to be dirty or whatever.

When I ask her what she thinks, she says, "I don't think it's like that, I don't see why." When I ask her what makes her want to masturbate, her answer keeps the possibility of her sexual desire in the shadows: "I don't know, it's probably just sexual arousal or something, whatever, I don't know." When I ask if that is something she feels, she responds, "Probably."

She is aware that there are different expectations and standards about male and female sexual desire; she disagrees with this state of affairs but cannot articulate why she feels this way: "well, you hear about men's desires and I guess it used to be thought that women didn't have desires, and I'm sure that's not, that people know that it's not true, but it's still not really admitted that much, I don't think." When I ask her why she thinks this inequity exists, Kim becomes completely discombobulated again: "I can't think, I don't know, usually this doesn't happen, I can't even formulate any thoughts, because these kinds of questions aren't usually asked, and since I've never been asked before, I haven't really thought about it that much, so." In her mounting efforts to try to "remember," to "think," not to "block," I begin to sense frustration on her part. She asks and then answers her emerging questions: "Why don't I know what I'm feeling? One reason is that people don't really discuss it that much, people don't discuss pleasure . . . it's not that I don't want to answer you, I just don't know, it's just difficult for me to answer." While Kim links her confusion to silence about girls' desire and pleasure, she also seems aware that it is not only what hasn't been said that creates a stumbling block for her.

Reflecting the social ambivalence she has picked up on, Kim lives out the disconnect that comes from not talking about sexuality. She says her mother has "never talked to me, she hasn't really mentioned the subject. She keeps telling me I should be dating right now, just, but I don't know why." When I ask her what she thinks about her mother not talking with her about sexuality, tears start rolling down Kim's cheeks. Abruptly, she tells me that her father has had an affair. Voice steady yet very soft, as tears slip down her face, Kim continues to speak; she does not seem to be aware that she is crying. I ask her: "Do you feel sad?" She says: "Um . . . I don't know." From the silence that surrounds her father's betrayal, Kim gets the message that knowing what she wants and needs can set her up for betrayal.

She tells me her father has "strong opinions" and "rape has been discussed." She explains her father's position: "he has always taken the side . . . well, women have to take some kind of responsibility for that too, and that it could be kind of their fault too." When I ask her what she thinks about her father's opinion, she says she does not agree with it. His point of view in fact raises a poignant question for her: "How do you know what situation you shouldn't get into or not? I've heard some people say that women shouldn't dress provocatively or something, but I don't know, I don't think it's very fair to say that, because it shouldn't provoke anything like that." Kim does not agree that the way a woman dresses should make her responsible for getting raped. Yet it seems hard for her to feel sure; her father's perspective makes the question of women's culpability in their sexual violation more confusing for her. If a woman—or a girl—can be held responsible for being raped, on what grounds does she make decisions about her sexuality? How can girls feel desire and be safe if being raped "could be kind of their fault too?"

Throughout the interview, in response to my questions about desire, Kim raises the potential danger of rape, violation, and hurt. In talking about how she feels walking around the city, she explains:

> I mean, you couldn't really be raped if you're just walking around the street, I mean you could, but like not so easily, because there's so many people around. I guess that doesn't really matter, but date rape I think is more scary, I mean, I'm not very scared when I'm walking down the street, but once I was scared actually, because it was over the summer and I was, I had just been out to dinner with a friend, and I was walking back and so when I was walking it was like 8:30, so it was dark, and this man started following me, and so I crossed to the other side of the street and he crossed over too, and I crossed back, and he crossed on that side too. And that was really scary, because there weren't too many people around, and so I was scared. I don't remember how I got out of it, he just walked off.

Finely tuned to the various dangers embedded in sexuality, completely on her own with these painful, frightening, contradictory, and confusing observations and experiences, Kim not surprisingly "solves" the dilemma of feeling desire and being safe by remaining unclear about whether or not she experiences sexual desire. Her extreme difficulty keeping track of her thoughts and her dissociated states in the interview, coupled with her keen observations of the pervasive silences about female sexuality and the dangers associated with sexuality for women, provide ample insight into why Kim suffers from a lack of clarity about her own sexual desire.

In his earliest case studies, Freud inadvertently told his own story. As a young physician, without any theories but with a strong curiosity to understand and an intense desire to help, he started out by simply listening to ill young women. These women—who prior to their illness were, as Freud noted, unusually intelligent, outspoken, and honest—had been diagnosed with physical symptoms that had no physiological explanation and had been deemed "hysterical."[5] Invariably, these symptoms involved the loss of feeling or movement in parts of their bodies. When these young women became conscious of and articulated their forbidden knowledge about sexuality, about abuse, and about their own desires—through the "talking cure"—the hysterical symptoms that had emerged in their bodies disappeared. The safe space that his office and this early form of therapeutic relationship afforded to these women enabled them to embody their desire rather than disembody themselves. For a time, Freud was able to ask and hear about these women's experiences of desire and violation,[6] and thereby appreciate that to deny women's sexual desire was to impair their psychological health.

How can the stories of girls who do not feel sexual desire inform our understanding of female adolescent sexuality? The girls who narrated silent and confused bodies did not experience their sexual desire as posing a dilemma; they lived it. They told of individual, often unconscious solutions to social problems produced by gendered sexuality. The girls in this chapter harbored a poignant distress or unhappiness about them. They found it difficult to communicate their feelings to someone else, at least in part because they were not aware of or could not figure out exactly what their feelings were. And they found romantic relationships frightening, confusing, or something that they simply tried to avoid. Hence the question of whether or how to integrate their own sexuality into their identity or their relationships was moot for these girls; sexual desire, sexual pleasure, sexual subjectivity— none of these notions was in their lexicons or their lives. In essence, these girls illustrate a kind of unconscious preemptive action: They avoid having to address the dilemma of desire by not having desire.

Within current constructions of gendered sexuality, it is easy to question the wisdom of making adolescent girls aware of their own sexual desire. But as the stories in this chapter reveal, girls who are not able to sense the presence or absence of their own sexual desire risk becoming dissociated from their own experience and from reality, thereby impairing their psychological integrity and their understanding of what is happening in the world around them. Such dissociation makes it difficult for these girls to know and name sexual exploitation. Jenny's silent body, for instance, kept her from being able to maintain the clarity of her "no" and insist that her word be respected. Fine and colleagues have observed that women who feel "entitled to their bodies and sexualities . . . question the 'rights' of male violence" and "refus[e] the passive position of sexual victim" (1996, p. 128). Jenny illuminates how difficult such questioning and refusal is without awareness of one's own desire. Meanwhile Kim silences her body out of fear that she will be responsible for being violated, and the constant dissociation she endures keeps her from saying what she sees and knows about a social world that makes her desire seem dangerous.

By omitting or penalizing girls' desire, the notion that girls' sexual subjectivity is suspect places them in a double bind. On the one hand, girls' inability to look to their own desire as a guide to their actions leaves them vulnerable in the worst case to coercion or at the very least to feeling bad about themselves in the wake of an uncomfortable experience. On the other hand, as media coverage of teen sexuality illustrates, girls' expression of desire also renders them vulnerable by undermining the credibility of their resistance to unwanted sex. Remember that the girls who were attracted to the members of the Spur Posse, who dated them and sought their physical attention, were labeled trash (Yoffe, Marszalek, and Selix, 1991). By expressing their desire and thus behaving like "bad" girls, they not only lost the approval and protection of their community but had to face the seeming justification of this injustice. Silent and confused bodies are one answer that leaves girls diminished but undoes or eludes the dilemma of desire. The girls who are aware of this bind and who do feel desire tell other stories.

> While too few safe spaces exist for adoles-
> cent women's exploration of sexual subjec-
> tivities, there are all too many dangerous
> spots for their exploitation.
>
> —Michelle Fine, "Sexuality, Schooling, and
> Adolescent Females: The Missing
> Discourse of Desire"

Although there continues to be tre-
mendous debate over how to conceptualize and deal with the various forms that sexual desire takes for women,[1] what remains clear
is that women's sexuality holds a fundamental contradiction under
current gender arrangements: It involves both pleasure and danger. As wide-ranging and variable as the dangers and harm that are
associated with sexuality for girls and women are, so too are the
potential pleasures and gain. When we frame sexuality only in
terms of risk and avoidance, as is the case most often for female
adolescent sexuality, not only are such pleasures obscured but consideration of the place of pleasure in sexual development seems
hedonistic and irresponsible. Yet to leave pleasure out or to deny its
importance is, quite simply, to misrepresent sexuality.

In adolescence, as girls begin to explore their sexuality, romantic
relationships, and identities, they are immediately and necessarily
confronted with this duality. Fine has suggested that "the adolescent woman herself assumes a dual consciousness, at once taken
with the excitement of actual/anticipated sexuality and consumed
with anxiety and worry" (1988, p. 35). She notes that girls' views

on sexuality cannot be separated from their perspectives on gender relations. Neither can these views be separated from girls' perspectives on, and investment in, norms of femininity.

The template for gender relations under the institution of heterosexuality is the master narrative of romance, which is premised on female passivity and male aggression and dominance, denoting appropriate feminine and masculine behavior in relation to the opposite sex. Romance provides a script not only for how males and females interact but also for expectations about female and male sexuality, including that resilient distinction between "good" and "bad" girls, as defined by the absence or presence, respectively, of sexual desire. Though it may seem somewhat outdated, research on adolescent sexuality consistently suggests that this romance narrative continues to be an important organizing principle in many adolescents' sexual relationships (Thompson, 1995; Kirkman, Rosenthal, & Smith, 1998; Tolman et al., 2002). Ultimately, the romance narrative provides girls with limited condoned pleasures buttressed by the constant threat of dangers. While a romantic relationship is held out as a safe space for girls to express their feelings, as Linda Christian-Smith notes, romance "discredits a girl's feelings and right to control her body" (1990, p. 32). In return for being feminine and "good," in this framework, girls are rewarded with the pleasures of male adoration, the chance to love, and the privilege of being protected.

In essence, the romance narrative entices and invites girls into trading in the full range of their real feelings, including sexual desire, taboo emotions, and knowledge of what is actually happening in relationships and reality, for male commitment, care, and attention. In this organization of heterosexual romantic relationships, patriarchal constructions of femininity are key. Not only does romance position girls as the objects of boys' sexual desire, but from the developmental perspective of adolescence, "the female gaze is trained to abandon its claim to the sovereign status of seer. The 'nice' girl learns to avoid the bold and unfettered staring of the 'loose' woman, who looks at whatever and whomever she pleases" (Bartky, 1990, p. 68). Becoming feminine requires that girls themselves learn to be "good" sexual objects, which precludes having desire of their own, and that process is deeply informed by the imperative not to become a "bad" girl, not only in the eyes of others but in the eyes of one's own internalized male gaze.

Most of the girls in this study did report feeling sexual desire. They described several ways of negotiating the dilemma of desire, premised on their experiences with and perceptions of the physical, relational, social, and psychological pleasures and dangers of desire. The majority of girls in the study, then, provide illustrations for the ways that mind and body interact in the realm of desire, in the various contexts of their lives. For the girls in this chapter, the dangers of desire loom so large relative to the range of possible pleasures that the girls resist their embodied desire, literally doing battle with themselves, as a way to stay safe, maintain relationships, and know themselves as "good."

DISAPPEARING DESIRE

Some girls resist their sexual feelings by making them go away. The girls who thus "disappear" desire may or may not be conscious they are engaging in this process. Some, like Ellen, juggle various kinds of desire—the desire to achieve, the desire not to get pregnant, the desire to protect relationships—and seem unaware they are describing the disappearance of their sexual desire. Others, like Rochelle, narrate a semiconscious resistance to their own sexual feelings, with awareness of the power and importance of desire but not of the multiple dimensions of the trade-offs they are making. And some, like Inez, talk about a conscious decision to stifle their desire; aware of the power, pleasure, and danger associated with

their desire, they choose safety above all else, with an understanding of the costs involved in this choice.

Ellen: Contradictory Desires

Like Janine, Ellen is soft-spoken; her intelligent eyes look bashfully
at me, from behind her thick glasses. She too has a sweet smile and
a quiet, shy way about her. Her mother "doesn't talk about that . . .
everything that I learned about sexuality, I learned on my own, you
know, you know, I had to find out on my own." She tells me she has
"all kinds of questions" about girls' sexuality, "and then I ask, you
know, how am I going to answer them, when I don't know the
answer. Then finally I forget about it after a while." The way Ellen
talks about her questions parallels how she describes her experiences with her embodied sexual desire: She has sexual feelings, she
is confused by them and overwhelmed by the dangers she associates with them, and then she makes herself forget about them.
Although she says she never talks to anyone about sexuality,
because "I'm afraid of what other people might think, what they
would say," by the end of our hour-long conversation, which she
characterizes as "strange, because I never thought about it before,"
she concludes that "it's pretty interesting, because it made me want
to think about it more, how I feel about it, you know, more deeply."
This ultimate wish to consider "more deeply" how she feels about
her own sexuality after having a chance to evaluate her experiences
and choices in the open air of our brief encounter is in considerable contrast to what she has to say about her sexual desire along
the way.

Ellen is evasive and tight-lipped during the first part of the
interview. Clearly wary of me and my questions, Ellen has not easily accepted the offer of a chance to talk and ask questions about
sexuality with an adult. When I ask if sexual desire is a feeling she
has experienced, she responds, "Ummmm, no." Her hesitation

makes me think that maybe she doesn't understand what I'm asking, so I try another approach—"A feeling of wanting?" She replies, "Yes." I observe the contradiction, "No, yeah?" and we both laugh. I hope that questions about specific experiences will shed some light on this contradictory beginning.

At first, when I ask Ellen if she can tell me about a time when she experienced sexual desire, she tersely describes a time when she started "thinking about [a boy] . . . having sex, kissing him." When I ask her if she can tell me more, she answers, "Umm, I can't, I just forgot about it, I really didn't." Ellen's story, a short story that ends abruptly because she "just forgot about it," repeats and reflects what sexual desire may be like for her. In "thinking" about "having sex" and "kissing," she begins a process in her mind that could lead to sexual desire in her body. Ellen tells me later that she does not "feel very much" in her body, yet she has experienced some embodied sexual feelings. She tells me that kissing someone she liked was pleasurable "all over my body." She talks about a dream in which a boy kissed her; in her dream she says it was "half and half, yes and no" pleasurable: "I didn't want it to happen, because my mother was in the next room and you know, 'cause I did want it to happen." Ellen tells me that she tried to figure out what the dream meant but couldn't, perhaps sensing a connection between the proximity of her mother and her ambivalence about her dreamed-of desire. Because she does know a little about embodied pleasure, she prevents her thoughts about sex from moving into her body by "forgetting" it.

In contrast to Janine and Jenny, she is curious about sexual pleasure; she wants to know "everything about it, you know, what happens, what do you do, you know, the reactions." She says she'd "probably" like to do "everything" when it comes to expressing her sexuality. What keeps her from this unfettered sexuality is that she has made a promise; a deeply religious girl, at age eleven, she made a promise to God not to have relationships, "particularly that kind of relationship," until she graduates from high school. Ellen's sexual feelings and her desire to know more about her sexuality constantly threaten to jump out of the lockbox she has put them in. She does not go out with boys because of her promise, but Ellen can articulate the interplay between physical and other kinds of attraction she has noticed in her experience: "most of the time it's physical, you know, the way they look, it's like half of the time, you know it's like the way the person thinks, you know, their reactions, certain things."

Ellen has a story about desire close at hand; she tells me about a time when she really wanted to kiss someone:

> E: You know we was talking quietly, we was on the bed and we was just talking, and I was thinking about it. I didn't do anything, we just kept on talking. What, you think I would ask him to kiss me? I wouldn't do that!
>
> D: Why not?
>
> E: I don't know, I'm not a forward type person [long pause].
>
> D: What do you think it would be like to do that?
>
> E: I don't know. He might not like it, that's the one thing, or I might not like it afterwards, or, we both might like it. Lots of things could happen! One was the reason I just told you, we might both like it.

The complexity of this simple story is startling. It is about desire for connection. It is about how there is no such thing as an innocent kiss, since any and all kissing is fraught and ultimately overshadowed by its position as a floodgate for all of the "things that could happen." It is about the vulnerability of being a wanting girl: running the risk of becoming "a forward type person," of provoking an embarrassing rejection or aversion. Ellen underscores the possibility that she, as well as the boy, "might like it." In letting

her psychological guard down for just a moment, imagining that
she does not dampen her desire, her mind goes immediately to the
danger of her liking it, for if they both like it, then who will stop
it? Ellen takes responsibility for her own protection by never taking the risk that she "might like it," since she knows that she must
be the one to keep sex, the inevitable outcome of a kiss, from
happening.

The logic of her promise not to have relationships that involve
sexuality and of her story of aborted desire becomes clear when
she switches gears. Ellen interrupts her own desire narrative with
another story, about how her friend wanted to have sex, got pregnant, was abandoned by the baby's father, and had an abortion.
She acknowledges to me, "see, I'm afraid of sex." Ellen has closely
observed the dangerous outcomes of desire and decided to avoid
them, explaining that she "didn't want that happening to me, just
because of a boy." And it is not just boys' desire that scares her. She
has seen evidence that girls' desire can be powerful and can inter-
twine sexual desire and desire for a child. Her younger sister
"wanted to experience [sex], she met a boy and she did, she started
liking it and so she started doing it often, and she got pregnant
because she wanted to have a baby." She says simply, "I don't want
to be in that situation."

I am not surprised to hear that Ellen's strategies are effective and
generally keep embodied sexual desire at bay. While much of what
Ellen says matches Janine's descriptions, the significant difference
is that Ellen does indeed know what embodied sexual desire feels
like and thus must engage in practices to stifle it, even though it is
not an experience she has frequently. In fact, Ellen's description
draws attention to the relationship between mind and body in the
production of desire: "I don't feel very much in my body, it's like
very few is physical. It's kind of strange, though. I don't feel it phys-

ically, but you know mentally I do. Maybe it might change." One example of the "few" times she has had "physical" feelings is when one particular boy is so persistent in his wish to be with her that it makes her want to break her promise; it is her "feelings" that threaten her resolve. This experience causes Ellen distress. She says:

E: I didn't like it. You know, well, I didn't want it to happen.

D: What's the it?

E: Sex, or kissing, or whatever, my feelings.

D: You didn't want your feelings to happen?

E: Yeah.

D: How come?

E: 'Cause, you know, it wasn't the right time, you know.

D: What was happening that wasn't right?

E: Um, liking the person so much.

D: What do you mean?

E: Umm, I'm afraid that, you know, liking the person so much, or um, maybe that something will happen.

D: Like?

E: Um, my desire, or that, um, I might act upon it, you know. I'm not ready, you know, I don't know, it might affect my life, a lot. What happens or my education.

Ellen is "afraid" that "something will happen" unless she extinguishes the tiniest flicker of her desire, because her response to her desire, if she were to allow herself to feel it, "might [be to] act upon it." Thoughts about sexuality and physical "needs" or "wants" do surface, however. As she explains, "it could happen anywhere, well, if I don't have anything else to think about, sometimes it just pops in my head, and I'm like, ohhhkay . . . and I just try to figure out why I'm thinking about it or how did I come to think about it." Ellen considers her own desire a serious threat to her education. It makes it hard for her to keep her promise and puts her future in jeopardy. Paradoxically, she also says that girls should learn about their own desire and pleasure "because it's important that they do know . . . to understand themselves more by that." Ellen is able to distinguish between feeling and acting on her own desire. And after we have finished talking, she plans to give her own desire, though not her promise, "deep[er]" consideration.

Rochelle: Distance Makes the Body Grow Fonder

A small, sweet voice and shy smile emerge tentatively from Rochelle, in stark contrast to her tall, full-figured body. Rochelle's narratives highlight how girls' sexual desire connects to other forms of desire—desire for a boyfriend, desire to complete an education, desire to be treated with respect and kindness—and to the myriad dangers it brings. Her descriptions of the different sexual experiences she has had underscore the extent to which the circumstances in which sexual feelings occur determine how girls make sense of and respond to them. Her stories about times when she did not feel desire serve as counterpoint and context for the times when she says she does have powerful sexual feelings, conveying the contradictory and quixotic quality of desire in her life. She speaks evocatively of both the pleasures and the dangers that she associates with her own sexual feelings. While evidence of her dissociation from her sexual feelings abounds, Rochelle can describe intense embodied experiences of sexual desire as well.

When I ask her about her experiences of sexual pleasure and sexual desire, the dual nature of her sexuality is immediately apparent. On the one hand, Rochelle says not only that she does "not like sex" as a general rule, but that she "hate[s] sex." Yet her understanding of desire emerges through her talk about hating sexual intercourse. For instance, she says that she likes "to be touched more than anything." Having had sexual experiences with

and without her desire, she has learned about how, when, and why
she might feel sexual desire:

> There are certain times when I really, really, really enjoy it, but
> then, that's like, not a majority of the times, it's only sometimes,
> once in a while . . . if I was to have sex once a month, then I
> would enjoy it . . . if I like go a long period of time without
> havin' it, then it's really good to me, 'cause it's like I haven't had
> something for a long time and I miss it. It's like, say I don't eat
> cake a lot, but say, like every two months, I had some cake, then it
> would be real good to me, so that's like the same thing . . . if you
> have sex moderately, then you have more desire.

Rochelle conveys a careful knowledge of her body's hunger, her
need for tension as an aspect of her sexual pleasure, but the pre-
dominance of her dislike of sex suggests that she does not feel she
has much say over when and how she engages in sexual activity.

She speaks about her sexuality with a detailed knowledge of how
it is shaped, silenced, denigrated, and still possible in relationships
with young men. Rochelle's stories about her sexual experiences
are also stories about her intimate relationships; her narratives
illuminate the complex interplay between gendered sexuality and
heterosexual relationships. Though such relationships have rarely
been a safe haven for her, she reveals how, as a sophomore in high
school, she had felt compelled to "get a boyfriend to make [her] life
complete." In this early relationship, Rochelle complied with the
mandates of romance, despite evidence that the promise of protection and adoration was undone by male dominance and arbitrary
action. She says her boyfriend "treated [her] like [she] was nothing" and was "real, real mean" to her. She narrates how the tem-
plates and scripts for relationships and sexual encounters offered
by romance disable her by cutting off her own feelings and encouraging her sexual passivity. Having sex for the first time "just

happens"; she did not "really" want to do it but did so to try to "please [her boyfriend]." When she is operating within this framework, her desire is not considered a factor by him or by her.

However, Rochelle has begun to discover what she does and does not want in relationships and in her sexual experiences. Relying on what she has learned from her own relationships with boys, both bad and good, she carves out the possibility of her entitlement to her own desire and pleasure. Her own algorithm is more complex than what romance has to offer, weaving female sexual subjectivity into the more conventional condition of having sex in a relationship that has lasted an unspecified "long, long time," for the unspecified but generally agreed-upon rationale that this "next step" may be necessary to keep a teenage boyfriend: "it depends on like if you enjoyed yourself when you did it or not, you know, it depends on how you feel, if you just do it with somebody you met at a party, then I consider that bad for you. But like, if you've been with somebody for like a long, long time, then that's special and okay."

Although she has a strong sense of the possibilities of pleasure, and its role in a genuinely intimate relationship, more often than not the dangers loom too large and have been too potently present in her own experiences for her to take a chance on pleasure. She often finds her own sexual feelings quite frightening, and with good reason. Rochelle's stories cover the entire gamut of dangers associated with female sexuality. In every account she articulates how and why she is motivated to not be a desiring girl. The physical vulnerabilities to which acting on her desire expose her are at the top. When she and her boyfriend are watching TV, she "see[s] AIDS and . . . always think[s], what if like ten or twenty years from now, I'd be diagnosed with AIDS and like I just think about it." While she "always" uses a condom, she knows that condoms can break. Once, in a committed relationship, she believed that she had the symptoms of a sexually transmitted disease. Since she had been faithful to her boyfriend, having such a disease would have meant having to admit to herself that her boyfriend had cheated on her and would also have made her vulnerable to false accusations of promiscuity from him.

Of the physical threats, the most recurrent danger Rochelle talks about is her fear of pregnancy. She explains that "for a teenager, babies is like the biggest issue." She tries to avoid sex, she says, because "I'm too young to be tied down with a baby." She realizes that she is not prepared to care for a child: "I don't really like having it, 'cause it's like, I'm going to college and stuff and I'm still a baby myself, I couldn't handle a baby." She also realizes pregnancy would threaten her education because she would have to sacrifice going to college. Rochelle relates the goal of education—at least high school, she hopes college—explicitly to security through financial independence from men; she wants to "have something of my own before I get a husband, you know, so if he ever tries leavin' me, I have my own money."

Social consequences weigh on her as well. She is afraid of being talked about and getting a reputation—"I was always scared that if I [had sexual intercourse], I would be portrayed as, you know, something bad." Whereas for some girls having sex within the context of a committed relationship provides a kind of safety zone from social ostracism, for Rochelle there is no such security. She astutely notes the precariousness of this protection—the capricious behavior of the boy involved—observing that she still "could've had a bad reputation, but luckily he wasn't like that." She offers her analysis of being a sexual object for someone else's desires rather than being treated as a person with her own feelings: "I don't know, 'cause like, I think when you have sex and the guy just, you know, has sex with you and doesn't like hold you and touch you, I feel like he's just using me . . . I always feel so bad if he did that to me, 'cause I was like, you know, it wasn't nothin' to him."

Along with being objectified comes vulnerability to violence (Tolman, 2000). Rochelle understands the connection between the absence of her own desire and male violence, because her first boyfriend "flattened [her] face" after she broke up with him when she found him with another girl. She is worried about other people, especially her mother, thinking she is immoral, a worry that discourages her from obtaining contraception: "When you get birth control pills, people automatically think you're having sex every night and that's not true." Although her mother has told her that "sex is not bad and that as long as you do it with somebody who cares about you and who you care about, then it's okay," she believes her mother told her these things when she thought Rochelle was still a virgin. She projects her struggle to figure out her identity as a sexual person onto her mother, and it ricochets right back at her.

Rochelle describes a time when simply feeling desire while a boy kissed her made her "so scared that I started to cry." It was not the kiss itself that scared her, but her own desire, the fact that she "wanted to have sex with him." Despite this overdetermined knowledge of the dangers of desire, Rochelle also appreciates the importance of the pleasures of desire and is thus on the path toward developing a clearer sense of who she is and what she wants in this part of her life. She finds herself "scared" to voice her true desires in response to her boyfriend's gentle inquiries into "what are some things [she] would want him to do": "I am like, 'Oh, nothing,' but in my mind there's something I wanna say but then I won't dare say." Though predictably and understandably "scared," Rochelle says that she is "curious" about sexual experiences besides intercourse, such as cunnilingus. While "sexual pleasure is the last thing on the list," she still wants to know about it: "I always wonder how you can tell if you did [have an orgasm] or not? . . . Does that make it more pleasurable if you come?" Given her fear of and dislike of sexual intercourse, discovering other forms of sexual expression may in fact be helpful to Rochelle as she moves through this time in her life.

With her dual consciousness of the pleasure of desire and the endless list of its dangers, Rochelle ends up, more often than not, unconsciously cutting herself off from her body. Yet she also has figured out how to jerry-rig safe spaces for desire once in a while. There is a hitch, though. She explains, "Most of the time, I'm by myself when I do." In other words, one strategy is to feel desire when she is alone. She tells a story in breathless tones about an experience of her own sexual desire just the previous night:

Last night, I had this crank call . . . At first I thought it was my boyfriend, 'cause he likes to play around, you know. But I was sitting there talking, you know, and thinking of him and then I found out it's not him, it was so crazy weird, so I hang the phone up and he called back, he called back, and called back. And then I couldn't sleep, I just had this feeling that I wanted to have sex so so bad. It was like three o'clock in the morning. And I didn't sleep the rest of the night. And like, I called my boyfriend and I was tellin' him, and he was like, what do you want me to do, Rochelle, I'm sleeping! [laughs]. I was like, okay, okay, well I'll talk to you later, bye. And then, like, I don't know, I just wanted to, and like, I kept tossin' and turnin'. And I'm trying to think who it was, who was callin' me, 'cause like, it's always the same guy who always crank calls me, he says he knows me. It's kinda scary . . . I can't sleep, I'm like, I just think about it, like, oh I wanna have sex so bad, you know, it's like a fever, drugs, something like that. Like

last night, I don't know, I think if I woulda had the car and stuff,
I probably woulda left the house. And went over to his house,
you know. But I couldn't, 'cause I was baby-sitting.

This story exemplifies how the eroticization of danger can play
out in women's sexual desire. Rochelle is visibly pleased when I
acknowledge that, while frightening, this experience has an exciting quality to it; as she says, "yeah, it's sorta arousing!" There is a
paradox in that she has these intense sexual feelings when she is
alone and essentially assured of remaining alone owing to the late
hour and her responsibilities. Alone, not subject to observation
nor vulnerable to physical or social consequences, Rochelle finds
freedom to experience the turbulent feelings that are awakened in
her body. In this moment, Rochelle's desire has not been obliter-
ated by her fear; desire and fear coexist.

Inez: Telling Her Body "No"

Inez, the girl who told me sex "just happened" in the first chapter,
says that the adults in her life talk to her a lot about sex. Inez's
description of what she hears about girls' sexuality exemplifies the
cacophony of voices that swirl in girls' minds, illuminating how
often adults warn them about sexuality and how rarely girls can
speak honestly or ask genuine questions about their desire. Inez
has been inundated with messages about the importance of her
virginity—messages that ring in her ears even though she has
already had sex—and about the hazards of pregnancy. While her
mother still thinks Inez is a virgin, she tells Inez over and over
again, "Be sure you don't get pregnant." In church she hears that a
girl is "supposed to be a virgin when she gets married. If you don't,
you're sinning." In school she is told about contraception, condoms, and avoiding pregnancy. Her father offers the most dire and
negative cautions, warning that her boyfriend "was gonna take my

virginity, and then he was gonna leave me, and I was gonna get pregnant, and I was gonna have a baby with no father and that I wasn't gonna have a job and I was gonna drop out of school." While talking about her sexuality constantly, the adults in Inez's life dwell on the dangers of pregnancy, sinning, and boys' bad behavior; no one says anything to her about her sexual feelings.

Recall that in telling a story about having sex for the first time, Inez does not name her own desire. She says that "everything just happened." Having sexual intercourse for the first time was not actually Inez's first sexual experience. In other stories she tells, she offers descriptions of her desire that convey her knowledge of its power, her experience of sexual pleasure, and how she has, on her own, come to make sense of and deal with these feelings. Her keen awareness of both the pleasure and the danger that come with desire filters through a story about a time when she had such a "conflict" between her body and her mind:

> Yesterday I was talking to my ex-boyfriend, and I was having a little conflict in my mind, 'cause he was kissing me and he was making me feel desire and, but he wasn't touching me, you know, he was just, he was just kissing me, kissing me on the back of my neck. And he knows where my weak spot is. That's my weak [laughs, points to her neck], that's my weak spot. And he was touching me on the back of my neck and I just felt a lot of desire . . . [and] my mind was saying yes no yes no! . . . I was like, come on, let's take a walk and it was real fresh air, it's like, I was like [takes deep breath in, out], oh God, Inez, I kept telling myself, calm down, please! Just calm down.

Inez calls a part of her body that, when touched or kissed, generates powerful feelings of desire her "weak spot." With full knowledge of the pleasure of desire, even of how it makes her feel connected with someone she cares about, Inez understands her

own desire as a source of tremendous vulnerability. She takes me
through the mind-body conflict that arises when she is in a "pleasure mood":

> My body does not control my mind. My mind controls my body,
> and if my body gets into the pleasure mood, my mind is gonna
> tell him no . . . because I said so, because I control you, and my
> mind is lookin' towards my body.

Inez describes a watchfulness that her "mind," reservoir of social
norms and rules and compendium of consequences, exerts over
her body. Not only does she describe her mind as chastising her
body, almost as if it were a recalcitrant child, but her mind is also
"lookin' towards"—protecting—her body, a body she experiences
as in danger and as a source of danger. She is very knowledgeable
about the physical dangers associated explicitly with her own
desire that make her vulnerable:

> Let's say you don't have no kind of contraceptives like a condom,
> and he has AIDS and you don't know that, you can get AIDS just
> by having sex with him, because your body said yes, your mind
> said no, but your body said yes.

As a result, Inez vigilantly controls her own sexual feelings. She
knows about and uses contraception, though it is unclear how
accessible reliable methods are for her. She knows also about using
condoms to protect herself from exposure to disease, though she
voices concerns about condoms breaking. And she alludes to other
forms of sexual expression, though she rejects some of them as
"nasty."

Inez protects herself from her own desire by keeping herself out
of risky situations—situations in which her desire might be
inflamed, situations in which she might know the joys of pleasure

and a feeling of connection with another person, situations in which her desire might "win" and inevitably lead to danger—and minimizing the moments when she will have to cope with this mind-body conflict. She deepens her knowledge with observations of other girls:

> Desire? Yes, because she's [a girl] probably in one of those, like let's say she's just drunk and she doesn't know what she's doin', and she's dancing with this guy, you know how they dance reggae, ever seen somebody dance reggae? How they rubbin' on each other? Well that gets a guy real, I'll say, hard. And it gets a girl very horny. And they could just be dancin' together for like five minutes, and all of a sudden [snaps fingers], they just, they, something just snaps in 'em and they say, "oh, let's go to the bedroom." And, it'll just happen, just because they were dancing. That's why I don't dance reggae with guys.

Inez does not frame the danger of dancing reggae as the lure of romance or the promise of a romantic relationship; this kind of dancing is sexually arousing for the girl as well as for the boy—the boy gets "hard," the girl gets "very horny." In this interview, Inez has told me that she enjoys dancing and describes herself as a very good dancer, which is something about herself that makes her feel proud. However, to avoid getting "very horny," Inez does not dance reggae. To keep her body safe, she keeps her body still.

Especially tuned in to social risks associated with acting on her desire, the danger of losing her reputation and of not being "respected," she is also fearful of doing or saying anything that might reveal her true wishes, thereby risking humiliation and a loss of dignity. She identifies talking about her sexual desire as a way to make trouble and reveals her intricate knowledge of how a confidence about sexuality can become "dangerous":

Let's say I trust my best friend, I trust her with all my might and I would say, oh yeah, I just had sex with my boyfriend yesterday, and I had oral sex. And [I] say, yeah, I been with him six months and it was the first time we did something and we had oral sex. And she says, wow, that's good, you know, and somebody else is listening in and they're saying goodness! They was like, that girl, she's havin' oral sex! . . . and she goes and tells her friends, oh yeah, you know, Inez has a boyfriend, she's been going out with him for six months and she's had oral sex. And then she'll go to somebody else and they say, yeah, you know that Inez has had three boyfriends in the past six months and she had oral sex? And they say, oh yeah, you know, and then they go to the next person and it goes on and on and everyone's like, yeah, you know that Inez did it with two [guys in a gang] and she had oral sex, it just like goes from one person to another, and let's say the first one when they hear it, they hear it exactly the way it came out, and they go to someone else and they say, yeah she has five boyfriends and she's had oral sex with three, and it can be the first time. But nobody knows that except for you.

Inez's description brings to life this nightmare scenario that she imagines will follow a careful story about exploring a new sexual experience told to a close friend, in confidence. Even though in this example Inez stipulates that she was talking about a committed relationship, an ostensible "safe space" for such experiences, she is keenly aware of how it can be spun into a tale of sexual promiscuity that has nothing to do with reality. As in a game of telephone, she has no control over what the final version will sound like. Once talked about in this way, a girl will have a hard time getting her version of the story accepted and reclaiming her status as a "good," nice, and "respectable" girl.

Having had a boyfriend who told his friends that he had had sex with her when he had not, she goes to extreme lengths to make sure that no one besides her two best friends knows anything about her sexual experiences. Her response to having been hurt and humiliated is to not trust boys easily or often (although she also describes girls as culprits in giving other girls a bad name). She also tries to exert ever more control over herself, even though in this instance she had not in fact had sex with the boy (although she confesses that "it was something I really wanted"). Inez can control only herself and not what others choose to say about her, so keeping her desire dampened does not keep her safe.

One thing she can do is be adamant that boys give her respect. To earn her trust, she says, boys "gotta respect me from the beginning, they gotta trust me with guys, they gotta respect me, not to touch me if I don't wanna be touched, not to kiss me on a first date, 'cause I don't kiss guys on a first date. Not to try to touch me anywhere that I feel uncomfortable or tell me stuff that's gonna make me feel uncomfortable . . . like trying to give me a hint like, yeah, let's have sex, I don't like when guys do that." She does not worry about getting a "bad name" because of her vigilance about getting respect. The logic of Inez's strategy—to get respect, she needs to keep boys, and their desire for her, at bay—requires that she forbid kissing on the first date. But what if she wants to kiss a boy on the first date? Inez has learned to circumscribe her desire as a way to keep herself safe but in so doing puts her ability to feel and to rely on her desire, to know if and how she wants to express her sexual feelings, in jeopardy. She wears the mantle of full responsibility for sexual episodes, not questioning why she should have to be put in this position in the first place nor seeing how unfair it is that she must be solely accountable or vulnerable to social sanctions in such situations. Her response to the anticipation of male sexual aggression is to protect herself from it; the question of how boys do or should handle their own desire is never formulated.

If Inez succeeds in fending off her own desire, she is still vulnerable to the desires of others and must continue to protect herself from being harmed, used, or taken advantage of. Without her own desire, Inez is reduced to being a sexual object, the object of another's desire. So while her strategy of silencing her body's "yes" may lower her risks in some ways, rather than create a safe space for her, it just keeps danger out. Whether or not she feels sexual desire and sexual pleasure, she remains at constant risk of being hurt, getting a "bad name," and never being able to make positive choices about her sexuality. Inez's sacrifice of her own desire and pleasure represents a logical yet ineffective attempt to protect herself.

AMBIVALENT DESIRES

The girls who "disappear" their desire sacrifice their sexuality for the sake of safety in a realm of their lives that feels suffused with danger. None of them questions this approach; the notion that it is unsafe for girls to have sexual feelings, premised on an assumption of male entitlement to unbridled sexuality, is deeply embedded in their response to their own desire. The other group of girls who resist their own sexual desire do not sound as decisive, nor do they sacrifice their desire in the same fashion. Both Emily and Megan have some awareness that they should be entitled to their sexual desire and so do not cut themselves off as a solution. However, they describe an uneasy balance between the power of desire and the threat of consequences. As they feel desire, apprehend how it connects them with themselves, and appreciate a mutual connection with another person, they worry about the price they will have to pay. In the circumscribed space they have allotted to their sexual subjectivity, vulnerability to being objectified and ostracized looms large. These girls also evidence a glimmer of a critical perspective on the institution of heterosexuality, which unfairly punishes desiring girls, yet they do not go so far as to push "good" girls off their pedestals or to elevate "sluts." Emily, who has a vague sense of her right to sexual feelings, is especially fearful of social consequences, while Megan, whose critique of the double standard is more evolved yet still falls short of rejection, has more comfort with her desire for boys. For Megan, the recent acceptance of her sexual feelings for girls is the front line of her struggle.

Emily: The Fear of "Being Used"

There is no question that Emily is ready, willing, and able to talk to me about her experiences with sexual desire. Woven through her vibrant, insightful, and at times brutally honest descriptions and stories are hints about the duality that characterizes desire in her life. I am especially taken with how engaged she is in our conversation and with this topic; it is clearly a key issue for her. Echoing other girls in the study, Emily does not tell a completely monolithic story of desire. Her ambivalence about her sexual desire is not immediately evident; it takes shape as she talks about the various ways that she has experienced it in specific contexts. Like a naturalist, Emily has made careful, specific observations about how her body works and what she feels like, both physically and emotionally, in various situations. She can talk about what does and does not give her pleasure, what piques her sexual desire and what dampens it. Her sexual desire plays a principal role in the stories she tells about her sexual experiences with her boyfriend of the last year, whom she "loves a lot," and weaves in and out of other stories she tells about her experiences with boys, relationships, and sexuality.

The first thing she tells me flies in the face of societal beliefs about adolescent sexuality. In describing how her current relationship evolved, she reflects: "I think I wanted to sleep with him more than he wanted to sleep with me at the beginning. He's not that type . . . And he wasn't really sure that he was ready, and so we ended up waiting like two more months." Her comments and questions about her desire have a sophisticated flair, as she describes being frustrated when she doesn't find some sexual experiences satisfying, curious about what an orgasm feels like and how to have one, puzzled and a bit miffed by the ease with which her boyfriend seems to experience "more intense" sexual pleasure than she does, experimenting with how to increase the power of her own feelings. It is also clear that this relationship is a safe space not only for her sexual desire but also for exploring how sexuality and intimacy work together in a heterosexual relationship in which the gendered power differentials are minimized. The way she has characterized her current relationship, and herself in that relational context, stands in stark contrast to the more familiar landscape of gendered sexuality that girls tend to describe and that she herself does in other stories she tells about her own desire. Emily has the good fortune of having a boyfriend with a genuine interest in an egalitarian relationship, who respects her feelings and her entitlement to safety and pleasure. But not all of her sexual experiences have been with boys who evidence such disinterest in the kinds of power that the institution of heterosexuality confers. And Emily herself finds reaching for equality and entitlement challenging.

Sheepishly elaborating aspects of her desire that she considers unflattering, she tells me that desire "is a big deal for me in terms of boyfriends. I think that the reason, this may sound really bitchy and really like awful, but the reason a lot of times that I break up with someone is because I'm not attracted to them anymore . . . if they're not attractive to me anymore then I just can't . . . if I'm not attracted to them I don't wanna fool around, it's almost like a chore." She describes this quality as "a criterion that I haven't been able to overcome . . . it's just kind of important to me." Emily demonstrates a sophisticated understanding of the central role that her desire plays in providing her with information about a relationship. This insight is coupled with her embarrassment over how important feeling "attracted" to a boyfriend is for her, calling her sentiments "really bitchy" and "awful," intimating that the loss of feeling attracted to someone is not an appropriate female "criterion" for breaking up. At the same time, she realizes that having a sexual experience when she is not attracted to her partner, something she is doing for negative reasons that do not include her own wish to "fool around," feels like a "chore" for her. Her sense that the absence of her desire is a problem collides with her knowledge of how its presence puts her at risk for being labeled a bitch. I begin to see the kind of no-win situation that Emily's desire, either having it or not, creates for her in the quicksand of aspirations of femininity.

Emily does not speak about sexual violence. She says that she does not worry about pregnancy because she is using contraception in a committed relationship, and she does not mention any concern about HIV. Although sex does not "just happen" to Emily, her own desire appears to be unreliable as a guidepost for her behavior. For instance, Emily does not feel entitled to explore her sexuality through masturbation because "it's not accepted for women to masturbate." Even though she knows that "girls should," and even though Emily has stated that she wants to understand and experience her sexuality more than she has been able to up to now, she "can't" engage in the simple act of touching herself sexually, the safest of all sexual practices, in private and out of range of the judgment of others. Thus it is not the rejection by others that concerns Emily; for her, the discomforts of desire come from inside.

The source of this discomfort lies in her ambivalent embrace of gendered sexuality. While on the one hand she can describe feeling and acting on her desire and how important it is to her to integrate her sexuality into her growing sense of who she is and how relationships go, on the other she is keenly aware of the potential danger that sexuality opens up for girls. She describes how she has been socialized into this view: "Maybe it's that all through growing up, [adults tell you] he's gonna try to get this off you, and he's gonna try to do, you know, when you're little, and he's gonna try to kiss you and you have to say no, you know, stuff like that, not that you have to say no, but be prepared for that, and stuff like that." She realizes that she often feels "self-conscious using 'I'" as we talk; she observes, "I don't like to think of myself as feeling really sexual . . . I don't like to think of myself as being like someone who needs to have their desires fulfilled." When I ask what she thinks about the contradiction between this self concept and her explicit descriptions of feeling desire as a positive part of her relationship, she expresses her ambivalence. She just does not feel comfortable acknowledging that she "need[s] this kind of a thing," despite also having a sense that "it's wrong [not to acknowledge her needs] and that everybody has needs." Emily has offered a picture of adolescent sexuality that does not include her sexual feelings. In fact, it requires her to protect herself from a boy's assumed desire for her; she is responsible for holding his feelings at bay. So it is not surprising that Emily feels "self-conscious" when she speaks about and claims her "sexual needs." Emily remembers hearing "he's gonna try to kiss you"; she does not speak of hearing that she might want to kiss him. She demonstrates a sophisticated understanding of how she has been guided through "societal" means out of her body and into "self-conscious[ness]," perceiving the vulnerability of girls who have needs in a world where boys are assumed to be sexual aggressors. Despite having a pleasurable sexual relationship with a boy who is not a sexual predator, and despite knowing that her feelings are or at least should be considered normal, she is unsure if she can have desire and be safe, given the constant threats of social repercussions and male sexual aggression that have been ingrained in her. The gap between "everyone has needs" and what she knows and fears happens to girls who do has not yet been filled in.

As she pursues her identity as a "good" and "nice" girl who is liked, respected, and not exploited, Emily lives in a constant state of fear that she will "get used" and feel like a "slut," that is, a "bad" girl who has no defense against being mistreated. Espousing the complementary belief that boys and men are sexual predators makes it hard to question the social, relational, or psychological dangers that are meant to keep her desire in check. When she capitulates to these interlocking gendered notions, she comes into conflict with what she knows about girls from her own embodied experience and about boys from her own relational experience. While strong feelings of desire do not sit easily with her self-image as a "people pleaser," who must discount her own feelings to avoid conflict, ironically, it is when she takes on this identity that she becomes vulnerable.

For instance, she describes pretending to have enjoyed a time when a previous boyfriend, in whom she was rapidly losing interest, put a lot of his fingers in her vagina:

> E: He was almost like hurting me, I just faked like loud and I just like made him come so the whole thing would stop . . . I was just getting almost bored, nothing was happening, I would just rather have been watching TV, I wasn't really attracted to him, I just didn't have the energy to put off his come-ons, so I just gave him a hand job and so he came and then it like ended.
>
> D: Why was it important for you to appear like you were enjoying yourself?
>
> E: I don't know, I think it's kind of almost mean, personally, I would feel mean and uncaring if I didn't, it was just one, I mean, it was no skin off my back to do it, so why not make him happy

by just pretending, it was no big deal, I mean, I wasn't getting hurt by it.

Describing herself as "bored," "[not] really attracted to him," and not "hav[ing] the energy to put off his come-ons" in this story, Emily renders her own sexual feelings irrelevant to, and absent from, the situation. Her sexual behavior is fueled by her desire to stop an unpleasant experience; her strategy for doing so is to fake her own pleasure and engage in a sexual behavior that is empty of feeling. She explains that this pretense of pleasure keeps her from feeling "mean" and "uncaring"—undesirable qualities for a nice girl who thinks of herself as a "people pleaser." It is ironic that to get a boy to stop hurting her in a failed attempt to provide her with pleasure, rather than asking him to stop or do it differently, she covers up her displeasure with pretend pleasure, which, she says, did not cause her to get "hurt."

It is when, and only when, her sexual subjectivity is discounted, by herself or by someone else, that her talk turns to being exploited or "used" or being considered a slut. This fear is a pall even over her current relationship; her uncertain reflection "I don't feel used, particularly," suggests her suspicion that having sexual experiences in which she does not feel "fulfilled" while her boyfriend gets "more satisfaction" might mean she is being used. In another situation, a boy she "fooled around with" one night at a party "jumped out of the bed and walked out of the room as soon as he had come." When I ask her why she might get into a situation like that, her explanation includes her lack of desire and her wish to avoid conflict: "because it's usually in front of other people and like, why you, I'll say no, no, the first time and then they'll do it again or something like that, and I'll just feel bad and I'll just say okay. I mean it's not a big deal to me, so in a way I'm letting myself be used." Not only does her resolve fold under the pressure of her wish to evade "feel[ing] bad" by embarrassing a boy "in front of other people," she also takes the blame for "letting [her]self be used," letting the boy off the hook for his coercive behavior. Interestingly, while she says that being used makes her feel like a "slut," she does not say she worries about getting a reputation. In a way, social repercussions are superfluous, since she beats her peers to the punch by being so punitive with herself.

Emily is negotiating a complex set of messages that do not line up neatly with her own experiences. Hearing that boys will assert their sexual needs is contradicted by her boyfriend's reticence about having sex. The notion that "everyone has needs" is challenged by how her sexual feelings are overlooked by others and her own ambivalence about them. The contradiction between being a "people pleaser" and a girl with desires of her own leaves her with no clear direction about how to deal with her embodied sexuality in a landscape that is dotted, inside and out, with the possibility of being a "slut" who will always and forever be in danger of being used.

For Emily, her own desire has led both to humiliating and scary encounters she regrets and to powerful experiences of connection with someone she loves. It has led to exciting, unexpected moments tinged with taboo and to frustrating, disappointing interactions that leave her confused. Emily is not sure if or how she can rely on her desire, or when it is and is not safe to do so. Yet these contradictory experiences of desire are not compartmentalized; each hangs over the other, casting shadows and shining light on possibilities for danger and glints of pleasure.

Megan: Confusion in the Face of Contradiction

Megan has questions of her own about girls' sexual desire, lots of them. Perky, enthusiastic, yet increasingly jittery as our interview progresses, she hits on the contradiction between her awareness of the social mandates for appropriate female sexuality and her awareness of the vicissitudes of her own sexual desire. She identifies herself as bisexual, having joined a group for sexual minority youth, where she is "exploring" her feelings for girls. Her descriptions of her experiences of sexual desire differ for boys and for girls. Regarding boys, she offers articulate and evocative descriptions of what desire feels like to her; it is Megan who says that her "vagina starts to kinda like act up" when she feels desire. For girls, however, she is in uncharted territory, her mind "block[ing]" her body out as soon as she notices she feels an attraction. She attributes this short-circuiting to the newness of her own acceptance of her desire for girls. We talk more about her heterosexual experiences.

She is fully aware of how "society" makes no room for girls to feel sexual desire, while boys are expected to feel "horny." Grounding her analysis in her acceptance of her own sexual desire, she thinks this failure to acknowledge or normalize girls' sexuality produces the pretense among most girls that they do not have such feelings: "I'm not more horny than the next one but [when talking with her brother about sex,] I'm open about it and probably other girls aren't open about it, so he's probably like, oh my god, but I think a lot of girls are like that and if a guy said it, it'd be fine, but you know, me saying it, it's different." Nevertheless, Megan cannot figure out how to put this awareness to use in her own life. Her consciousness of girls' embodied desire and her refusal to buy into the notion that it is immoral or abnormal yields an astute social analysis that "maybe reputations like keep you in line, like maybe [girls would] just do whatever the hell they wanted to do if there was no reputation they would get or something." While she understands the dynamics of social control at play, she does not go so far as to reject this social stigma. While Megan is an avid and critical reader of gendered beliefs about adolescent sexuality, she struggles with her wish to fit in and to be considered, as well as feel, normal under current gender arrangements and mandates that leave her actual feelings out. Her ambivalence about what she knows and what to do about it are tangible.

Megan has had a few boyfriends and a number of heterosexual experiences and has had a range of reactions to and questions about them. Talking it over with her mother, Megan has decided that she is "too young" and wants to wait until she has a "good relationship" to have sexual intercourse.

> It's better to do those kind of things with someone you really care about, you know, it just makes it better, and you just like it more, you know? And that makes sense. I don't want to like ruin my first experience with someone that I don't know at all . . . I'm just not old enough to have sex . . . I still have a lot more exploring to do before I do that, you know? I wouldn't wanna rush it. It's just not worth it.

Megan's choice not to have intercourse is grounded not in the constraints of femininity but in practical considerations about her maturity and her values. Like the majority of girls her age, at this point in her life, her sexuality is in fact not about sexual intercourse, it is about experiencing sexual desire and "exploring" the contours of her sexuality outside the danger zone of intercourse. Therefore, even her mother's advice, which guides her to make responsible decisions and also to have positive expectations about sexual intercourse with boys, does not help her understand her sexual feelings when intercourse is not the issue. Reflecting on a time when she and a boy were kissing and touching each other, she says:

> I don't know what I wanted. I was so confused the next day, it was like why did I do that? I mean it felt good when we were doing it,

so why wouldn't you just wanna keep going on and on and on? I stopped him, it felt good, but I am so young, and you just don't do that . . . I mean, are you just supposed to ignore those feelings?

Megan is left to her own devices to figure out how she might deal with her desire: Is she "supposed to ignore those feelings?" And the contradiction between her feelings and societal messages confuses her:

It's so confusing, 'cause you have to like say no, you have to be the one to say no, but why should you be the one to, 'cause I mean maybe you're enjoying it and you shouldn't have to say no or anything. But if you don't, maybe the guy'll just keep going and going, and you can't do that, because then you would be a slut . . . I mean so many of my friends have done it and in a way it's kinda good if you, like my friends who haven't ever kissed a guy or they've just kissed or something, that's not cool either, you have to be kinda in the middle, you know, you have to like know what you're doing but not go that far . . . There's so [much] like, you know, stuff that you have to deal with and I don't know, just I keep losing my thought.

Although Megan knows the logic offered by society—that she must "say no" to keep him from "going and going," which will make her "a slut"—she is also aware of what is missing from that logic, that maybe the girl is the one who is "enjoying it." The fact that she may be experiencing sexual desire renders the response she is expected to have—to fend him off—virtually nonsensical. The rule does not address her actual question; it precludes such a question. She also has the additional burden of trying to figure out what "be[ing] kinda in the middle," having some but not too much sexual experience, actually is. Because she does feel her own desire and can identify the potential of her own pleasure, Megan asks the next logical question: "why should you be the one to [say no]"? She knows the answer that gendered sexuality supplies: because she will be called a slut if she doesn't apply the brakes, while there are no negative consequences for boys. Because she does not actually pose this question to anyone else, she remains confused by a system that does not make sense, if her own sexual desire is part of what actually happens.

Her questions about the double standard enable her belief, at least in theory, that she is as entitled to sexual pleasure as boys are. Alone with her questions, relying only on herself for answers, she finds that it is hard for her to feel comfortable acting on these countervailing convictions. She tells me, "I do stuff, I feel like I wanna, I wanna do stuff, that I wanna do, but I know that isn't right for me societally." When I ask her for an example, she offers masturbation, indicating how the conflict for her is not only with the external social world but also inside herself: "Sometimes I stop myself from masturbating, but usually not. You just kinda, I just kinda struggle with that, you know, I mean, you feel guilty but, so what? No one knows. Except you [laughs]. And, you know, [I read a teen] magazine that said it was okay [laughs] so [laughs]." Laughing through her discomfort with the contradiction between knowing that desire is not acceptable for girls and reading a magazine that says it is okay, Megan ends up masturbating but struggling with her guilt about it.

Not only has she observed the ways that messages about girls' sexuality, in their ubiquitous focus on preventing sexual intercourse, leave out or condemn her embodied feelings for boys and even the possibility of sexual pleasure through masturbation, she is also keenly aware of the pervasiveness of cultural norms and images that demand heterosexuality:

Every teen magazine you look at is like, guy this, how to get a date, guys, guys, guys, guys, guys. So you're constantly faced with, I have to have a boyfriend, I have to have a boyfriend, you know, even if you don't have a boyfriend, just [have] a fling, you know, you just want to kiss a guy or something. I've had that mentality for so long.

In this perfect description Megan brings the concept of compulsory heterosexuality to life, capturing the pressure exerted upon her to have a boyfriend, which produces inevitable conflict with that other mandate: to say no when with a boy who is supposed to be trying to have sex. She is aware of how her psyche has been shaped into a "mentality" requiring any sexual or relational interests to be heterosexual, which contradicts how she actually feels. Megan explains how compulsory heterosexuality comes between her and her feelings, making her vulnerable to dissociation from her feelings under this pressure.

Megan tells far fewer stories about her desire for girls. Becoming friends with a lesbian girl this year and joining a youth group for sexual minorities "really helped me to, you know, talk about it, just made me feel so much better, like I read my diary from before and I just remember, I came back from this basketball game where I had liked this girl and I was just like so . . . confused, I don't understand, why do I like this girl, why does this always happen, you know? And I just didn't like myself for doing that." Acknowledging her feelings, and having those feelings accepted and validated, has diminished the negative feelings Megan had about herself and her attraction to girls when she was living, as she describes it, in a more "homophobic" environment.

In contrast to Megan's clarity about her embodied sexual feelings toward boys, her desire for girls is much more elusive. She is aware of her own psychological resistance:

I mean, I'll see a girl I really, really like, you know, because I think
she's so beautiful, and I might, I don't know. I'm so confused . . .
But there's, you know, that same mentality as me liking a guy if
he's really cute, I'm like, oh my God, you know, he's so cute. If I
see a woman that I like, a girl, it's just like wow, she's so pretty,
you know. See I can picture like hugging a girl; I just can't picture
the sex, or anything, so, there's something being blocked.

Megan links her confusion and "being blocked" to the absence of
images of lesbian sexuality, in contrast to the heterosexual imagery
all around her: "I think that there's always that little thing in here
that, you know, you need a guy, in my head, sometimes I just can't
tell where the line is or whether, you know, I mean physically wanting a guy or mentally. Or a girl . . . there's never that mentality to,
you want a girl, you want a girl, you want a girl, so I never think of
that. But then I'll see a girl and I'll like have a crush on her, you
know . . . But I can't imagine kissing them."

She posits a connection between her lack of sexual experience
with girls and her lack of clarity about her desire for them: "my
vagina doesn't act up when I just see a guy. More of like when I'm
close to a guy, touching a guy, kissing a guy, and I haven't done that
with girls." Yet she has been in a situation where she was "close to" a
girl and narrates how she silenced her body in its first stirrings:

There was this one girl that I had kinda liked from school, and it
was like really weird 'cause she's really popular and everything.
And we were sitting next to each other during the movie and,
kind of her leg was on my leg and I was like, wow, you know, and
that was, I think that's like the first time that I've ever felt like sexual pleasure for a girl. But it's so impossible, I think I just like
block it out, I mean, it could never happen . . . I just can't know
what I'm feeling . . . I probably first mentally just say no, don't
feel it, you know, maybe. But I never start to feel, I don't know.

It's so confusing. 'Cause finally it's all right for me to like a girl,
you know?

Megan details her resistance to her embodied sexual feelings,
describing how she "mentally" silences her body by saying no, pre-
empting and dissociating from her embodied response. Echoing
dominant cultural constructions of sexual desire, Megan links her
"blocking" of her desire for girls with fear: "you can picture yourself kissing a guy but then if you like a girl a lot and then you picture yourself kissing her, it's just like, I can't, you know, oh my God,
no [laughs], you know it's like scary . . . it's society . . . you never
would think of, you know, it's natural to kiss a girl." Megan's fear
about her desire for girls is different from the fears associated with
her desire for boys. Although being too sexual with boys brings the
stigma of being called a slut, she has a fundamental belief in her
entitlement to heterosexual desire. Given what she knows about
the heterosexual culture in which she is immersed—the pressure
she feels to be interested in "guys"—and also given what she knows
about homophobia, there is an inherent logic in Megan's response
of confusion to her feelings for girls.

For Megan, a keen awareness of compulsory heterosexuality
undergirds her fear of rejection. Megan keeps herself from feeling
the feelings that could lead to disappointment, embarrassment,
frustration, or even retaliation, keeping her safe from these negative consequences. But at what price does she buy this temporary
stay on her desire, this momentary safety? If Megan has to constantly engage in an active process of denying her desire, like Inez,
then not only is her ability to develop a healthy sexual self impaired
but she must funnel a lot of energy into maintaining this silencing,
into keeping herself cut off from the reality of her own feelings. If
she were able to acknowledge her feelings in relationships with her

peers, she could think about rather than think away what her feelings are, what they are like, and what she might choose to do in response to them.

As Teresa Bernardez (1988) has observed about anger, another feeling regulated out of the repertoire of femininity, cultural prohibitions on powerful embodied feelings in women turn into psychological inhibitions, which "prevent rebellious acts," with the result that women come to feel complicit in their own misery, and in fact do in some sense become complicit. Society's dominant cultural construction of femininity encourages girls and women to be desirable but not desiring. The association of femininity with the absence of hunger incites in girls a wish for what Elizabeth Debold and I have called a "no-body body" of femininity, "an image [that] is flat, has no feelings, is silent . . . can have no appetite, no hunger, no desire, and no power of its own."[2] This wish is substantiated and supported by the rule book of gendered sexuality, by the carrot of romance and the stick of a maligned reputation.

The girls in this chapter negotiate their own personal dilemmas of desire by resisting their sexual feelings. While they are aware—some more, some less—of the power, pleasure, and possibility embedded in their sexual desire, they feel acutely vulnerable to its dangers. The more dangerous they feel desire to be for them, the more unequivocally they resist their desire. Working within the institution of heterosexuality, they do not hold boys or social conventions accountable for making sexuality dangerous; rather, it is *their own sexual feelings* that constitute both the problem and the answer. These girls all evidence awareness, at some level, that if they bring their desire forthrightly into their relationships, they will be in conflict with others in their lives, and with themselves. Some, like Inez, resist consciously: she tells her body no. Others,

like Rochelle, respond more psychologically and reflexively, as
when her own desire frightens her to the point of tears. Still others,
like Emily, vacillate between a recognition of their own desire and a
painful discomfort with accepting it as a normal feature of who
they are. Megan voices an acute frustration with her resistance to
her desire for girls; perhaps her experience of desire with boys
offers her a foothold for identifying her difficulty with desire for
girls.

Why is their formulation of their desire as a route to danger a
problem? Why should we worry, for example, that Ellen and Inez
silence their bodies in response to their own desire? After all, for
Ellen, this is the road to staying safe until she completes her education, and for Inez, it is a way to gain respect and avoid sexual intercourse. Given current arrangements, this strategy not only makes
sense, it even conveys a certain wisdom. But if we anchor our
assessment in the belief that having sexual desire is normal, we ask
a different question: Why should the girls' responses have to be so
extreme? Why should they have to cut themselves off from themselves simply to stay safe, complete their education, maintain their
reputations?

The girls in the previous chapter did not feel desire and thus, in
essence, described an unconscious response to the denial and denigration of girls' desire. The girls who feel desire but resist it are
more likely to cast it as an individual problem they have to figure
out. Because they have internalized the notion that girls' sexual
desire is anathema, they do not talk with anyone about how they
might deal with these feelings. Embodied desire, which Inez recognizes and knows can bring her pleasure but feels she must silence,
is not part of the lexicon of how anyone—her friends, her family,
her school, or her community—talks with her about sexuality.
These girls' internal focus, illustrated so well by Inez's microman-
agement of her own sexual feelings, distracts them from asking

what might become obvious questions if they felt entitled to their own sexual feelings, including the question Megan is on the verge of asking: Why do I have to protect myself from boys' sexual desire? Why aren't my feelings accounted for, inquired about, responded to?

5   PARAMETERS OF PLEASURE

> For some, the dangers of sexuality . . . make
> the pleasures pale by comparison. For oth-
> ers, the positive possibilities of sexuality, ex-
> plorations of the body, curiosity, intimacy,
> sensuality, adventure, excitement, human
> connection . . . are not only worthwhile but
> provide sustaining energy.
>
> —Carole Vance, "Pleasure and Danger:
> Exploring Female Sexuality"

While it is almost a cliché to say that
the personal is political, listening to all of these girls struggling
with the various incarnations of the dilemma of desire reminds us
just how personal the political actually is and how political the personal is. Calling attention to the possibility and importance of
pleasure and passion rather than focusing exclusively on the need
to diminish danger and threats brings the political nature of gendered sexuality to the fore. This double-edged quality is at the
heart of the politics of female sexual desire.

In the last few years, resistance to societal denial and denigration
of adolescent girls' sexual desire has been brewing, among adult
activists and scholars and among adolescent girls themselves. Web
sites, magazines written by and for girls, "zines,"[1] and books such
as *Deal with It! A Whole New Approach to Your Body, Brain, and Life
as a gurl* provide information about female adolescent experience
that has traditionally been taboo or unconventional. In some zines
girls write "rants" about their fury at being objectified, violated, or

abused, and about their right to their own sexual desire (see, for example, Carlip, 1995). Such girls consciously claim an explicitly politicized perspective on beliefs and master narratives, which serve to normalize the denial of girls' desire and sexual subjectivity within and through the institution of heterosexuality. These girls are "resist[ing] the temptation to . . . simply correct . . . for male perspective [which makes] the framework . . . invisible" (Gilligan, 1990, p. 509). Specifically, they can discern how "reality" is shaped to make a desiring girl a "bad" girl, and, because they can identify the pressures they are under to adopt this point of view and how it does not serve their interests, they are able to resist it. In so doing, they gain a standpoint from which to see how concepts such as "femininity" and "slut" function to keep them from acting on, feeling entitled to, or even knowing about their own sexual feelings. What is necessary for such resistance, however, is the ability, courage, and willingness to see and critique these highly institutionalized processes that work because they are so hard to pin down.[2] It requires an awareness of the politics of desire and a community dedicated to changing the situation, because resistance in isolation is extremely hard. When girls can say what they really know and experience to others in relationships, this knowledge becomes more stable.

Feminism and the sexual revolution have obviously made significant inroads in revealing and undoing women's and girls' sexual oppression but just as obviously have not fully solved the problem (Jeffreys, 1990; Ussher, 1997). Listening to the girls in the previous chapters reveals how entrenched gendered sexuality and the double standard continue to be (see also Kamen, 2000). The sexual revolution began to challenge the demonizing of women's desire, but complete freedom for female sexual desire was not won.[3] The good girl–bad girl dichotomy has been challenged but not dismantled. In fact, it has become even more confusing because it is now riddled with caveats, such as girls should not be sluts but they should not be prudes. In this context, girls are now expected to be sexual, but primarily in ways that cater to boys' desire rather than to their own (Wolf, 1997); stringent and shifting social constraints upon their desire remain in place. The girls in this chapter describe experiences that reflect the advantages and limits of this destabilized situation.

In contrast to the girls in the previous chapters, all of the girls in this chapter are certain in their belief that they are entitled to their sexual desire. Rather than negate their bodies or try to juggle mixed or truncated messages about girls' sexuality, these girls narrate their attempts to work around the social, physical, relational, and psychological implications they are well aware await them if they refuse to give up or feel uncomfortable about their sexual feelings. Like the girls who have silent bodies or resist their own desire, however, most of these girls also experience their desire as a dilemma of personal proportions.

Like the girls in Chapter 4, this group of desiring girls have differing assessments of the specific contours of their dilemmas. Their choices, more and less conscious, of how to work within, around, or despite gendered constructions of sexuality are evident in their strategies for dealing with the dilemma of desire, transforming consequences into opportunities. Although they share a conviction that they deserve their desire, they differ in the extent to which they appreciate the politics of female sexual desire, in particular, the sexual double standard.

ENTITLEMENT MANEUVERS

To claim safe spaces for their desire one group of girls utilizes the degrees of freedom they find within the conventions of romance, maneuvering into secure spots and around minefields that go along with that territory. Some seek refuge in long-term heterosexual relationships with boys who defy characterization as sexual predators; others consciously manipulate the role available to them. All make choices that allow them to express their sexual desire but only in circumstances where the dangers of desire can be muted. These girls speak of a kind of freedom to question and to get to know their own bodies and the parameters of their own pleasure, and they also describe experiences of both equality and mutuality in their different manifestations of this kind of relationship. Entitled to their sexual feelings, they strain against the limits of the good-girl category without shattering it. In a sense, these girls are figuring out how to have it both ways. They reach the limits of this arrangement and find that it affords only partial protection for certain forms of desire rather than for the full range of their feelings. Yet they also reproduce the distinction between girls whose desire is "worthy" and those who should be demonized and devalued for not living up to their standards of "purity." Without an explicit politicized perspective on their sexual subjectivity, their stories reflect how the parameters of pleasure thus remain constrained for them.

Eugenia: Desire with a Safety Net?

Tall, slim, blonde, and fair, Eugenia, like Jenny, fits the image of the desirable "good" girl that is readily available in magazines and on television. As we begin our conversation, I am struck by her intelligence and her authentic interest in participating in this project. Eugenia offers detailed knowledge of and comfort with her own desire; her embodied sexual feelings are simply a part of who she is. The "emotional part" is a feature of her sexuality to which Eugenia refers often. In contrast to Inez, who describes how her mind and body "fight" about her desire, Eugenia is aware of the connection between her mind and her body in producing and sustaining sexual desire: "like it kinda starts off just like in your mind, but somehow it, it works out so that it goes to your body too [laughs]." In contrast, she can also speak articulately about what it is like to have sexual experiences without any desire of her own: "like when [my first boyfriend] would do things, like he fingered me, and it was just so, I could've done my homework, you know, I, it was just so, there wasn't any like fulfillment out of it." Juxtaposing the pleasure of desire with the boredom of being a sexual object, Eugenia grounds her objection to being denied her sexual subjectivity in her experience of what she feels entitled to want, "fulfillment."

A key feature of Eugenia's descriptions of her sexual desire, and her sense of entitlement to these feelings, is the context in which they occur. She has experienced desire exclusively within what is the sanctioned and safe space of a long-term monogamous heterosexual relationship. As Eugenia remarks, "as long as you're with [your boyfriend], then it's not a big deal." Under current gender arrangements, such a commitment can indeed enhance a girl's social and emotional safety and diminish the dangers of desire, while garnering her the rewards of the institution of heterosexuality; in this sense, such a relationship does double duty. Yet at the same time it provides space, it delimits what kinds of desire are acceptable for girls, offering some slack without dropping the reins. The politics of Eugenia's desire are unconscious insider politics. She claims her right to desire and pleasure without any awareness that she occupies a privileged position by virtue of her circumstances. She explores the contours of her feelings for her boyfriend, emotional and physical, without fear of social stigma or tainted identity and, in so doing, reproduces and supports the institution of heterosexuality.

Eugenia does not experience and does not see or critique the two-tiered system that encourages male sexual freedom and constrains female sexuality. Yet she still operates under the entrenched, if somewhat updated, moral code of appropriate sexual behavior for "good" adolescent girls by which she, like Emily, judges other girls quite comfortably. Eugenia says that she feels safe from getting a reputation and so doesn't worry about it. But she notices girls who go out "with some guy one night and then . . . there's always another guy"; girls who "seem to do it . . . like just to do it," who are "just like horny," "dirty," or "loose" girls whose desires may be out of bounds and who thus do get "labeled." From her morally superior, privileged, and in a paradoxical sense sexually liberated position, Eugenia cannot understand why a girl would be sexual in a way that would result in others calling her a slut. She herself thinks that "maybe it has something to do with like, not finding the right person or not, feeling um accepted or loved." She articulates more pity than disgust but is willing to categorize such "horny" girls as "dirty" nonetheless.

Eugenia knows that it is not only acceptable but virtually "assumed" that, since she and her boyfriend have been together for a long time, they are having sexual intercourse. Yet she offers clues that she is aware of the fragility of her safety net, of the instability of her status as a "good" girl who can have sex because she is in a relationship. She had promised to tell her best friend when she first had sexual intercourse, "but then, when it happened, I didn't think I wanted to, and it wasn't like I myself felt bad about it, but I just didn't want, 'cause I felt good about it, and I didn't want anyone else passing judgment on me, that's what it was." In the course of explaining her wish not to talk with her friend, she reveals her awareness of the bottom line within this unchallenged arrangement of gendered sexuality: that any girl who has sex is, in the end, vulnerable to others "passing judgment" on her. Given her own feelings for girls whom she denotes sluts, it is no wonder that these concerns are not dismissed by assurances that having a boyfriend can in fact shield her from such harm.

Eugenia's descriptions of and stories about this relationship suggest that it may stand as a counterpoint to the more conventional
gender hierarchies other girls have described. Some of the ways she
talks about her boyfriend intimate that, like Emily's boyfriend, he
is not fully invested in gendered sexuality. There is a theme of egal-
itarianism that runs through her reports; rather than feeling like
the object of a boy's desire, she expresses her sexual subjectivity
and alludes to a kind of even playing field on which they are,
together, exploring sexuality and intimacy. For instance, she associates the pleasure of their first kiss not only with how "sensitive" it
felt, with the physical pleasure of it, but also with the sense of
equality she felt in the experience: that "we both wanted to do it
but we both weren't really sure" is what "made it really nice." She
knows she has a voice and feelings of her own, which she can safely
bring into this relationship and which will be respected; she feels
"comfortable" and "secure." Given how she has described earlier,
unpleasant sexual experiences with other boys, there is evidence
that a kind of mutual connection has been instrumental in her
developing sexual subjectivity (Miller & Stiver, 1997).

She had not, for example, given a boy oral sex prior to this relationship, and she describes how "he knew" how she felt because
they talked about it: "and I said it was something like when we first
started going out, I don't know, that, that you know, that I wasn't
sure of, and then it wasn't 'til like a year later, and then, so he just
left it alone, you know, and it wasn't a big deal, and um, and so then
like a year later, I just, I totally wanted to, I just was totally curious,
I just wanted to try it." In the context of this relationship, they have
agreed to carve out a space for her desire to develop and flourish;
they waited until she "totally wanted to" because she was "totally
curious," after having been together for a year. Though she "feel[s]
perverted saying it . . . it's just something that I, one of those things

I really enjoy doing now, like one of those things that doesn't like physically pleasure me, as like, you know, if I had sex myself but that, but it's something that I really enjoy doing a lot, I feel totally comfortable with it." Eugenia distinguishes the pleasure she feels in giving her boyfriend pleasure in this way, on her own terms, from her own physical pleasure; at the same time, she recognizes that she is not supposed to find this activity pleasurable, that such pleasure must be "perverted." It is a judgment that she does not allow to get in the way of what she actually feels but that she also does not question, even though it is at odds with her own experience.

In contrast to the stories of so many girls, whose experience of first sexual intercourse "just happened" and whose desire and active choice were absent, Eugenia's story about having sexual intercourse for the first time is unequivocally a story about her desire:

I started feeling like it was something I wanted to do and, you know, so we talked about it like a lot, and finally I decided . . . I definitely wanted to do it, and so . . . it was a big deal in that I wanted to make sure that it was with like the right person? You know, and I felt comfortable? And so, well, I talked to my mom about it, and she took me to the gynecologist, and we talked about birth control. But I also wanted to make sure that I didn't wanna, like, have any regrets about it at all . . . And, I mean, I loved my first time, it was like [laughs] one of my favorite times ever having sex, and I heard that some people say, you know, that you shouldn't get your hopes up, because sometimes it can be really awkward or whatever, but it was such a great experience like . . . I think I was really, like, pleasantly surprised that it was just, that it did feel good, you know? But um, so maybe that's what helped to make it more enjoyable, 'cause, or maybe I was just lucky, 'cause I just really was. It's like even if, you know, we got, you know, started hating each other and then broke up, it's like I'd never regret that time, just 'cause I knew that I wanted it so badly, and like, you know, it was so great then.

Eugenia identifies both the physical pleasure and the fact that it was her idea as making it one of her "favorite" sexual experiences. Within the safety of this relationship, with her mother accepting and respecting her well thought-out decision, and taking full responsibility, Eugenia does not have sex that "just happened" to her. Her first experience of sexual intercourse comes after a lot of other sexual experiences, also pleasurable and reflective of her own desire, with this particular boy, whom she trusts and loves, who helped to make it safe for her to act on her desire.

So how is desire a dilemma for Eugenia? If she is making safe choices in a mutual, committed relationship, isn't that an ideal context for adolescent sexual expression? In trying to explain a time when she did not communicate her discomfort with a sexual experience to her boyfriend, pretending to feel pleasure instead and then feeling bad about violating their trust, the outline of her dilemma emerges. Her story turns the usual explanation for "faking" on its head, because the dilemma lies with her disquiet about having pleasure and knowing her body rather than with sacrificing her feelings to make him feel good for pleasing her. In an example of remarkable communication (as much so for adults as for adolescents), her boyfriend had asked her how he could touch her so that she would have an orgasm. She explains that she could not answer his question: "I don't exactly know how to like make myself have an orgasm. I mean, we've kind of talked about that once, and 'cause he asked me to, we were just talking about it, and he said, 'well, why don't you show me?' And I said, 'I don't really know.'" Eugenia says that she has had orgasms during sex, but only when it "kinda just happens" because of "how your bodies are fit together." While she feels entitled to sexual desire in her relationship, it is only in that context that she feels this way about her sexuality. It is safe for her to feel and respond to her desire when chaperoned by her boyfriend, but it is not when by herself.

Outside that limited domain, Eugenia is filled with questions, concerns, fears, and worries that keep her from exploring her own body or other aspects of her desire, which also limits her pleasure and connection in her relationship. All other situations are suspect and frightening, not necessarily in the eyes of other girls or boys or adults, but in her own eyes. Eugenia's struggles are with "dangerous" desires that are in fact intensely private: masturbation, something she "can't just let myself relax enough just to, you know, put everything aside and just like think about myself"; and also phone sex with her boyfriend. Not feeling able but wanting to masturbate is particularly disturbing to her: "I do think that somehow like society does say that it's wrong. I mean it's not something, it's not something you, ah, like in health class not something you ever come across really either." She believes that being able to "be" with herself in a sexual way will strengthen her knowledge of herself and improve her "confidence," which in turn will enable her to have a more authentic and joyful connection with her boyfriend. The pressure not to acknowledge what she knows—that masturbation is "natural," and that it can enhance her sense of self and her sexual subjectivity—renders the topic contentious and difficult, something about which Eugenia thinks a lot but does not feel safe discussing with anybody else.

Some of her thoughts "intimidate" her—imagining the possibility of sex with another girl, fantasizing about having a sexual experience with two boys at the same time, having a one-night stand. While she is confident that she can "control" her desire when she is with her boyfriend, and keep it within what she believes are acceptable or normal contours, she finds her own desire scary when she imagines sexual experiences outside this safe zone. For Eugenia, it is not that these desires might become evident to other people; her thoughts and feelings are not visible and thus not judged by others. It is the internalized Other (de Beauvoir, 1961), what Dana Jack (1991) has called the "Over-Eye"—a moral code or order that defines and enforces the rules of femininity, in this case delimiting female desire—that keeps Eugenia's desire in check unless it occurs in the sanctioned space of conventional sexual behavior in a specific type of heterosexual relationship.

Sophie: Desire Weaves and Bobs

Lithe and energetic, Sophie is the girl who feared she had been selected because I had somehow discovered she was a "bad" girl. Much to my surprise, she is completely engaged in our interview. She has a playful, impish quality about her and exudes a comfort with herself that is contradicted by her habit of adding a question mark to the end of many sentences, as if she is not sure about what she says or is hedging in case what she knows is somehow suspect. She has not yet had sexual intercourse or "a really big relationship." Whereas many of the girls think about their sexuality in terms of whether to have intercourse, Sophie explains that she "enjoy[s] the feeling of being attracted and the sort of fun little games that you can play, but it doesn't ever have to come to anything. And you can just enjoy it that way?" In contrast to her distress about a girl who had sex to "join the club," her sense of entitlement to her own sexual desire is striking; as she says, she chooses to "fool around" with someone because "I just feel that way."

Sophie's ability to speak so straightforwardly about her sexual feelings is extraordinary. Her compass is her own desire. She has never faked pleasure; it doesn't make sense to her: "I don't see any reason, the whole point of sexual things is enjoyment and fun." She tells me how some of her friends feel "guilty" if they do not have an orgasm when a boy is doing something intended to yield that response, a feeling she does not share: "I'd never feel guilty. And I don't feel like it's my responsibility." She is one of three girls in the study who say they masturbate, and she "can't understand if somebody can't do it." She argues, "this is your body and if there's anybody that you're closest to, it's yourself." She is also the only girl who answers my questions about oral sex in terms of cunnilingus. She describes fellatio as "fun" but says that "when it gets to be too much [for me] I don't keep doing it. Because I wouldn't want him to sit there and be unhappy with it, then I would just like go on with my hand or something like that." She believes that a girl's not knowing what she wants sexually contributes to her vulnerability: "I don't think [a friend who has a lot of sex out of relationships] knows what she wants? I think that's part of the problem . . . she's just willing to do what the people around her are doing." She believes that sexual experiences should be "exciting" for girls, "either physically good or emotionally good." Sophie has not yet experienced these two aspects of sexuality working in tandem.

Sophie is waiting to have sexual intercourse. She has watched her peers make this choice and knows she dislikes the idea of being "sneaky," because "that's almost what makes it seem like it's bad?" She is impressed with a friend who is "really in a relationship and everything seems really nice," who has told her mother about her choices. She never wants to have sexual intercourse in order to feel she fits in, which she thinks is a "pathetic" reason, as well as "stupid" and "slutty." She believes that "being in love" and having "an ongoing thing" would constitute a good reason. She also believes that "it's okay to like fool around with somebody that you're just attracted to . . . having fun is a good enough reason [to fool around], but having sex is more of like a commitment to me." Because she has never had sexual intercourse, she notes that she has never worried about getting pregnant "and stuff like that. So for me, it's always kind of been more like a fun experimental thing?"

At sixteen, Sophie feels she is not ready to have sex and chooses, instead, these "other ways of having fun." That she has fun on her own terms intimates that if she does choose to have sex, her own desire will be a key part of her decision. Her description of how she takes control of sexual situations, by providing boys with the information they need to give her pleasure, suggests the same thing. Because "it's different on everybody," she says,

> when you show them then, it's almost like when you say something, it's almost like they feel like they could say, well, where does it feel good? And you could say, well, like right there? . . . well, I don't know if it feels good to them, if you kind of say, well, where do you like it, and they kind of show you, then you know that you're not just making them completely miserable or if you were that they would speak up? . . . I don't know, maybe I just like to talk, I'm really talkative.

While able to assert herself and be a responsive partner, immediately after recounting what would be sophisticated communication for anyone, never mind an adolescent girl, Sophie "takes back" this description of her sexual agency by referring to herself as merely "talkative." Her backtracking sheds light on her constant efforts to balance being a desiring girl with avoiding the negative judgments she fears in retribution for her sexual subjectivity. She tells me she is worried that, if she reveals experiences that weren't "wise" to me in this interview, I might "think bad things about [her]." Sophie is extremely aware that many of her experiences have had a public quality to them, occurring at a party or a "busy place," and that she is thus constantly at risk of being "judged," because she does not confine her sexual exploration to long-term relationships.

Sophie says she has not had a relationship because she hasn't "met anybody" who has the qualities she seeks: being able to share a lot and to be really open. Although she says she thinks she will feel "more secure" in a relationship, none of her actions suggest that she wants one. She avoids conventional relationships in favor of sexualized friendships and flirtations, in which she describes feeling and exerting a sense of power and control. Her desire to avoid a relationship that affords protective custody or cover for a girl's desire seems to be both a product and a mainstay of her sense of entitlement to her sexual desire on her own terms. Resisting this part of the institution of heterosexuality while wholeheartedly embracing the division of girls into good and bad categories is the heart of her dilemma. In part, Sophie finds this arrangement distressing because, while she embodies and enacts resistance to gendered sexuality, she has no consciously articulated critique of what is wrong with it or realization of its social foundations, which she is experiencing and dealing with as entirely personal.

Despite worrying about the risks, particularly the social ones, that her choices invite, she knows being "bad" can be part of the fun:

> feeling like somebody's attracted to you, I don't know, feeling like you're not in control but kind of, like, feeling like you have the power to make them feel attracted and to feel like you have power, I guess . . . it's almost like that kind of adventurous stuff can make you feel sexy? Stuff that you like to do that maybe isn't your mom's dream come true [laughs] for you to do. Maybe it's almost being bad that can be, feel sexy . . . It's just almost feeling like good about yourself, in a certain way?

For Sophie, feeling sexy is being a sexual subject, not a sexual object, who "feel[s] good about [her]self" in part because she is having an adventure and feeling "power," aware that both constitute a trespass and are in part exciting because they do.

Sophie still works within social conventions to pursue her desire without invoking too much risk, either sexual or emotional, while garnering pleasure from the experiences she chooses to have. In telling a story about a flirtation with a boy, she describes how she takes up the scripted role of a girl who is not supposed to have sexual desire but is supposed to be the object of a boy's affections. Sophie narrates how she reworks this position as the proverbial damsel in distress, maneuvering within it to make space for her sexual subjectivity, and how she is completely conscious of what she is doing. She goes to elaborate lengths to disguise her desire from the "handsome" young man:

> My friend [Allison] was on the phone, and he was like chasing me around, like we were totally joking. He was like chasing me with some like bat or something like that? And I like went to get away, and he like pinned me down. It sounds like cruel and like ferocious, but he was like holding me down, and I was like, Allison! But I was literally like, I was like, Allison! But she knew that I liked him [laughs], so she was just staying on the phone. And he was just right above me and had both my arms down, and it was like, I knew that I was acting like I just wanted to get away, but really I just would've wanted to just totally kiss him or something? And it is those great brown eyes, he just looked right at me, and he's just so—it's that sexual desire thing, you just feel a certain way, and it was just like, it's almost like a waiting feeling?

By her own admission, this performance of passivity is fueled by her desire. She has, she admits to me, "provoked the first move" and disguised her real feelings with predictable and scripted fake cries of distress. Yet she is not conscious that the script she is using to her advantage is problematic—she "does not know" why she did this—and instead she attributes her behavior to "just the way [she is]," a claim that rings rather hollow in light of what else she has told me about her sexuality. The vulnerability embedded in this role is also evident, though only indirectly and not necessarily to Sophie, in her description of this boy's "cruel" and "ferocious" behavior. In fact, a melding of fear and excitement is evident in Sophie's story and makes sense in a culture that eroticizes danger and women's, especially girls', vulnerability. Sophie's story illustrates once more that just a tinge of danger, especially with the safe proximity of a friend, is a kind of thrill. She has only a fleeting hold over this scenario as it unfolds. In telling this story in this way, Sophie seems both to know and at the same time not to know (or not wish to know) the potential for danger—other than what she is consciously trying to elude, being seen as an assertive, desiring girl—that is braided into pleasure for her in this situation.

Given that girls her age are "supposed" to want to be in a romantic relationship, the fact that Sophie does not sets her apart. Why not take advantage of this safe space carved out of her social landscape for exploring her sexual feelings? Why risk the judgment that being a desiring girl outside a relationship, in her eyes and the eyes of her peers, brings? It is quite possible that she has, simply, not met anybody yet. This choice could reflect her unwillingness to get so serious with one boy at her age. There are those who might argue that she is uncomfortable with or not ready for the intimacy that goes along with a serious relationship, that she has a "problem." Normalizing the wish for romance pathologizes her rejection of it. Under the institution of heterosexuality, a girl who does not want to be in a relationship is weird or abnormal, has something wrong with her. An alternative possibility is that Sophie has noticed that with long-term heterosexual relationships comes pressure to have sexual intercourse, which she does not want to do. Her concerns could be even broader, that her current freedom to anchor her sexual experiences in her own desire may be difficult to sustain in the kind of relationship that promises some semblance of safety for her sexuality. For now, being the mistress of her own desire is Sophie's top priority. Without a critical perspective on why this choice is one she should be but is not actually wholly free to make, Sophie weaves and bobs through her dilemma of desire.

DESIRE UNDER COVER

The second group of girls in this chapter also feel entitled to their sexual desire and deal with the dilemma of desire in a way that privileges and protects their sexual subjectivity, but at a price. Like the girls who are overwhelmed by danger, these girls too have a highly heightened awareness that their desire can get them into trouble. Excruciatingly aware of the dangers of their desire, they are just as keen about their entitlement to their own sexual feelings. Their strategy is to try to manage the circumstances in which they experience sexual feelings to mitigate danger and to create space for their desire on their own terms, while keeping it obscured from others. The logic underpinning their psychological and relational processes is that if they can keep what they know to be their own desire out of the view of others, then they can avoid incurring consequences for having or acting on their feelings.

In studying the role of relationships in girls' psychological development, Lyn Brown and Carol Gilligan (1992) suggested the notion of an "underground" as a kind of safe psychological space, comparable to the secret safety provided by the Underground Railroad for bringing slaves into freedom. Brown and Gilligan found that some early adolescent girls take their true thoughts and feelings into such a conscious psychic retreat, remaining aware of what they actually think, feel, and know but keeping it to themselves and out of their relationships. This is one way girls respond to their developing sense that "certain" thoughts and feelings are not considered acceptable for girls to have or to express to others, and that if they do not comply with or capitulate to the norms of femininity, negative consequences, such as conflict, humiliation, or rejection, await them. This practice has both psychological and behavioral dimensions, such as girls acting friendly to someone who has hurt them in order not to incite the anger or antipathy of the other person, which requires that they cover up their own distress. While effective in the short run, this strategy can be costly over time. Brown and Gilligan suggested that when girls take their true thoughts and feelings out of relationships, they risk losing the ability to see and know, to discern the chasm between what is said about them and what they actually experience.

Some girls engage in a similar practice when it comes to their sexual desire. Rather than simply hiding their true feelings, though, the girls who take their desire under cover are acting on it covertly. At the level of their own embodied experience, the girls who utilize this strategy resist the societal suggestion that their sexual feelings are immoral, not normal, or just too dangerous to have. Yet, while they can identify and reject the social denial and denigration of female adolescent sexual desire, they continue to orchestrate their behavior and appearance out of their concern about the repercussions they know can result if others find out that they are desiring girls. These girls take great pains to obfuscate their actual sexual feelings, reacting to and acting upon them but making certain that their secret is safe.

Trisha: Context Is Everything

Trisha's advice to other girls who wish to learn about their own desire is this: "if you feel a certain way . . . [go] with your feelings, instead of listening to what everybody else says, go by what you feel, inside of you." In the context of an ongoing relationship, Trisha feels free to express her desire or make it evident to a person whom she trusts, whom she believes "know[s]" what she wants, and who can read her signals. Although she will not "come out and say" to her boyfriend that she is feeling desire or what she wants to do, she is willing to act on it: "If I just, if I want it, I'll just go after it, I mean I'm just, I'm just like that [laughs]. If I want, like um, if I ever wanted to kiss my boyfriend, I'd just go right over to him and start kissing him, I mean, I have no problem with it." Unsolicited, Trisha tells me she believes "one hundred percent in birth control . . . always," noting that seeing her friends pregnant and with babies makes her "scared."

Knowing what she does enjoy and feel comfortable with, and why, she can say what sexual experiences she does not want. For instance, she is not interested in oral sex: "the way TV always made it seem, it was gross and it was dirty and all this, and it just, it kinda makes you think, you know, just thinking about it just makes me feel uneasy, I just, I've never had it done to me, I've never done it to anybody else, and I refuse, I just, that's just not me. I think if you were meant to do something like that, you'd be three feet high. To be honest, to be honest with you, I just, I just don't like it." Even though she was molested as a child, Trisha believes both that she deserves to have pleasure and that she has the right to say no: "if the person's doing something you don't like and you don't want them to do it, you'll tell them to stop and if they don't stop, then it makes you, you know, not want it anymore, it takes the pleasure right out of it." She offers an example of how she feels no compunction about interrupting and correcting a sexual experience that is not working for her:

> Sometimes when you're having sex with someone, I don't know if it's ever happened to you, but you really have to go to the bathroom, and I mean like he's inside of you, and then he's hitting your bladder, and it's just like you just want him to stop, so you'll scream, "Get off! Get off! It hurts, you're on my bladder" . . . a couple of times I had, I would literally have to force him off of me and say, "I have to go. Now." You know, whether or not he got off on it or not is his problem, I have to go, I'm goin'.

Trisha reports that she has never faked pleasure, and she finds this idea funny; while other girls in the study brought up the infamous "deli scene" in *When Harry Met Sally,* in which Meg Ryan gives a virtuoso performance of faking an orgasm as something they could relate to, Trisha thought it was "stupid." For her, not feeling pleasure is a sign that there is a problem. Unlike other girls, Trisha does not conclude that something is wrong with her if she does not have an orgasm nor does she feel guilty. Instead, she takes it as information: "I mean, if you don't, I mean it, something's wrong, 'cause I think something would be wrong. I mean, if you don't, then either he's not doing it right or it's not somebody that you wanna be with, because if you don't, then, what's the sense, I mean, it's like sitting there, I don't know, playing cards with somebody [laughs]. You might as well just sit there and play cards."

The most salient and overriding context for her sexuality is her keen awareness that girls are vulnerable to getting a reputation. Although Trisha says that she does not "particularly care what others think about [her]," she also tells of one time that did bother her, when she herself experienced the negative effects of being the victim of a rumor mill that had "switched around" an innocent experience, going for a canoe ride in a boat with a boy and another girl during the day, into having gone with him alone at night, with the implication that they had had sex. This false story was a problem for her, because it was difficult for her to refute. She believed that it made others think, "oh she's easy, I can get off her anytime I want, you know, they're gonna think you're easy, so everyone else is gonna try it. And then your friends are gonna think of you lower, so it's like, you wanna try to keep your reputation good." While acknowledging the limit on how much she can control what others say about her, she takes action on her own behalf. She explains that "it was one of the first ones that had went around me, so it bothered me and I was just like, I'm gonna put an end to this one. So then I did." Trisha felt both entitled and able to override the rumor with the truth of her experience, and did in fact prevail.

Given her own experience, and sense of entitlement to her own desire, one might imagine that Trisha would reject the categorization of some girls as "bad" and others as "good." Trisha nevertheless evaluates herself and other girls in these terms by making a crucial distinction between undeserved and deserved reputations: A girl cannot be held accountable for untruths that are said about her, but a girl who acts on her desire is taking chances:

> If it's by your own desire and pleasure, then that's your own fault, I mean you're just, you're just literally saying, say this about me . . . If it's kept in, then that's, you know, then there's nothing wrong with that, but then if it bleeds out, then you're just gonna end up getting yourself into trouble. You just better chill. Slow it down a little . . . if you know that the person's gonna say something, you better—well, I wouldn't say you better but—try and make it so that they're not gonna say anything. Like um, if it was me, I'd just be like, I'd have to be with the person for a long time, knowin' they're not gonna say anything.

Because girls who act on their desire are choosing to put themselves at risk for getting a bad reputation, Trisha offers several strategies for how girls can protect themselves. She can "chill," that is, not act on her feelings, or find a boy who's "not gonna say anything."[4] She says that her own strategy is to express her desire and pleasure with someone she's been with "for a long time," whom she has judged to be trustworthy, "knowin' they're not gonna say anything." But this is not her only approach to having and protecting her desire.

Trisha knows context is everything. In fact, she has an entirely different way of protecting herself when she has sexual feelings outside a long-term relationship. Well aware of the social risks of acting on sexual desire in this unsafe context, she tells me, as if in a confessional, "I've had my share of one-night stands, and I don't think I'd ever go through it again, 'cause it makes you feel kind of, I don't know, kind of slutty, I guess. I've had them, yeah [laughs]. I'll be honest, I've had them." Not only is she at risk of being called names under these circumstances, she in essence thinks of herself as a "bad" girl; rather than saying this choice makes her feel vulnerable, disappointed, excited, guilty, or scared, she says she feels "slutty." If having a one-night stand makes her feel "slutty," if she feels safer having sexual experiences within the context of a relationship, then why does she do it? When I ask her what is in it for her, she explains:

> Oh, I don't know. Just to, I guess just to see what the person's like. I hate to say it that way [laughs] but, um, if I'm with my friends and we're at a party, and I just look up, and there's like a guy there that I want . . . And then I'll start talking to him, like if I know the person, or someone else knows him, we'll start talking and then, you know, nothing will, I don't think any sparks will start flying until, you know, he asks me a question that's gonna like, start, I don't know, I mean, wanting him, just by [pause] him . . . and I know it's just gonna be one of those one-night stand type of things, I'll get myself trashed, and I'll be just like, but I will still, I won't be to the point where I'm, I don't remember anything, just, I just, I want that person, I mean just, he's getting to me. I'll just have a few drinks, I mean, to the point where I get flirty, 'cause I won't do it if I'm straight [laughs]. I have to wait 'til I get flirty and then I'll just say, let's go [laughs] . . . and then I can blame it on the alcohol and say, oh, it was because I was drunk.

Trisha says she has one-night stands "to see what the person's like," and because she has met "a guy that [she] want[s]." She does not say that she wants to or will have sexual intercourse with him, but she does want to explore her sexual feelings and, in so doing, learn something about herself and how she feels about this other person. If a boy were to explain his decision to act on his desire under these circumstances, it is unlikely that either Trisha or any-one else would think ill of him. But Trisha is aware that, for a girl, this choice is a risk. She then articulates why it is worth the risk and how she manages it. She acts on her feelings in a public situation, a party, which offers both protection (her friends are nearby) and vulnerability. But she takes her desire under cover by choosing to hide behind alcohol.

Trisha sees and uses getting herself "trashed" as a form of pro-tection from getting what she would judge to be a deserved reputa-tion for acting on her sexual desire. When she is drunk, Trisha becomes a desiring girl whom she "can just deny and say I never did anything," because being drunk obfuscates her own desire and provides her with a way to claim that she did not know what she was doing. Blaming "it" on the alcohol muddies the question of responsibility and thus excuses her from culpability, for others and for herself. Trisha explains that she is careful to drink enough but not too much, not to "the point where I'm, I don't remember any-thing." She drinks as both a public performance and a private salve that screens her sexual desire in unprotected, unsanctioned cir-cumstances. By working within the framework that some girls are sluts and all girls are vulnerable to being thought of (or thinking of themselves as) sluts, Trisha limits the degrees of freedom for her desire. Not willing to give up her desire yet seeing no alternative but to think of desiring girls, including herself, in these terms, the best solution she can contrive is to keep her desire under the cover of alcohol.

Barbara: (Not) Feeling Like a Fool

Barbara works hard at balancing what is said about girls' sexuality with what she knows about her sexuality from her own experience. She articulates first an awareness and then a critique of how girls' sexuality is controlled by the threat of social repercussions. She

observes that girls but not boys are socially chastened for expressing their sexual feelings, which for her does not make sense and is
not fair: "the fact is that a girl, if she sleeps with a hundred different
guys, she's considered a slut, but if a guy sleeps with a hundred different girls, he's the guy, you know, he's macho . . . if a girl wants to
have sex, she has every right just like a guy. It takes two to do this,
so neither one is any wronger than the other one, is how I view it
[laughs]." Unlike Trisha, Barbara refuses to put girls into either category. When boys, or girls, call another girl a slut, she won't "listen
anymore, it's like, you know, you guys don't have a right to label
her, you can't judge her for what she's done. You've done the same
thing." Yet she also notes that opting out of this system is not completely within her control. With resignation, she explains, "I just, I
have to live with it, but I kind of work around it."

Barbara's rich and insightful descriptions of her sexual feelings illuminate her success in "work[ing] around it." She offers a
multidimensional analysis of the factors involved in her sexual
response: "[girls'] bodies are very sensitive and when you get into
having, you know, you're making out one night, your whole body
can feel good depending on what they're doing, but it's kind of,
it just depends on the mood." She links her sexual feelings to
her partner's ability to communicate, her level of comfort and
ability to concentrate, and her and her partner's knowledge about
her body:

> It can be pleasurable, but if it goes on for too long, then it can be,
> it can get overwhelming, so they, that's when you have to really
> kinda be able to communicate to one another saying, look this is
> enough, I can't take any more of this [laughs] and at the time,
> that's when, 'cause he was always very open with me, and I tried
> to be very open with him, and so, not so much the first time, but
> this time, the second time that we had done this, I was able to

communicate more, and I said, okay, enough [laughs], it's beginning to be too much here.

Barbara has a highly sophisticated understanding of the embodied and relational processes involved in her sexual desire and pleasure. She offers a realistic rather than a romanticized description of having an orgasm, which she says "was wild . . . oh wow, it blew my mind basically." Her sexual subjectivity comes through in her explanation of how she has chosen not to have more than one "so far." Noting that "it's not easy . . . to have one" and "there's a lot of work involved in it," she emphasizes that it is her own lack of patience rather than her boyfriend's ("he can sit there all the ding dong day") at the heart of her choice.

Barbara keeps careful track of the vicissitudes of her sexual feelings. But this focus is quite recent. A survivor of childhood sexual abuse, which she reports "happened for quite a few years" prior to her current relationship, she explains that even after having "counseling" she "had a lot of problems with just being able to kiss [boys], it's like, no, get away." She had to make conscious efforts to, in essence, get her body back,

> because I wanted it to be that way. I wanted to be able to feel pleasure. And, 'cause in the back of my mind, I knew that I couldn't just go on being this way, 'cause if I got married, I was never going to enjoy it. And I wanted to be able to enjoy it. And so I worked upon it myself a lot, with one of my friends, and we worked around it. I began to open up to myself and look at, well, this was what was done in my childhood. This person did this to you, but that doesn't mean everybody else is like this. And as I got, and as I began to try and open up to people, especially to guys, um, and let them try things, and I'll try things, and got used to it, and began to trust them, I was able to get over that

particular barrier. Even though it'll still come back now and then, but it's like, it hasn't for a long time.

Not only is Barbara able to feel and speak about her own sexual feelings, she has fought to have them, winning back her sexuality from the disembodiment that followed profound violation.

Despite this hard-won sense of entitlement, Barbara is not free from the dilemma of desire. While she has observed that a girl has a certain leeway for exploring her sexuality in the context of a relationship, and rejects the social risks that dominate so many girls' management of their sexuality, for Barbara it is the interpersonal and psychological risks associated with her own desire that loom large. Rather than worry that her peers will label her a slut, she fears that if she does not take care in negotiating her desire in her relationship, she might be shamed or lose her relationship if her desire is perceived as abnormal.[5] She explains how she keeps her desire under cover, until she is sure that it is safe to let her feelings be known, as she did with her current boyfriend "before [they] had sex, 'cause [she] wasn't sure how he looked at sex":

> There was this time, he was giving me a back rub, and all I could think about is what I wanted him to do besides have back rubs [laughs], and he has to rub my body, forget the back, just do the whole body . . . it was a very strong desire just to have him rub all over, and that was the one time I can think of I've really had it bad [laughs] . . . I'm laying there thinking this, and I didn't want to tell him that, 'cause I didn't know him that well at the time, and it's like, noooo, no, we'll just wait [laughs].

"Laying there" as her boyfriend rubs her back, having thoughts and feelings full of desire to be touched "all over," Barbara enacts the kind of passivity that is expected of her, keeping her actual feelings disguised. Like Inez, Barbara responds to her "very strong desire" by telling herself "noooo, no"; yet unlike Inez, rather than trying to make her desire disappear, she plans to "wait" until she has specific evidence that there is a safe space for her sexual feelings in this relationship. Once she feels she is on safer ground, she expresses her desire slowly and carefully, taking the initiative only if she is shielded by "subtlety":

> I didn't know him well enough. I subtly like to initiate, I don't like to come outright and say, oh let's go do this, I just like doing things very subtly, 'cause I'm not a very, when it comes to sex, the first few times with the person, I'm not very forthright about anything, until after I've gotten to know them, and I trust them a little bit more, and I know that they're not going to look at me funny when I say I want to do something like this.

Barbara is concerned that the form her desire takes could be construed as indicating she is somehow not normal; she protects herself from the risk that this particular boy might "look at [her] funny" when she brings her desire out into the open. Barbara operates as a kind of secret agent, avoiding being "forthright," making sure she can cover the tracks of her desire by behaving in a way that is not readily identifiable as such. Although the pervasive threats to girls who are sexually assertive do not lead her to deny her desire, her personal experience of having once made her desires known prematurely keeps her cautious:

> That was like with oral sex, I never thought I would meet a guy that didn't like oral sex, and I met a guy. 'Cause I hadn't had oral sex with this boyfriend, but the boyfriend before that I was wanting to attempt that, and he would have no part in that. And so I was kind of, you feel really embarrassed after you've asked to do something, and it's like, and then they're, "oh no, no, no, get

away." And so I came to this boyfriend I'm thinking, I was very [laughs] subtle about doing this 'cause I wanted to make sure I wasn't going to make a fool of myself.

Barbara has learned that even in the supposed safe haven of a relationship, making her sexual wishes known can be humiliating. Rather than finding the relationship automatically safe, Barbara needs to assess how a specific boyfriend will react to determine whether and how she will respond to her own sexual feelings, which persist even if she decides to hide them.

This constant monitoring, caution, and fear take its toll, a psychological cost for keeping her feelings under cover. Regarding her choice not to tell her boyfriend about her desire to be touched, Barbara reflects, "it's kinda depressing in its own way afterwards, 'cause you're like sitting there, well I, you know, I should have said something or, you know, actually left and gone home, you're laying there, well, I should have said something [laughs briefly], 'cause later on it's like, well, I didn't fulfill it [moans, laughs]." She is filled with regret and frustration at having kept her real sexual feelings under wraps. Perhaps precisely because Barbara keeps her desire under cover rather than silence her body, she understands the costs of doing so.

Melissa: A Minefield of Desire

Dressed in a flowing gypsy skirt, her skin pale against the lively colors she wears, Melissa is clear about her sexual feelings for girls, claiming a lesbian identity. Unlike many gay and lesbian adolescents (Savin-Williams, 1998), Melissa has felt safe and free to be open about her sexuality with her family. Yet despite her comfort with her own sexual feelings, the dilemma that desire raises for Melissa is the lack of opportunity to explore or express it. Most often, Melissa associates feeling sexual desire with frustration; she explains that she "find[s] it safer to just think about the person than what I wanna do, because if I think about that too much and I can't do it, then that'll just frustrate me." Living in a world defined as heterosexual, Melissa finds that "little crushes" have to suffice: "I don't know very many people my age that are even bisexual or lesbians . . . so I pretty much stick to that, like being hugely infatuated with straight people. Which can get a little touchy at times . . . realistically I can't like get too ambitious, because that would just not be realistic." She feels stuck and isolated, having little access to other lesbian adolescents and thus to sexual relationships or experiences. Having only straight friends to talk with, Melissa worries constantly about saying or doing too much.[6]

In speaking of her desire, Melissa names intense embodied feelings of "being excited" and "wanting." Cognizant of pleasure, Melissa is just as aware that she is vulnerable to harm. Not only is the question of how to respond to her feelings difficult, Melissa realizes that even the existence of her sexual desire for girls can lead to anger or violence if others know about it: "Well, I'm really lucky that like nothing bad has happened or no one's gotten mad at me so far, telling people about them hasn't gotten me into more trouble than it has, I mean, little things but not like anything really awful. I think about that and I think it, sometimes, I mean, it could be more dangerous." Melissa describes the various ways that she keeps her true feelings in a private and lonely but safeguarded place. Her stories about the tension between her desire and her need to mask it exemplify how keeping one's authentic sexual feelings out of the ebb and flow of relationships can put a girl at risk of losing touch with how she really does feel, thereby sacrificing the chance for authentic relationships.

As intensely as she feels her desire, Melissa also knows that it could interfere with her friendships with other girls. Although she is "out to a lot of people," it is not public knowledge in her school that she is a lesbian. By keeping her sexuality secret from others, she explains, she is able to express her desire covertly by being physically affectionate with other girls, a behavior that is common and acceptable; she can "hang all over [girls] and stuff and they wouldn't even think that I meant anything by it." Yet Melissa describes herself as "hat[ing] having secrets from people and hiding things." She tells a story to show how she sneaks her desire in where she knows it is not exactly welcome but where she has a chance to express some of her pent-up feelings:

> But there's especially this one girl that I used to have this huge infatuation with, and she . . . didn't drink that much [at parties] but when she did she always drank, like, as much as possible . . . But she was [laughs] so cute, even when she was like that and I would just, sort of, follow her around, and especially maybe it was nice that she was like that 'cause she didn't notice as much. And I mean I was sort of out to her so it wasn't like she would have noticed, but I just remember just like following her around and just like making sure like I could just touch her and stuff, not a lot or in any special way. But, and I kept like, when I was leaving that party and, I'm like, I'm like kissing her on the cheek and trying really hard to just keep it [laughs] on the cheek, and, and like I love you, Mary! [laughs]. And she was like, I love you too! And I was like, and that made me so happy, and I mean of course she was like completely drunk, she didn't even care about it at all, but it made me happy, but I really didn't [laughs] wanna leave.

Some of Melissa's heterosexual friends also sense that her desire for girls could cause problems. She describes how they monitor her at parties, for instance, keeping track of how much she has had to drink, to make sure she is, in their words, "not gonna do anything stupid" or "say anything bad to anyone." While Melissa "think[s] it's really nice of them, 'cause I know that they mean well, and I know that they just want to, like, protect me," there is something about their behavior that she finds "annoying." Melissa is thus not the only one keeping a lid on her desire; others around her police her sexuality to make sure that she keeps her feelings to herself.

At the time of our interview, Melissa is in her first sexual relationship, which began when a close friend, a girl who is several years older and ostensibly heterosexual, expressed a sexual interest. Melissa was surprised because she had not "been thinking that" about this friend and, in fact, was not sexually attracted to her.[7] After a history of having to hold back her sexual desire, of feeling "frustrated," of being "hugely infatuated with straight people" and not having the chance to explore her sexuality, Melissa felt she "should take advantage of this situation":

> And I was like, kind of thrown off by it and I didn't know what I should do, because I was kind of like, I mean I really love her a lot, 'cause we're really close and she's a really great person and everything, you know, it's just like hmm, well, I don't know, I should take advantage of this situation [laughs] and, you know, and I really do like her and I think, I sort of, I don't know [laughs], how I feel at the moment, I mean because, first she was just like well, you know, I just wanna take care of you, and then later on she was, it was kind of clear that that's not the only thing she wanted. And, so, I mean it became physical and, now, I mean I'm not really sure if, I, I mean I kind of think that I just really love her a lot and I really, I mean it's such a good feeling to have someone love you that way. And I just really wanted that and I don't know how much I'm really like attracted to her [laughs] personally.[8]

Feeling something is missing, as we talk about her desire in our interview, Melissa is struggling with a conundrum that comes from having had to keep her desire hidden and unexplored for so long; if she is not sexually attracted to this girl and "it's just sort of like I just wanted something like this for so long that I'm just taking advantage of the situation," what should she do? She knows she has feelings of want yet suspects that they are not sexual, and her hunger for a relationship is apparent—"I really wanted someone really badly, I think, I was getting really sick of being by myself . . . I really need someone." The desperation in her voice, and the sexual frustration she has described elsewhere, suggest that she has "wants" and "needs" that are both sexual and relational; while perhaps related and occurring simultaneously, these desires are not the same.

Accustomed to keeping sexual feelings under wraps, Melissa has not had much experience sorting out her sexual feelings and determining whether they are *present*. In response to my questions about her body, her desire, her experiences with this girl, Melissa realizes that her own desire is actually missing from these first sexual adventures, enabling her to clarify her discomfort with her new girlfriend and illuminating the importance of being aware of both the presence and absence of sexual desire. Having kept her desire under cover for so long, she is finding this distinction unexpectedly difficult. As we talk, Melissa becomes more certain that, while she is anxious to explore her sexuality, she would like to do so on her own timetable and in response to her own sexual desire. She feels ready for kissing and exploring another girl's body but not for the more intimate experiences her girlfriend has initiated with her. Even though she didn't "know how [she] was supposed to feel" when her girlfriend "started putting her hand down [her] pants," she did know that "[she] didn't really wanna do that" and that she "was pretending that it was more fun than it was." Sorting out what is and is not happening for her in this relationship, Melissa concludes,

I don't really think I'm getting that much pleasure from her, it's just, I mean it's almost like I'm getting experience, and I'm sort of having fun, it's not even that exciting, and that's why I think I don't really like her . . . because my friend asked me this the other day, well, I mean does it get, I mean when you're with her does it get really . . . exciting? [laughs]. But it doesn't, to me. It's weird, because I can't really say that, I mean I can't think of like a time when I was really excited and it was like really sexual plea- sure for me, because I don't think it's really like that. I mean not that I think that this isn't good because, I don't know, I mean, I like it, but I mean, I think I have to sort of realize that I'm not that much attracted to her.

Wanting both a relationship and sexual pleasure, a chance to explore closeness and her sexual curiosity, and discovering that this relationship leaves out her sexual desire, Melissa is again frus- trated: "I sort of expect or hope or whatever that there would be some kind of more excited feeling just from feeling sexually stimu- lated or whatever. I would hope that there would be more of a feel- ing than I've gotten so far." The absence of her sexual feelings in this relationship has left her with a conflict: "I'm not that attracted to her and I don't know if I should tell her that. Or if I should just kind of pretend I am and try to . . . anyway . . ." When I ask her how she would go about doing that, she replies, "I don't think I could pretend it for too long." Melissa speaks often of feeling guilty about her sexual feelings: guilty about having desire for girls who are not accessible because they are heterosexual, guilty about not having sexual feelings for girls who desire her. It is not desire itself that causes Melissa to feel discomfort; it is finding it so difficult to play out her feelings authentically that makes her feel bad.

DESIRE POLITICS

A third and very small group of girls stand apart from the others in this chapter and from the others in the study as a whole. While making unapologetic claims on their desire, these girls also speak about desire in a matter-of-fact way, as an aspect of their experience that they simply expect to have. They offer sophisticated and critical analyses of gendered sexuality as the context in which they deal with their own sexual desire. Fully aware that they are not supposed to be desiring girls, and fully aware of the consequences for doing so, they simply refuse to deny their feelings. Not only do they feel entitled to their own sexual feelings, since they believe such feelings are normal and acceptable, they think that the "reality" of gendered sexuality is a con of immense proportions. Thus, there is a conscious political edge to their resistance to gendered sexuality, tinged with their outrage at being unjustly muzzled. They understand how their sexuality is perceived from a "male gaze" but do not embody it. Instead, they embody sexual subjectivity as a form of resistance with both psychological and political contours. They are agile at consciously "working within the system," as a kind of guerrilla tactic to maintain their integrity, or just rejecting it as unfair and oppressive. Their resistance is thus both overt and political.

Rather than accept the limits of unreliable pseudosafe spaces for their desire, these girls defy the very categories of good and bad, recognizing how this hierarchy separates girls from one another and diminishes and undermines them all. They are outspoken, irate, and defiant about their right to their own desire and pleasure in mutually acceptable circumstances. The girls tell stories about balancing pleasure and danger, refusing to be hemmed in by the fear of a bad reputation, insisting on taking appropriate precautions to protect themselves from physical consequences, and making active decisions about what sexual experiences they want to have and doing so in the relational contexts that make them comfortable. They not only are aware of the double standard but also know what is wrong with it; and they not only see that it is unfair but also pinpoint what is unfair about it. Though they do not use the word themselves, these girls are adamant *political* resisters.

That is, they are engaging in a conscious refusal to comply with constrained constructions of who they can be and insisting on breaking rules they know to be unfair in order to be authentic and have integrity with themselves and others (Brown & Gilligan, 1992). In the realm of sexuality, overt political resistance constitutes a girl's unabashed claim to her own sexual desire and sexual subjectivity. And it risks dangerous reactions from people or institutions that are threatened by such a refusal to accept condoned conceptions of normality and morality (Freire, 1970; Lorde, 1984; Taylor, Gilligan, & Sullivan, 1995). Refusing to engage with the framing of their desire as a personal dilemma, these girls understand that the problem they are dealing with is not simply their own but one with deep social roots.

Paulina: The Power of Desire

Paulina looks me straight in the eye as we sit down to our interview. She is serene but with an air of defiance. Having emigrated from Eastern Europe five years earlier, Paulina speaks quite excellent English, with a strong accent but an unwavering clarity about what she observes, knows, and feels. Her answer to my first question, about what she has heard regarding girls' sexuality in her family, resonates with many other girls' responses: "I would say [my family is] not very open about it, I mean, they don't want to discuss it, or talk about it, my grandmother just doesn't bring up the subject, and if it ever comes up, she just ignores it. Like it doesn't exist." But Paulina is quick to follow with her critique of social norms that silence female adolescent sexuality. Having her sexuality framed as "trouble" or the road to pregnancy or even something that "doesn't exist" does not jibe with what Paulina herself believes and knows about girls'—and her own—sexuality. This message from her family directly contradicts her own experience. Clearly grounded in her own body, Paulina has no trouble describing what her own desire feels like; when she feels desire, she "feel[s] really hot, like, my temperature is really, really hot . . . And my body would have like, I would like have a feeling going up my spine."

Paulina conveys how her sexual interactions include and express *her* feelings; she links her sexual experiences and choices to her feelings about her partner and her acceptance of her body and comfort with what she is doing. She thinks that "it depends how, how a girl feels about her body, for her to enjoy it . . . I'm not ashamed of it, I'm just, that's the way I am." While she notices that other girls avoid oral sex because they are worried about how someone might react, she does not think that is a good reason: "Because there's a lot of girls that I know who just wouldn't do it, they're kind of like, they wouldn't have oral sex with somebody because the person might think something of them. And I don't really care what the person will think, because the person will know me well enough, so if I want to, I just do it." When I ask her why, she answers simply, "Because I would want to." Like Eugenia, she had sexual intercourse for the first time on her terms, with her current boyfriend, who had been a friend before their relationship became romantic: "In the beginning when he would like try to do anything, he would ask me and I would say no. And if he would touch me I was just like, I don't think so. Then like one day, I thought about it a lot and, and I said like, if you use precautions and everything. I just wanted to, because I wanted to see what it was like."

Paulina does not take her sexual freedom for granted, however. She makes a rebellious claim to her sexual desire, angrily telling me how she refuses to participate in the usual double standard:

It's okay for a guy to have any feelings. Usually a guy makes the first move, not the girl, or the girl's not supposed to do it, the girl's supposed to sit there going, no, no you can't. I [won't] do that . . . I mean the guy expects the girl to be a sweet little virgin when he marries her, and then he can be running around with ten other women, but when he's getting married to her, she's not supposed to have any relationship with anybody else. You're supposed to be holy . . . and pure . . . I just don't think so . . . I think she can, a woman can do whatever they want to, why shouldn't they? I mean, they have the same feelings, they're human, why should they like keep away from them?

Her sense of entitlement is grounded in a critique of current gender arrangements and strengthened by her outrage at what she considers this imposition on girls' and women's humanity: "I think that women have the same feelings as men do, I mean, I think it's okay to express them too." Throughout the interview, Paulina conveys her conscious and constant resistance to a politics of desire that denies her own feelings.

Paulina brings this sense of entitlement to her views about sexual reputations. Like the other girls, Paulina observes, "Guys, they just like to brag about girls. Oh, she does this, and she's a slut because she slept with this guy, and with this guy, but they don't say that about guys. It's okay for them to do it, but when a girl sleeps with two guys it's wrong, she shouldn't do that, she automatically becomes a slut." Other girls in the study note this inequity, but when I ask them why they think this distinction exists, they all say, "I don't know." Even as they know that this distinction is unfair, they worry about being called a slut. In contrast, Paulina has an analysis to offer. She has made the link between gender and power: "I think males are kind of dominant, and they feel that they have the power to do whatever they want, that the woman should give in to them."

From this amazing perspective, which is more sophisticated than those of many adult women, she can explain why she has made a conscious choice not only to ignore but to defy what she realizes is a form of social control over her sexuality. And she puts this analysis to work in her own life. Even when in platonic friendships with boys, she has had to contend with knowing looks and assumptions that all relationships with boys are sexual. Paulina understands that what she actually does or even says does not matter, that anyone can say anything they want about her: "I just realized that they're gonna talk anyways, that it doesn't make, even if you say a word to somebody, they're still gonna talk, they're gonna still make up something." She also realizes that for this threat, which so often has nothing to do with her actual behavior, to work she has to care. To dissipate this control on her sexuality, Paulina— unlike Trisha and Inez, who also understand that such talk is beyond their control—has "just stopped caring." She refuses to let fear of this label interfere with her right to choose with whom and what sorts of relationships she will have. Like Barbara, Paulina also refuses to participate in enforcing this inequity. She does not shun girls who get called sluts and stays friends with girls who have bad reputations, despite the personal consequences: "I don't care what they are, they're my friend, but it doesn't always get accepted in the community, and if I'm friends with that person, they're looking like, oh she's probably the same way. They just assume it, they don't know me, but because somebody does something that obviously I must too."

In a similar vein, Paulina chooses not to read romance novels, because she finds them

too fake, the guy usually ends up with the girl, and they end up with each other and everything. It's not real. And they never had any serious problems, I mean, there'd usually be something that happens or something, but they would get solved, and the problem would be over. I just switched to horror . . . I don't know, they just talk about the feelings a person goes through in life, because romance books, they don't say how she felt, what she really thought about.

Paulina knows that relationships usually entail "problems" that need to be "solved"; that endings are not always happy or predictable; and that girls have thoughts and feelings that do not appear in any "real" way in romances.

Like Eugenia, Paulina tells of a time when she resorted to pretending to have desire as a way to avoid offending her boyfriend or making him think she "didn't care" about him. But she also tells of a subsequent time when she told her boyfriend that she did not want to have sex when he did, which did upset him, just as she believed it would when she pretended:

> He's just like, you don't want to. I said, no, I don't want to do anything, so I'd rather not. He just stopped and did not do anything. And he got mad, and he wouldn't talk to me. He just felt that I didn't like him, or maybe I was with somebody else. But, later on, I just explained that I just, it just didn't feel right, it just was a time when I didn't want to. He was upset, though . . . I just felt that . . . I didn't [want to] hide anything from him. I just felt, uh, I don't want to go through that again. Might as well tell him, whatever way he takes it. If he loves me, he obviously, he'd be able to deal with it, if he doesn't, then . . .

Her experience of being inauthentic in a sexual situation went against the grain of her commitment to herself and to having an honest relationship. Her fears about how her boyfriend would respond if she did act on her feelings were in fact realized; he "got mad," "wouldn't talk to [her]," thought she "didn't like him," and suspected that she was cheating on him. What Paulina learned from her earlier faking experience, however, is that she would rather have no relationship than not be able to "tell him anything."

She also links her sense of entitlement to act on her desire, and not act in its absence, to her refusal to allow her boyfriend to "have any power" over her or to "control her." She demands equality in this relationship and is willing to walk away if he will not agree to these terms.

This sense of entitlement to her sexual desire provides a kind of protection against making sexual choices driven by a wish to fit in or to please others. Paulina has had a "bad" sexual experience with a boy whom she had thought of as a friend. In the interview, she describes a time when this male friend tried to force her to have sex with him:

> There was one experience, the guy wanted to have sexual inter-course and I didn't . . . I didn't have sex with him. He, he like pulled me over to the couch, and I just kept on fighting . . . I was just like begging him to like not to do anything, and like I really did not have like much choice. Because I had my hands behind me. And he just like kept on touching me, and I was just like, "just get off me." He goes, "you know that you want to," and I said, "no, I don't. Get off me, I hate you."

When the phone rang, he let her answer and, in her native language, she asked her friend to come over. Unwilling or unable to continue to coerce her when her friend arrived, the boy finally left. Paulina's assailant attacked her both physically and psychologically. Lucky to have eluded actual violence, Paulina was able to resist his attempts to coerce her because she was so familiar with her own desire and thus fully aware that she did not in fact "want to."

Paulina reports that she gets called "pushy" and "bossy," but she claims, "I don't really care what people say." Yet I am struck by how Paulina maintains a kind of active program of not caring, how hard won her entitlement to her desire actually is. Even as she nar-rates her defiant sexual subjectivity, her story is often interwoven

with a certain defensiveness. When describing her experience of
having an orgasm, she interrupts her own story to assert: "I liked it,
and there's nothing wrong with it. I mean, if guys can feel it, why
shouldn't girls?" While Paulina does not directly experience her
own desire as a dilemma, the social dilemma that girls' desire is set
up to pose suffuses her personal experience of repudiating gendered sexuality.

Amber: Doing Desire

Amber defies neat sociological categories. Both of her parents
abused drugs, and neither is in her life at the time of our interview.
She has lived in foster homes and currently stays with conservative
family members. She has dark blonde hair, lively brown eyes, a
quick smile, and a twinkle in her eye. She is loud and outspoken.
Amber "gets" my project: "the first thing I said [to my guardian]
when I got the letter was like, wow, you gotta do this. She's like,
what is it? I'm like, it's an interview on sexuality and desire, and
she's like, on what? and I'm like, sexuality and desire, and she's like,
why would you want to do that? I said, because this is something
that no one ever talks about, and it would be good to do this."
Amber is able to articulate her experience of sexual desire especially well in her descriptions and stories. She describes sexual
desire as "kind of like a fire that needs to be put out, [laughs] definitely. Kind of like an itch that needs to be scratched." While she
has considered masturbating, she is not intimidated by any prohi-
bition on it but chooses not to because "by touching myself or
[using a device] I'd be achieving an orgasm, but I think my desire is
more to be with someone than to have an orgasm." Amber has had
a number of boyfriends but has had protected sexual intercourse
with only one, with whom she had a long and intimate relationship. Unlike in other relationships, when "I wasn't sure if I had
wanted to," she says that "when I did, I was sure I wanted to, I mean,

I really liked the kid and I wanted to." Her method of birth control is condoms—she emphasizes that she uses "one of those spermicidal lubricated condoms"—and she explains that she has chosen this particular method because "I'm not that sexually active."

What stands out most in Amber's stories about her sexual experiences is her agency, and the explicit link she makes between her agency and her own sexual feelings. She tells a story about a time when she felt desire for her now ex-boyfriend: "he looked really good and I just missed him so much and that just combined, I really really wanted him really bad, I actually did get him." And then she proceeds to tell a story of seduction: her seduction of him. "I forgot what I was wearing, but I had like some kind of skimpy top underneath, and I took it off and I went over to him, and I started putting lotion on my legs . . . I just like was really close to him, and I was whispering into his ear, and he turns to me 'cause I kind of startled him, and I kissed him, and then it just went on from there." In this story, Amber is an agent of her own desire. Rather than manipulate him into taking the lead, she takes it herself: "I kissed him." When I ask her what it was like for her to do that, Amber replies, "I think I became more confident, I mean, it definitely builds my confidence level, the part of me that makes me outgoing, like brave to face the world, to be able to say things to different people without worrying what they were going to say back, or how they are gonna react." Amber experiences her sexual agency as building her overall confidence, linking her experience in this domain of her life to other relational situations in which she might take a chance by expressing her true feelings.

This story also exemplifies how Amber works around a system that positions her as a sexual object, by refusing to experience herself in this way yet also using her object status to her own advantage. She has astutely observed that there is power available to her in this system: "I think that women have the power, I think that men 5 percent of the time, I mean the men are really like weak in that sense, they can't seem to turn down an offer from a girl, you know." In the end this decision born of desire does not produce the desired or anticipated results for her. Reflecting on the event, she says, "I had wanted him back, and I felt that if we had sex that would bring us closer, but you know, it didn't work, I'm like, oh my God, I don't like it, I can't believe I'm doing this, it's actually very boring, I'm like, when is this over . . . there wasn't anything mystical about it or, you know." This is not sex that "just happened." At the beginning of the story, Amber is a desiring girl. However, as her desire evaporates, "I kissed him" becomes "when is this over." With the loss of her desire, Amber becomes a "bored" object. Because Amber feels entitled to and expects her own desire, when the experience becomes "boring" and not "mystical," it is a signal to her that something is amiss. Amber is garnering information she did not have prior to having, and losing, her desire: that she did not really want to be with this boy after all. Refusing to wait passively for a boy to be the agent of desire differentiates Amber from other girls:

> I'm always the one to say like, "Jimmy, I want you" . . . I think maybe other girls aren't really as forward with talking about sex, I mean I've seen a lot of that in girls, my sister is one, she says, "oh wow, I really wanted to do something, he won't do anything, he doesn't kiss that good." I said, "well, Lizzy, why don't you pull him aside and say, you know, if it were me and somebody didn't kiss well, I'd be well, do this, do that, or I'd give them hinters and 'cause I mean I just wouldn't sit there and wait for him to pick up on it, he doesn't know what he's doing, you know, maybe he's not aware."

Yet she is also aware that being sexually assertive can get a negative response from boys: "I think it's pretty good for, you know, some men feel like the lady is being overly aggressive when they [make the first move], but I've been lucky enough not to have any of those men, but I mean I think it's good for a woman." Amber is aware of the dangers associated with her sexual agency, possible rejection—or maybe worse—by angry guys. She is also aware that she could get a bad reputation, although that does not stop her from "talk[ing] about sex a lot, but it doesn't mean that necessarily I go through with things and talk about them, I mean I could have gone through with them, it doesn't mean I go through with them continuously, and no, I'm not worried at all." Amber's disregard for getting a reputation is, like Paulina's, grounded in her sense of justice. Because she realizes that no one else can really know what her talk about sex actually means, she knows that if she did "go through with them [sexual behaviors] continuously," she could be vulnerable to this consequence. But for it to be an effective consequence, Amber would have to care about getting a bad reputation.

Like Paulina, Amber has a critical perspective on the double standard, about which she is passionate and outspoken: "My [relative] would talk about whores as if it was the lady's fault and that the lady shouldn't be thinking about sex, that the man is the one that should be thinking about it and they have a right to. I think that's wrong [laughs]. I think that ladies should be more forward in the conversations about sex, and definitely do what they feel they would like to. I think it's really up to the lady. You just don't want to put up with that, I mean I know myself, if I were to talk about those things, my friends might turn and say, 'Ssssh! don't speak too loud, someone might hear you,' and it shouldn't be like that at all, I think it should be open to talk about it." Amber has gone so far as to develop a transgressive identity for herself as the girl who says her "perverted" thoughts out loud. She sees herself as providing a service to her peers, "kind of like relieving the pressures of other people, because other people don't like to talk about it, and they see me talking and they come and they join the conversation." At once the bad "perverted" girl and the helpful nice girl, Amber eschews these distinctions as she embodies and speaks as the girl who is a desiring subject.

She notes that when girls' sexuality is discussed in church or school, the message is that "girls that have sex get in trouble, you know, get pregnant, have AIDS, chlamydia, but I mean usually it's nothing positive." Amber observes that female adolescent sexuality is considered entirely negative. Because her own experiences have been positive, she criticizes this perspective. She goes on to deplore the lack of information about abortion available to her; and she critiques our interview as keeping the conversation about desire private, demanding from me recognition of the need for public acknowledgment and talk about girls' desire. Amber lays claim to her desire with aplomb. While she has a critical perspective on the double standard, as Amber has herself explained, she is an individual, brave, and brazen girl, "unique" in her ease with her desire. Although Amber knows she is refusing to comply with a construction of girls as not having desire of their own, or not acting on their own desire, unlike Paulina, she cannot answer the question of why girls' desire is forbidden and maligned. Her stories cry out for an answer beyond simply turning into a guy. Even within the comfort of her own desire, Amber is aware that her social context considers her "perverted," a construction she transforms by appropriating it as a fun identity.

The stories told by these desiring girls illustrate how feeling entitled to their own sexual desire can enable them to make active choices in their relationships. Comfortable with their own embodiment, they narrate sexual subjectivities that are compelling and enlightening. These girls' stories clarify how sexual desire, like all other forms of desire, can be empowering, instrumental for girls' confidence in themselves, and essential to their overall ability to act on their own terms. Sexual desire becomes a compass for making decisions about relationships and sexuality, and a road to knowledge about oneself and relationships, an empowering force in girls' lives. The more entitled they feel to desire, the more they speak of balancing pleasure and danger. These girls exude a vitality and a psychological robustness not seen in many of the other girls in the study. With the exception of Melissa, whose distress is due to the quality of her feelings rather than to the existence of them, these girls are happy to be alive, connected to themselves and to others through their embodied feelings.

The differences in how the girls in this chapter experience and manage their entitlement to desire call attention to yet another view on how girls' perspectives on gendered sexuality inform and are informed by their dilemmas of desire. The girls who premise their entitlement to their desire on operating within the restricted zone of one kind of relationship—long-term, monogamous, heterosexual—illuminate both the importance and the limits of this potentially safe space. Eugenia's experience exemplifies society's partial accommodation of female adolescent sexuality within a mutual relationship. Her stories show how sexual subjectivity and sexual desire fuel emotional connection, a sense of safety, and responsible decisions. Yet this context does not defuse her dilemma of desire; it simply shifts it to the other arenas of Eugenia's sexuality. Sophie's stories of maneuvering her desire around relationships serve as counterpoint. The relationship haven does not accommodate her desire to explore her sexual feelings with different boys on her own terms. Since Sophie does not want to have sexual intercourse, entering a committed relationship may make her feel vulnerable to pressure to have sex. But because such a relationship is a requirement rather than an option for being safe as a desiring girl, Sophie is constantly monitoring her risk for being thought of as a "bad" girl.

Although the girls who take their desire under cover show a certain ingenuity, the limitations and vulnerabilities of this strategy are readily apparent. This approach buys these girls some space for their sexual feelings by keeping them out of view; in the moment, they are able to protect themselves from the repercussions they fear. Yet this response requires sacrificing authenticity and real connections with others as Barbara's regret signifies, and can lead to situations and choices that are risky, such as Trisha's use of alcohol to hide her desire. Melissa can hardly find breathing room for her doubly anathema desire; keeping her sexual feelings under cover is the best way she has found to lessen the isolation she feels.

The only girls in the study for whom desire was not a dilemma was the small group that actively engaged in "desire politics." Paulina and Amber described comfort with their desire, willingness to take the chance of losing or disrupting relationships in order not to overlook their feelings, and refusal to be intimidated by man-made threats. Their defiance of the dilemma of desire rests on their critique of gendered sexuality and their insistence on not buying into the categorization of girls as good and bad.

The differences within this group of girls make clear that gendered sexuality alone does not function to keep girls in check. The variability in their stories points to the vital role the related practice of categorizing girls plays in limiting adolescent girls' experiences of sexual desire. Its power is most evident in the stories of the few girls who refused to participate. Amber and Paulina have figured out that they have the power to refuse to care, and have chosen not to care, *because* they understand and reject the inequity of a system that gives desire and entitlement to boys and keeps it from girls. They make what is a risky choice to stand apart from the institution of heterosexuality. They use their knowledge and affirmation of their own bodies to defy categories that are meant to keep them out of relationship with themselves and with other girls. They will not enact this form of social control by regulating themselves or policing other girls. Yet the stories of the girls in this chapter illustrate that, just like the girls who dissociate from or resist their sexual desire, these girls too are finding individual solutions to a problem not of their own making.

> History has divided the empire of women
> against itself... Black and white women
> have not suffered equally under the spec-
> tacle of symbols, which construct sexuality
> and gender.
>
> —Nancie Caraway, *Segregated Sisterhood*

Growth spurts, learning to think com-
plexly and abstractly, the emergence of breasts and pubic hair, and
the onset of menarche are expected events in adolescent development, even a source of distress if they do not occur in a timely fashion. Yet, while just as inevitable, we find it extremely difficult
to think about emerging adult sexuality as a "normal" part of adolescence for girls. When we think of female adolescent sexuality,
our minds immediately categorize. Scanning the covers of news-
magazines or the advertisements for the television equivalents,
we see two recurring images. The first has been prevalent since
1976, when the Alan Guttmacher Institute (one-time research affil-
iate of Planned Parenthood) announced that the United States was
facing an "epidemic" of teenage pregnancy.[1] It is the pregnant adolescent girl, black or Latina and thus assumed to be poor (Painter,
1992), or poor and white and thus deviant (Brown, 1999). These
images serve to feed the racist fears and beliefs of society's powerful. These girls' pregnancies are irrefutable evidence of their sexuality; the illnesses of their progeny (the only babies we are shown)

are evidence of their drug use and HIV infection and thus confir-
mation of their immorality. And they live in segregated places,
most often in the "inner city," where teenagers are, of course, out of
control and, we are smugly if not always directly assured, getting
what they deserve for being irresponsible and irrepressible.

The second image is newer or newly revived. It is the white,
middle-class girl who lives in the suburbs, the supposedly safe
haven from the fallibilities to which urban girls are prone, the protected place where the daughters of society's powerful live. Evidence of her sexuality leaks out, and we are stunned and horrified.
Recently, in a well-off, white suburban community, a notable number of syphilis cases led to the discovery that young adolescent girls
were engaging not only in sexual intercourse but in a range of sexual activities (fellatio, girls having sex with multiple male partners
simultaneously). This incontestable evidence of their sexuality was
considered so strange and unnerving that *Frontline* made a docu-
mentary, "The Lost Children of Rockland County," to determine
how these events could have possibly happened. It was assumed
that some heinous problem within the community had produced
an aberrant group of teenage girls. To emphasize their deviancy
and thus salve white, middle-class parents about the sexuality of
their teenage girls, the girls involved in the scandal were pigeon-
holed as "bad," "defective," or "victims" of mothers in the work-
force instead of at home. From the perspective of the dominant
white, middle-class society, whereas the poor, pregnant urban girls
of color were never even eligible for the category of "good" or
"normal," these white girls lost their privilege to occupy it.

These stereotypes of urban girls as sexually out-of-control and
of suburban girls as sexually innocent populate the public imagination, though of course they are recognized as the projections of
anxiety and fantasy they truly are by many people. Thus far, I have

focused on what the girls in this study share: a set of adolescent female souls and bodies that are coming of age within the institution of heterosexuality. That is, I have focused my analysis on their shared gender. Weaving together their stories into a larger narrative about how girls' sexual desire is socially positioned and personally experienced as a dilemma for virtually all of them, I have underscored and highlighted how gendered constructions of sexuality work against female adolescent embodied sexual desire and sexual subjectivity, and identified several ways that these girls as a group manage the dilemma. This approach might suggest that there is a single, monolithic story to tell about female adolescent sexual desire. Of course, there is not; the girls' bodies and souls are not interchangeable. Indeed, while profiling one aspect of female adolescent experience, I left other, relevant, shaping forces out: their unique circumstances; their family structures; the cultural constructions of sexuality specific to their communities, ethnicities, religious affiliations, and acculturation status; and the complex interplay of all of these features of growing up sexual and female.

In this chapter, I turn to another aspect of the multifaceted context that informs the meaning and experience of female adolescent sexuality. Like twisting a kaleidoscope so that the pieces fall into another pattern, I will analyze the narratives told by these girls from an angle that reveals how the geographies of their lives shape and embed their experiences of desire. Because where girls live is such a prominent organizing principle in how we as a society conceptualize female adolescent sexuality and ultimately how we think about, treat, and limit our support for girls,[2] it is another logical building block in constructing the phenomenology of female adolescent sexual desire. It is important to note, however, that these girls are also negotiating constructions of their sexuality within and from outside their cultural communities.[3] The black and

Latina girls in the urban group have to deal with a battery of specific racial and ethnic stereotypes in the dominant culture that form the backdrop (or the foreground) of the development of their sexuality, as does each of the poor and working-class white girls. Each of the girls in the suburban group must work within and against the racial and ethnic stereotypes that characterize her—what is believed about the sexuality of Jewish women, Mediterranean women, women who descended from the Puritans. Before listening for differences in how the urban and suburban girls experience sexual desire, I will flesh out the diametrically opposed societal conceptions of urban and suburban girls' sexuality and how they have served the institution of heterosexuality.

STICK FIGURE A: THE URBAN GIRL

Fantasies and fallacies about the sexuality of urban women—poor, working class, and white, African American, Latina, or Asian—developed in response to the shifting social hierarchies produced by rapid demographic change in cities at the end of the Civil War and significant influxes of immigrants into urban environments at the beginning of the twentieth century (Walkowitz, 1980; Peiss, 1983; Odem, 1997). These views continue to be sustained and exploited by selective and skewed media portrayals of urban life. Our current notions about the lives of girls who live in poor, urban areas are anchored in this history. As a society, we hold certain negative beliefs and assumptions about urban girls that emphasize their sexuality. The stereotypical Urban Girl is assumed to be poor, of color, "out of control . . . at risk and at fault. She embodies the problem of teenage pregnancy . . . she *is* female adolescent sexuality" (Tolman, 1996, p. 255).

The Urban Girl seems to be a container for the most egregious sexualization of marginalized groups of women, an unrealistic stick figure in the social psyche of dominant white society. Demeaning conceptions of black female sexuality are found in the hyperbolic controlling images of the castrating matriarch, the overly sexual young Jezebel, and the welfare queen or cheat, or in the utterly desexualized image of the black mammy.[4] Some of these images present sexually out-of-control instigators and temptresses, "bad" girls and women who therefore can never be sexually vulnerable or protected (Caraway, 1991; Painter, 1992; Wyatt, 1997). Latinas are often eroticized as exotic, sexually alluring, and thus available; stereotypes of sexual promiscuity and fantasies of proficiency in appeasing male desires are projected onto them.[5] By deconstructing this Urban Girl, we can see the ways that racial and class differences have been used to produce different forms of oppression against all women in general, and by white, economically privileged women against poor women and women of color in particular.

STICK FIGURE B: THE PERFECT GIRL

The mirror image or flip side of the Urban Girl is an equally insidious though far less visible assumption about female adolescent sexuality. The icon of white, middle-class or monied womanhood has been described by Lyn Brown as a "perfect girl," who is the embodiment of "nice and polite" (1991, p. 79). It is this girl who holds another conflation of race and class and is expected to appear on the sidewalks and schools of the suburbs, segregated from the Urban Girl. Subtly coerced and invisibly invited to take up dominant society's norms of femininity, which press girls to discount their own thoughts and feelings for the sake of avoiding conflict and maintaining relationships, this Perfect Girl is not surprisingly disembodied and ascribed no sexuality in the public imagination.[6] As Brown (1999) has noted, it is both race and class that anchor these conceptions of what is and is not proper femininity.

The Perfect Girl has a history as well, in what were known as the purity campaigns of the nineteenth century. The Industrial Revolution produced a middle class that separated the spheres of public life, occupied by men, and private life, supervised by women, creating the newly minted "angel in the house" (Smith-Rosenberg, 1985). This white, middle-class woman took up the position of morally superior savior both to men who could not control their base desires and to women who had turned to prostitution—usually out of economic necessity due to the dearth of ways women could support themselves outside heterosexual marriage (Degler, 1974; Walkowitz, 1980). She was entitled to this privileged position because of her "passionlessness."[7] From the perspective of dominant society, it is only this Perfect Girl who is even eligible for the category of "good" girl (Tolman & Higgins, 1996). She is also thus at constant risk of falling off, or getting knocked off, this precarious pedestal and being branded a "bad" girl.

Because our society is so stratified and segregated by race and class, it is easy to be seduced by what we see, or are shown, about life in urban communities,[8] and what we know, or do not know, about suburban life—and thereby to find credible these beliefs that categorize girls. This stratification of women is instrumental not only in the production of the Urban Girl but also in the production of stereotypes about middle-class white girls' sexuality (Collins, 1990; Caraway, 1991). As I have noted elsewhere, "[i]n a misogynist culture that offers dubious rewards to virtuous women and unequivocally punishes even the presumably errant, a (white) woman knows her 'goodness' by knowing she is not the Other . . . This complex interplay of oppressions depends on keeping women divided into good vs. bad, normal vs. out-of-control categories, coded by race and class" (1996, p. 256). The asexual "good" (white, middle-class) girl cannot exist without the hypersexual "bad" (poor, of color) girl to prop her up.

FLESH AND BLOOD GIRLS

When I consider the differences between how the urban girls and the suburban girls frame their sexuality, another pattern of girls' experiences with the dilemma of desire falls into place. Both the urban and suburban girls in this study narrated their own sexual desire as a dilemma, because both groups of girls acknowledged feeling sexual desire, were conscious of dangers associated with sexuality in general and their own desire in particular, and knew of the physical, emotional, and relational pleasures that their desire can usher in. They all talked about the caution with which they negotiate this dilemma and the precautions they take, both unconscious and conscious, to protect themselves from the things they fear could or would happen in the wake of acting on or in some cases simply feeling their desire.

Virtually all of the girls held themselves responsible for what occurs in heterosexual relationships, especially sexual events; with the exception of Paulina, few in either group held boys or men accountable for their sexual aggression. Controlling their own desire constituted the finger in the dam that kept male sexuality at bay and adolescent sexuality from running amuck. Moreover, all of the girls in the study voiced concern about the consequences of their desire for their relationships, with mothers, fathers, boyfriends, girlfriends, peers and friends, teachers, and other adults in their lives.

Despite these similarities, there are discernible differences in *how* urban and suburban girls spoke about their experiences that are vital for building the necessarily complex picture of adolescent girls' sexuality.[9] The landscape of adolescent sexuality is not an equal opportunity zone for all girls; geography, among other social markers of difference, positions these girls differentially, particularly with regard to sexuality. Differences in the implications of their desire, and thus in the meanings of their desire, are striking. While girls from both the urban and suburban schools spoke about the range of consequences they associated with their own sexuality, some repercussions were more salient in one group than in the other. The way in which some negative consequences were perceived to function as social controls differed as well.

For the urban girls the vulnerabilities associated with desire are immediate and ubiquitous, lit upon regularly in their classrooms, visible in the lives of their friends, recurrent on the evening news. Like the urban girls in Michelle Fine's ethnography (1988), these girls talked about receiving constant and solely negative messages about their sexuality. There was rarely anything mixed about the messages they received from adults; they told of adults painting rigid, one-dimensional tales of woe that rarely acknowledged the complex development of relationships and identities manifest in the girls' stories. However they dealt with the dilemma of desire, they were looking over their shoulders and operating under the assumption that, if they did not take preemptive action, something dire would happen. Even Paulina, who so overtly rejected gendered sexuality and proclaimed her right to desire, was watchful. Yet these girls were not passive; agency in the service of self-protection was a theme throughout their stories of desire (Tolman, 1994a).

Although sexuality poses certain physical dangers to all girls and women—the possibility of pregnancy, the vulnerability to disease, the reality of sexual violence—the varied dangers associated with female sexuality are in fact not equally distributed. As a group, the urban girls made constant references to vigilance and caution, suggesting how present and real the entire range of dangers was for them. On the whole, their stories held and reflected the reality that they had few degrees of freedom in this part of their lives. They tended to talk about multiple threats to their well-being; Rochelle's litany of fears is the most intense example of this pattern. But their own sexual feelings were, for the majority of them, a part of their experience of adolescence. Most of them characterized their experience of desire itself as strong and pleasurable, a positive part of their lives, while only a few of the urban girls found the experience of desire itself frightening or unpleasant. The urban girls who described their experiences as attempts to balance danger and pleasure revealed a kind of resilience and resourcefulness that stood out; the safe spaces they found or chiseled out were often tiny and hard-won but notably creative.

Whatever their approach to dealing with their own desire, the urban girls made explicit and frequent connections between their sexual desire and physical danger. More of the girls who silenced their bodies, experienced the feelings in their bodies as confusing, or cut off their desire as a way to stay clear of danger were from the urban school. All of them spontaneously mentioned their worries about pregnancy, and a number of them spoke directly about how their fear of contracting HIV made them uncomfortable about relationships and any form of sexual expression. The potential of male violence and aggression was central to their understanding of the vulnerability to which their sexuality could expose them. Yet for the most part, they were having romantic relationships that included their sexuality, though not necessarily intercourse. For some girls, like Ellen, these risks felt too potent, as if opening the door to intimacy a crack would set her on an inevitable path to danger and doom. Those urban girls like Trisha and Paulina, who engaged in various forms of resistance to the denial or denigration of their desire, talked about their use of condoms and contraception, as well as getting to know or befriend a young man, like Barbara did, prior to sexual experiences that could invite such risks.

Much has been made of the centrality of the master narrative of romance for girls in organizing their sexuality and romantic relationships, but for the urban girls, there seemed to be another fundamental organizing cultural story at play. A master narrative of sexuality as the road to ruination always figured in the stories their mothers, sisters, teachers, and others told them about where their sexuality would lead them and thus was always present in their experiences and choices. Some girls, like Janine, were ruled by this narrative of ruination; others, like Rochelle, tried to figure out how to hold the tension between romance and ruination. Still others, like Inez, seemed to recognize the potential for ruination but not espouse it as the central tenet of their experiences with relationships and sexuality.

In all cases the wish to be thought of, and to think of themselves, as "good" and not "aggressive" sexually, to comply with norms of femininity regulating their bodies and their behavior, was evident. Most of them talked about their fear of getting a bad reputation, whether they were engaged in sexual activity in any context or not. For the urban girls, this anxiety was very personal; they themselves felt at constant risk of being labeled a slut, though many of them realized that they could not control this outcome, as Inez demonstrated with her perfectly pitched rendition of how rumors get started. For some, labeling was a barrier to sexuality, while for others it was a pitfall to be skillfully avoided. What this peer policing did lead to, though, for all of the urban girls, was an especially intense fear of talking to anybody about anything having to do with sexuality.

One of the ways the girls talked about their fears of getting a bad reputation was in terms of respect. Demanding respect from others seemed to ensure that they would not get branded "bad," as Inez explained. Niobe Way has observed that what girls call self-respect has become a key dynamic in how racially and ethnically diverse (including white) poor urban girls negotiate their hetero-sexual relationships (Way, 1994), a dynamic also audible in some of these girls' narratives. It is of note that, without the message that girls are entitled to sexual desire, self-respect usually translates into a girl's resistance to giving in to a boy's desire; the self in question should not by definition have her own desire. And boys who respect a girl do not engage her on sexual terms.

Struggling with poverty and racism, getting few opportunities for second chances, having little access to quality education, bear-ing the burden of governmental surveillance and interference, and encountering high levels of overt violence, the urban girls had little room in which to develop a sexual identity. What was missing from most of their stories and likely from most of their lives was a cri-tique of how their own desire gets set up as the "straw man" when there are other such systemic factors at play. These girls have to deal with the impact of racism and poverty on the lives of others around them as well as on their own, including the pressures on men of color to construct masculinities with few resources, higher rates of HIV and AIDS in their communities, and others' expecta-tions that they will become teen mothers. Carrying these burdens, the urban girls may find entitlement to pleasure especially hard to come by.

Many of the suburban girls were surprised that I wanted to talk to them about their sexuality; it was as if, despite comprehensive sex education in their health classes and pamphlets about contracep-tion readily available outside the office in which we were talking, no one had taken this part of their lives seriously. Although these girls did mention in passing the physical dangers associated with sexual activity, usually in the course of telling me how they pro-tected themselves from these outcomes, they did not, as a group, emanate an intense fear of the potential bad outcomes associated with their sexual desire.[10] Some of these girls had had personal experiences with sexual violence; but even those who had showed no sign they were worried about being harmed by a partner. Some girls, however, told stories like Sophie's, revealing an unconscious awareness of the potential for male violence. And the phenomenon of becoming tongue-tied was more pervasive among the suburban girls who had silent bodies, confused bodies, or bodies cut off from their desire than it had been among the comparable urban girls, suggesting that the suburban girls were dealing with the complexities of sexual desire at a more unconscious level.

None of the suburban girls associated their sexual desire with material threats; none of them felt they had to "trade in" their sexuality to ensure their education. Reflecting their access to a material safety net, they did not feel their well-being was at stake. There was no master narrative of ruination underlying these girls' stories about sexuality. Instead of hearing relentless tales of sexuality's woes, the suburban girls told of receiving mixed messages about sexuality from adults and peers. Some, like Emily, said that their mothers or another adult in their life had talked in a positive way about female sexuality; yet they had also picked up and internalized negative constructs of desiring girls. She struggled consciously with this contradiction. The narratives of some of these girls suggested that being told they are entitled to their sexual desire did not mesh with the ways girls and their sexuality are pictured in the larger landscape of television and teen magazines, or with the experiences they observed or heard in their friends' lives. It is hard to hold on to the contrary notions that girls' sexuality is normal but that girls who step over an invisible and unstable line get tarnished with a bad reputation. Missing was an analysis of how this categorization of girls functions to keep all girls in a state of sexual anxiety. The tension exclusive to the suburban girls, between the new idea that "girls can do anything" and the enduring ways they were expected to limit their sexuality, was as unspoken as it was pervasive.

More of the suburban girls framed their sexual desire as something to which they were simply entitled, as Amber did. These girls' stories about their desire, and their struggles with their embodied feelings, signal that they were trying to explore the interplay between emotional and sexual intimacy. As we saw in Eugenia's struggles, the roadblocks for them derived more from within themselves than from the social world populated by female friends and male partners. In contrast to a lot of the urban girls, few of these girls spoke of much older boyfriends, suggesting that the gender inequities may be less pronounced when not amplified by age differentials. Several girls talked about the egalitarian nature of their relationships with sensitive boys, boys whose roads to success were already paved for them. Space for sexual curiosity seemed more readily available to these girls.

Almost all of the suburban girls talked about how girls perceived to be desiring girls are vulnerable to getting a reputation. Working within the framework of romance, though, these girls felt fully protected from being labeled a slut if they explored their sexuality in a long-term monogamous relationship. Within this safe space, the concern about getting a reputation was not an especially personal one. The notable exception to this rule reveals the price that is exacted most pervasively from the suburban girls: If, like Sophie, they strayed from or rejected the strict boundary on their desire stipulated by this single option, then they were fair game for being deemed a slut. While these girls, like most of the urban girls, participated in this policing practice, they were less likely to frame girls whom they labeled in this way as malevolently bad; rather, they saw girls who put themselves into this situation, which virtually none of them felt they had done or would do, as "pathetic" or having "low self-esteem." They were often puzzled about why a girl would expose herself in this way, volunteering possible explanations, such as that the girl wanted to fit in with her peers who had had sex or that she had a pathological need for attention; but none of them embraced these motivations as their own.

Here the romance narrative served them well; most of these girls framed sexual experiences, particularly intercourse, as expressions of love and caring, by themselves and their partners. The romance narrative was prevalent in how they talked about their sexual experiences and the resulting problems. For example, an interesting paradox was their frequent admission of faking sexual pleasure as a way to please their boyfriends. When I invited them to consider that it might be a bit curious to pretend to have pleasure to make someone else happy, some of them were able to see the paradox. But diminishing themselves for the sake of pleasing boys was more often than not seen as a normal act for these girls, a manifestation of the institution of heterosexuality they did not apprehend.

Perhaps because the physical dangers associated with their desire were less salient to them as a group, the suburban girls tended to consistently worry about maintaining their identities as "good," appropriate, and normal girls, and they feared that important people in their lives, especially their mothers, might not regard them in this way. Jenny provided the most extreme example of this concern in her dissociation from her desire; all of her narratives indicated a virtually complete internalization of the Perfect Girl, the girl who wants to be popular and have friends (ergo has sex to fit in, like Jenny thinks she may have) but wants to be a "good" girl (thus feels uncomfortable, like Jenny does, at the thought of having been bad, disappointing her mother, and possibly sullying her reputation). There is no space within herself to recognize or accept her desire; it is not in the mold. Yet Jenny's formulations and disembodiment were not the rule among the suburban girls. While they felt desire and many knew, at some level, that it was normal for girls to have sexual feelings, these girls spoke of an internal conflict, between their idea about who they felt they were supposed to be (not a desiring girl) and the problem of actually having such sexual feelings. This tension often surfaced when discussing masturbation. Most of the urban girls flat out rejected masturbation as inappropriate for girls, though a few believed girls (other than themselves) did indeed masturbate. The suburban girls took the opportunity afforded by talking about masturbation to articulate the sense of discomfort they felt about having sexual feelings when not pleasing a boy in the context of heterosexual behavior.

A comparison of the urban and suburban girls' descriptions of their dilemmas of desire reveals that what was present or most salient for one group of girls illuminated what was more muted in the other group. The suburban girls spoke less frequently than did the urban girls about their vulnerability to sexual violence. Being more consistently structured by the master narrative of romance that plays subtly with but does not distinctly define the connection between pleasure and danger, the suburban girls' stories suggest that they know unconsciously but do not have conscious awareness of the real dangers they could encounter and, for a number of them, have encountered.

In the balance of pleasure and danger, the suburban girls talked more about the pleasurable aspects of their sexual desire. They were more likely to be open to and open with their sexuality than the urban girls were; absent from their narratives was the constant feeling of impending disaster. The girls who felt entitled to their desire were more likely to be those from the suburban school; even in the group that associated sexual desire with danger, the suburban girls tended to accept an ambivalent truce rather than cut desire off entirely, as the urban girls were prone to do. With race and class privileges seems to come more opportunity for safe spaces, though for some girls, like Kim and Jenny, these were still hard to come by. Vigilant with themselves in a different way than the urban girls, the suburban girls struggled to hold the contradictions that seem more evident in their social landscape rather than attempting to erase them by ridding themselves of desire. While the streets of this suburban community felt relatively safe, life in the suburbs harbored dangers around sexuality that are in fact present but less a part of the girls' everyday lives and stories. The dangers of desire seemed less evident than in the urban community. Or they just were not discussed. For instance, Kim said that a girl in her school had gotten pregnant and had the baby, and was distressed that no one ever said anything about it. No other girl in the study mentioned this event.

Conversely, the urban girls less frequently referred to the more psychological dimensions of their experiences of desire and their sexual curiosity. The presence of the master narrative of ruination seems to eclipse these real features of female adolescent sexuality. So completely aware of the physical and material dangers embedded in their experiences of desire, the urban girls as a group had a harder time carving out psychic or relational space for the possibility of pleasure. In some sense, the stakes simply are different for these two groups of girls.

Further analysis of the differences between the stories about desire told by the suburban and the urban girls yielded new insights into the geographies of desire. Coding all of the girls' narratives for whether they were primarily about pleasure, primarily about vulnerability, or about both pleasure and danger, Laura Szalacha and I (1999) found a statistical difference in the narratives told by the urban and the suburban girls. Where the urban girls told over three times more desire narratives about their vulnerability than about their pleasure, the suburban girls told equal numbers of pleasure and vulnerability desire narratives.[11] The suburban girls told significantly more narratives about pleasure than the urban girls did.

SEXUAL VIOLATION AND GEOGRAPHY

Pregnancy and disease are not the only forms of physical danger to which sexuality makes girls vulnerable. In this study, nine of the thirty-one girls told me they had experienced some form of sexual molestation, abuse, or violence in childhood or in adolescence, when I asked them if there had been anything bad that had happened to them regarding sex or relationships; one other girl was not sure she had been raped, and two others had escaped attacks. Both the urban and the suburban girls reported such incidents. The girls who did speak of sexual violation were distributed across the groupings of ways girls spoke about desire. Statistics indicate that sexual violence is prevalent in the lives of all female adolescents (Silverman et al., 2001). When we evaluated whether these reports were associated with how the girls talked about their sexual desire, Laura Szalacha and I (1999) discovered that having reported a history of sexual abuse, attack, molestation, or violence in a romantic relationship had an impact on the likelihood of telling narratives about sexual pleasure for the suburban girls but not for the urban girls;[12] that is, the suburban girls who did not report sexual violence told significantly more pleasure stories about their own desire, compared to any of the other girls in the study. The other three groups—the suburban subgroup that had reported violation and both of the urban groups—told many more narratives of desire being associated with vulnerability than of desire being associated with pleasure or of pleasure and vulnerability figuring equally. For instance, suburban girls who had not reported sexual violence were almost six times more likely to tell a narrative about their own desire with a central theme of pleasure than were urban girls who had not reported sexual violence.

How do we make sense of this differential impact? We concluded that, in contrast to the suburban girls, the urban girls encountered constant and pervasive violence in their lives.[13] Shootings in a nearby subway station, neighborhood violence connected to drugs, domestic violence that was audible through thin walls of apartment buildings, a metal detector at school—violence was in the air they breathed, not sequestered in the realm of their sexuality. These differences highlight the conundrum of sexuality for all girls and women in this society: to be sexually empowered—that is, to feel entitled to act on one's own sexual desire responsibly—is at the same time to be in danger in a society that resists women's empowerment. But it is such empowerment that is required to identify and fuel the social change necessary to diminish and dismantle these dangers.

There were also nuanced and important differences in how the girls from each of these groups talked about their experience of desire. In particular, the suburban girls who had not reported sexual violation described desire as an interplay between their minds and their bodies. The narratives told by these girls offer a way to understand how sexual desire is not only a matter of physical feelings or sensations but also a conjunction of embodied feelings and thoughts and emotions. Sophie, for example, was able to explain that desire happens "both mentally and physically. Because your mind knows that you want that, but what triggered that was like the feeling in your body." Amber's description resonates with Sophie's: "It evolves from the head, definitely, it's kind of like head to vagina, it's like a little direct signal, but [pause] I think that the heart's involved too, depending on how much you like this person." The other suburban girls, and most of the urban girls, spoke of a disconnect between these two aspects of the self.[14] Recall Inez's mind fighting for control over her body. Alexandra observed that "when you're in a situation and your body's saying one thing, you don't really consult your mind all the time." For Nikki, desire was "all in my head . . . my body has nothing to do with it . . . pretty much it's in what you think about."

Within the group of urban girls who had reported sexual viola- tion, however, there were exceptions to this pattern. Some of them sounded more like the suburban girls who had not reported sexual violence. Barbara talked about feeling desire "emotionally wise, because you can feel it in your emotions, as well, especially if you really care about that person, then it becomes emotional as well as physical." All of these girls narrated a sense of entitlement to their sexual desire, and some of them described how, through their own efforts or through support from others, they had consciously developed the capacity for embodied sexual desire.

GENDERED GEOGRAPHY OF DESIRE: A WORD ABOUT SEXUAL MINORITY GIRLS

Although I cannot make comparisons between the few girls who identified themselves as lesbian or bisexual and the heterosexual girls, who constituted the majority in this sample, the experiences and perspectives of these lesbian and bisexual girls add insight. These girls were more conscious of their sexual desire than many of the other girls; it was not only a significant but also an especially defining feature of their adolescence. While it might seem as if girls who feel desire for girls or both girls and boys are somehow exempt from the institution of heterosexuality, in fact they stand in a very different and threatening relationship to it, by violating its most core principle: that we are, by nature, attracted to the opposite gender only. Like other women who do not enter into the socially sanctioned heterosexual relationship—women who are single, di- vorced, or widowed, or nuns—these girls have an "uncontained" sexuality that heightens social anxiety and thus instigates violent reactions (Weitz, 1984). While true in some sense for all adolescent girls, girls who desire girls instigate intense alarm. They commit a double violation: they feel sexual desire, and it is for girls.

Overall, their stories sounded more like those told by the urban girls. They spoke of multiple dangers, fear of physical harm, and complete loss of relationships, rather than damage through disappointing others. They were highly aware that a lot was at stake for them because of their desire. Even though it was a shaping force in the experiences of all of the girls, unlike the other girls in the study, the sexual minority girls had a unique awareness and ability to articulate the power of compulsory heterosexuality. These girls spoke about being particularly isolated, noting how their isolation lessened the chance of diffusing their confusion about or discomfort with their desire.

Bisexual and lesbian girls have particularly potent, frightening, and complicated challenges in their relationships with their parents (Savin-Williams, 1998, 2001). For instance, Megan told me of her mother's concern when she found out Megan was going to a support group for sexual minority youth, because, Megan reported, her mother "worried that they wouldn't say I was straight, that these adolescents were unreliable." Her mother's fears contradicted Megan's actual experience in the group, confusing her as well as upsetting her. While Megan understood her mother's difficulty— "no one wants a gay daughter"—she did not disconnect from her desire and stayed in the youth group. Her mother grew to accept Megan's bisexuality, even though "it was hard for her," according to Megan. Like the urban girls, girls who think they may or do desire other girls face overt threats of violence, rejection, and punitive lashing out from the adults in their lives and their friends.

A consideration of how the girls in this study, taken together as a group marked "girls," responded to the dilemmas that their own desire produced shows the continuities and similarities between urban and suburban girls. At the same time, a search for differences yields another dimension of the variability in adolescent girls' experiences of sexual desire. The topologies of these two geographies of desire reflect the relative instability and danger of urban life and the relative conventionality and safety of life in the suburbs. These findings are somewhat surprising, upending the Urban Girl and the Perfect Girl, the stick figures that organize our thinking about female adolescent sexuality. The girls whom society has marked as sexually out of control were the girls whose experiences were suffused with worry and caution about material and physical consequences. The girls who have been categorized as not sexual were the girls who felt freer to explore their sexual curiosity. That is, none of them were overly sexual, and none of them, even the girls with silent bodies, were asexual. How could we have gotten it so wrong, so backward? Breaking the silence about female adolescent sexuality not only reveals the impact of gendered sexuality in the lives of individual girls, it also reveals how readily we can make and impose assumptions about female sexuality when it has been silenced.

Your mama told you to be discreet
and keep your freak to yourself
but your mama lied to you all this time
she knows as well as you and I
you've got to express what is taboo in
    you . . .
and share your freak with the rest of us
cause it's a beautiful thing
this is my sexual revolution!

Macy Gray, "Sexual Revolution"

Misty, who identifies herself as a "riot grrl," referring to the national group of girls who actively defy conventional, constrictive constructions of femininity, writes in a zine called *Suck My Dick,*

> In American society, wimmin are novelties. Objects. A body part. Something to use for convenience. Wimmin need to learn that power is not given, we have to take it. We need to realize that we don't have to stand around and be treated like this. Don't let anyone control you or dictate your life to you . . . We need to break free of our own stereotypes. No one can save you from your oppression except yourself. (Quoted in Carlip, 1995, p. 58)

Misty's words resonate with the observations of Audre Lorde, who wrote that in this society, women have been systematically kept from the power of the erotic, because it makes women dangerous: Women so empowered will challenge an oppressive status quo

187

(1984). Girls' and women's knowledge is dangerous because it threatens to reveal that power differentials and abuses are not simply the way things should be.

At a time when we are told that there is a "war on boys" and that girls are just fine, the voices of the girls in this study sound a different note, reminding us that being a girl, living comfortably in a girl's body, is neither easy nor especially safe. When asked directly about their experiences of sexual desire, the girls in this study talked about these powerful feelings as well and as clearly as any of us can. Inquiring from a perspective that acknowledged the ways that the institution of heterosexuality is organized to preempt, prevent, or punish their desire, I heard how girls respond to the personal, relational, and social challenges they come to associate with their desire. These girls' stories underscored how the institution of heterosexuality makes it hard for them to know and validate the complexity of their own sexual feelings; most of them struggled with whether or how to integrate these feelings into a sense of themselves and whether or how to bring these feelings to bear on their decisions about what to do—and not to do—in sexual situations. They narrated ways to deal with the dilemmas that seemed to spring from their desire, which frequently kept them from being comfortable in their own bodies and from authentic relationships with other people in their lives (boyfriends, girlfriends, parents, peers).

When I invited girls to talk about their experiences of their sexuality, what emerged was the socially manufactured dilemma of desire, which pits girls' embodied knowledge and feelings, their sexual pleasure and connection to their own bodies and to others through their desire, against physical, social, material, and psychological dangers associated with their sexuality. This dilemma of desire is a poignant and powerful illustration of how girls can easily misdiagnose their problems as theirs and theirs alone, and then attempt to devise individualized solutions, which are neither answers nor routes to changing the social circumstances that produce the dilemmas in the first place. Many of the strategies these girls reported may be effective in the short run but are very costly and ultimately not effective in the long run; in fact, these coping mechanisms in essence support the system that makes them necessary. Michelle Fine has suggested that denying female adolescent sexual desire "may actually disable young women in their negotiations as sexual subjects. Trained through and into positions of passivity and victimization, young women are currently educated away from positions of sexual self-interest" (1988, p. 42). Without the big picture of why they deserve and are being denied their desire and how or why it is rendered so difficult for them *as a group*—not simply as individuals—they are limited in what they can devise for themselves. The lack of a framework for calling the very need for these struggles into question was evident. When articulated by a few of the girls, the power of being able to identify, deconstruct, and resist gendered sexuality and the division of girls into good and bad camps was compelling. It is reflected in their defiant claims on their desire, their ability to use their own sexual feelings to apprehend their relational worlds and make safe, responsible choices about their sexuality.

Like the political resisters in this study, Misty is right to be indignant at being objectified, to insist that girls refuse to be boxed in by stereotypes that leave out them and their feelings. And to some extent, she speaks the truth in her righteous claim that "no one can save you from your oppression except yourself." But Misty's call to action misses a key point: that girls should not and cannot be expected to, alone and in isolation, recognize and resist powerful social forces that make their own sexual desire into what ends up feeling like a personal dilemma. To support their healthy development, we need to make it possible for girls to gain the critical perspective that fuels Misty's outrage at being treated as the object of someone else's desire and Paulina's empowerment as a desiring girl. It is crucial that we not leave girls alone to engage in this difficult and necessary resistance. It is our job to make it possible for girls to gain such a perspective on their sexuality. We need to carve out safe spaces in which girls will be able to talk with each other and with adult women about their experiences with, and their questions, thoughts, fears, expectations, and hopes about, their own sexuality. We need to take responsibility for joining girls in making their sexual revolution.

Women listening to each other in consciousness-raising groups three decades ago began to realize that what was being said about their sexuality was out of sync with their actual experiences. What they knew had been covered over, left out, medicalized away, actively dismissed, and punished (Irvine, 1990). Through speaking with one another they understood that their own experiences had been systematically distorted and discounted, and that what seemed to be a personal problem was in fact a larger, societal phenomenon. The suggestion that girls need to speak with women and with one another sounds almost "retro" in the light of the early twenty-first century. Yet the stories these girls tell of the dilemmas their desire continues to pose attest to the necessity of going back to an old practice of speaking to one another about our real experiences.

Consciousness-raising groups in the 1970s more often than not centered on women's sexuality, on how women's experiences were at odds with what was being called "reality." Now it behooves us to create these conversations with and for girls, at a difficult time in their lives, and to make room for them to initiate these conversations safely with one another. Hearing the words of girls and women makes it possible for other girls to voice and make sense of their experiences, their justified confusion and fears, their curiosities—to live in our female bodies with an awareness of danger but also with a desire to stay connected with ourselves. Speaking the truths about female sexual desire—both the pleasures and the dangers—and acknowledging the reality of the complexity of girls' and women's sexuality in a patriarchal society is a truly attainable educational and psychological goal—and a most crucial one.

GIRLS SPEAKING WITH WOMEN

A place to start is for adult women to speak with girls about sexual desire and girls' entitlement to sexual subjectivity as they are developing into women. Sharon Thompson (1990), for example, found among the four hundred adolescent girls she interviewed about their first sexual experiences a small group she calls "pleasure narrators." Like Eugenia and Amber, these girls described their own desire and pleasure as key aspects of their first experiences of sexual intercourse. These girls were unique among the girls Thompson interviewed in that they talked with their mothers about female sexual desire and pleasure. Their mothers shared what they knew about the sexual feelings their daughters would experience, validating and even celebrating this embodied knowledge. Some feminists have interviewed girls about their experiences in relationships (Brown & Gilligan, 1992; Brown, 1999), specifically about the ways in which gender weaves in and out of their relational worlds (Fine & Macpherson, 1995). Janie Ward (2001), in her research on the political socialization that African American families engage in with their children, notes how vital it is for these children to have families and communities in which they can have ongoing conversations about the differences between the realities of their lives and what is said to be "reality." The girls in this study push us to ask: In a patriarchal society, what can make it possible for girls and women to speak about, feel, and act upon their sexual desire, and its absence, fully and freely?

At the end of each interview, I asked the girls in this study whether they had talked to anyone before about their sexual desire, their experiences with sexuality, or their own bodies. Jenny, one of the girls who said she did not feel desire, observed, "it's just not something that's really talked about, like what makes you feel good. It's not like a normal topic of conversation." Trisha explained, "I've never had a conversation like this [laughs], I've never been asked direct questions, so it's kind of like fun." Megan said, "it's okay, it's uncomfortable, it's just not normal, you know?" As Inez finished telling me a story about desire, she commented after a long pause, "it's weird . . . it's weird to speak about that, I, because I don't talk to anybody about that . . . if it wasn't because you was doing this little research thing, I wouldn't be speaking to you about it right now." The paucity of safe spaces for girls to sort out the contradictory, complex, and confusing mandates about their sexuality is palpable, and the need to initiate conversations about sexual desire, sexual entitlement, and sexual subjectivity is obvious.

Even the simple act of talking in positive ways about adolescent girls' sexuality is easier said than done, however. As noted by a number of the girls, talking itself constitutes a risk. While some of them would not talk to me about it, the majority were eager and relieved to explain to an adult what dealing with their sexuality was really like for them. Jenny and most of the other girls in the study realized, from their experience of speaking about their sexuality in the interview, that talking about it not only helped them but also offered an alternative discourse through which to sort out their sexual experiences; talking "made me think about different things that I've never really thought about before . . . like pleasure and like what makes you feel good and what you like and what you don't like."

The question of whom girls can speak to is also a vital one. Mothers often ask me how they should speak with their daughters about sexual desire. There is no simple or standard answer to this difficult question. Not all daughters want to speak with their mothers about sexuality; not all daughters have this choice. For instance, Sophie told me that she does not talk with her mother about sexual things; she believes "they make [her mother] uncomfortable." The African American concept of "othermothers" (Collins, 1990) is useful to consider here. Othermothers are adult women who serve as additional caretakers of children who are not their own but with whom they have a close and caring relationship. Women speaking to girls about desire, then, does not mean solely mothers speaking with daughters.

A few girls had had positive and helpful experiences speaking with other adults. Emily spoke about a young female teacher whom she felt "understood" rather than "judged" her and her friends, who offered straight talk about sex as well as her own opinion that sex is better for women when they and their partners are older and thus more knowledgeable about women's bodies and sexuality. This opportunity to talk and ask questions about sexuality without getting the response "just say no" enabled Emily to seriously consider the possibility that she wanted to postpone having sexual intercourse and led her to begin to ask herself, as she reported back to the group, "why am I really doing this?" in sexual situations. Focusing on her own feelings and motivations offered an alternative perspective on earlier unpleasant and in the end unwanted experiences that had been motivated by her wish to be perceived as nice and not to make waves. It became evident, when I asked the girls in the post-interview what they thought of the experience of talking this way about their sexuality, that participating in this one disruptive conversation, which offered an opportunity for speaking about their real feelings, provided a framework for them to reflect on their own desire. Megan specifically commented, "God, I know like the next time I'm kissing a guy I'm gonna think about all this stuff [laughs] that I'm talking about, I'll have to call Deb and tell her [laughs] what, exactly what I'm feeling." Megan's reference to her phantom call to me underscores the importance to girls of bringing these thoughts and feelings, their erotic voices, into a relationship they can then internalize, making such internal conversations possible. Jenny concludes that girls need

> somebody to make them think about [their own desire and pleasure] . . . I mean it's just a perfect example, I mean I wouldn't probably never thought about it unless I had this interview. Girls just have to like think about it, I don't know how you would do that, but make them actually think about it and ask the questions to themselves . . . I mean, I know what I do and what I don't do, but I've never like sat down and thought about it with myself, I mean what I definitely enjoy, what I definitely don't enjoy, and just like, I don't know why. I think it's good for girls to know themselves and what they're thinking. I mean it gives me a better handle on myself, it just makes me understand myself more, I guess, what I feel.

The diverse voices in this study are a wake-up call to the adults in their lives: We may not be ready to talk about or listen to the real questions girls have about the world of sexuality and romantic relationships they are entering, but *they are*. Many of the girls in the study, when asked, advised adults to give them the opportunity to discuss, explore, understand, question, and challenge the ways that their sexuality is framed for them and experienced by them.

We can continue to pretend that we do not notice girls' developing sexuality, and hope that it will go away or that they will "wait" long enough, but such pretense is not only unhelpful to girls, it is a hindrance. Although it is difficult to figure out how to talk to girls about their sexuality when there are real dangers attached, we have no choice; they need us, and we had better catch up.

GIRLS SPEAKING WITH OTHER GIRLS

The challenge of talking with adults about their sexuality is magnified tenfold when girls consider speaking to one another. When Barbara and her friends share their sexual curiosities, experiences, and knowledge, she knows that they are taking a risk: "you don't want [those things] all over the place, because of the way the society is, and looks at it. Then you end up with this rep and all of this other nonsense that runs around, like, and that's why a lot of girls don't talk about it, 'cause they are afraid of getting this reputation that they are sluts." Because the pre-interview meeting had not worked at the urban school, I scheduled no follow-up group discussion there. Recall that when I asked in the interviews why the girls had not participated in the first group, they said they would not speak in a group of their peers; that is, they could not trust one another. The dangers associated with speaking to one another outweighed any potential gain.

This problem of girls not trusting other girls with the realities of their sexuality is not limited to urban settings. Even Eugenia, who was so comfortable with her own sexuality and with talking to close friends and her mother about it, said, "I just wish somehow, like, where you could totally trust everybody, and it'd be such a, you know, confidential thing. But I don't know if I ever just trust, um, trust people like that." As long as the good-girl and bad-girl categories remain intact and as long as girls do not understand

how this mechanism of keeping girls and women out of relationship with one another does not serve us, it will be nearly impossible for girls to be able to trust one another.

Yet the power of being able to talk with peers about sexuality in
an authentic way did come through. Two of the girls in this study
were already participating in conversations about desire. They
belonged to a gay and lesbian youth group, a group designed to
bring out into the open and challenge how anathema homosexual
desire is to mainstream society. The theme of talking about sexuality with others weaves in and out of these girls' interviews.
Although Megan and her friends talked about sex, she considered
their talk quite limited and wondered out loud why this might be
the case: "we're so new [at sex] that we're worried about, like,
pleasing our partner and not ourselves? But, I don't know, but I
think that's kind of, like, in a way I'm demeaning us because I think
that we do have a lot more, like, feelings and thoughts about it, but
we just, I don't know, we just don't, like, acknowledge them or at
least we don't share them." A few other girls spoke about new conversations they were having with one another, and with close
friends whom they trust, about their sexuality in the wake of participating in the study.

One particular conversation struck me as a powerful example of
how girls, if they bring their real questions about their own desires
and pleasures into their relationships with one another, can discover that they are indeed not alone in facing these problems and
that these problems should not make them feel ashamed. Eugenia
reported that she and Sophie, who are close friends, had "never
ever talked about [masturbation], it was just one of those things
that, you know?" After I introduced the topic in the interview, they
began to talk about it: "after all those years it just popped up, you
know?" commented Eugenia. "After all those years," a taboo subject
had been made possible to talk about in their relationship in a way

that Eugenia described as being new, different, and ultimately helpful to her.

I learned about such aftereffects in the follow-up group interview with the suburban girls. In contrast to the silence and suspicion that characterized the pre-interview meeting, the follow-up interview was marked by lively conversation. Some of the girls began to talk, to me and to one another, about the aftermath of their interviews. In particular, they discussed how they had begun to notice that their boyfriends attempted to name their own experiences: One girl related how she and her boyfriend had actually had a fight about whether or not *she* had had an orgasm (he said she did, she said she did not). It was clear that one result of the interviews was a new attention to their own bodies while having sexual experiences. Not all of the girls spoke, but those who did seemed to receive affirmation from the other girls in the room.

GETTING BEYOND DILEMMAS OF DESIRE

Speaking the unspeakable, naming the reality, and validating the normalcy of girls' sexual desire are certainly crucial first steps in defusing girls' dilemmas of desire. But to come away from this project with the simple agenda of just talking to girls or encouraging them to talk with one another would be naive and misguided. Simply talking about or declaring entitlement to sexual desire for girls may be fraught with the same limitations as telling girls they can do or be anything they want when, in a world that continues to objectify and degrade them, that is not in fact true. Difficulties abound when we challenge the status quo. Telling a daughter that she should be entitled to her sexual subjectivity, without identifying the societal forces that work against her doing so, is not enough. Recall that Rochelle's mother encouraged her not to have sexual experiences unless Rochelle herself wanted them, but Rochelle got no actual guidance about how to determine what she wanted and no assurances that her mother would support her if she ultimately chose to have sexual experiences. Girls need help developing resistance strategies and living with the consequences of violating sexual norms. It is crucial that neither we nor girls deny the reality that when girls and women resist oppressive institutions and relationships, heels get dug in deeper. As women who were part of the second wave of feminism and those who were part of the early years of gay liberation can attest, the response can be unpleasant, frightening, dangerous, and even deadly.

To enable girls to speak about their sexuality and us to listen to them we must become conscious of the existence of heterosexuality as an institution, of the enduring power of patriarchy in organizing our lives. Sara Ruddick (1989) says that developing a feminist consciousness is essential to recognizing the existence and impact of conventional gender stereotypes. About mothers in particular she writes,

> They come to recognize that the stories they have been told and tell themselves about what it means "to be a woman" are mystifying and destructive . . . In unraveling these . . . stories, mothers acquiring feminist consciousness may well be prompted to explore undefensively their ambitions and sexual desires . . . Hitherto silenced voices, edging toward lucid speech, are developing voices, transformed by new experiences of seeing and saying. (pp. 21–23)

Ken Plummer writes in *Telling Sexual Stories* that sexual "stories become more and more likely to challenge authorities and eclipse one standard telling . . . Once stories become more self-conscious, recursive, and are told to distinctive audiences, then the stories given from on high are seen to be artefactual. The foundation collapses, and authoritarian stories are only one amongst many" (1995, pp. 137–138). In the foreword to *Adios, Barbie*, Rebecca

Walker observes "a crisis of imagination, a dearth of stories, the shocking lack of alternative narratives" to societal pressures and "the [resulting] hysteria to control and commodify an image of ideal beauty" for girls and women (Edut, 1998, p. xiv). This book of essays presents the resistant and resilient experiences of young women who, in "bar[ing] their insecurities and self-hatreds, as well as their determination to work through them to moments of self-awareness and bona fide self-acceptance" (p. xv), produce such competing stories about their relationships with their own bodies, grounded in what they know and feel, regardless of how they know they are supposed to feel about their bodies. This model is a useful one for the realm of female adolescent sexuality.

Even to acknowledge the dilemma of desire, we have to be aware both of our strong, embodied, and passionate sexual feelings and of the limited and oppressive ways these feelings are discussed or ignored in our own communities and cultures. It is crucial that girls understand that their desire *feels* like a dilemma as a direct result of social constructions of gendered sexuality. Many of the girls in this study identified the sexual double standard as unfair but had no idea why girls and not boys got called sluts. Not only do girls need a discourse of desire to support their embodied experiences and sense of entitlement in their relationships, they also need what Celia Kitzinger has called a "discourse of power" (1995, p. 194). They need to see how our conceptions of male and female sexuality are social constructions that produce privilege and oppression. The importance of developing this knowledge in the context of supportive, trustworthy relationships cannot be underestimated.

When we begin to speak about the experiences of "girls" and "women," the race and class contours of the challenges and constraints on different girls' opportunities and challenges speed to the surface. While the suburban girls were challenging the belief that they did not have sexuality, the girls at the urban school had to deal daily with a barrage of messages implying they embodied female adolescent sexuality, which constantly threatened to become unbridled. The specific instantiation of institutionalized heterosexuality and how women and girls deal with it will likely have different contours depending on how each racial and ethnic group constructs, constrains, or enables female sexuality. Cultural conceptions of gendered relationships will thus affect what women can or should do with girls to enable them to stay embodied and also stay safe.

The complexities for women in speaking to girls about their sexual desire should not be overlooked. By the time we are adults, most women have made compromises in relation to our own bodies and desires (Haag, 1999). Carol Gilligan writes that when listening to girls, "women may encounter their own reluctance to know what they know and come to realize that such knowledge is contained in their body" (1990, p. 531). To "be there" for girls, we have to be willing to consider our own experiences with sexual feelings. That is, we have to be prepared to delve into our own psychological remedies for living in our female bodies, textured by race, class, religion, and ability, within a patriarchal society.

In looking back over my own adolescence, the impetus of this work, I believed that desire had not been a dilemma for me. I never experienced or thought about my own sexual feelings as bad, abnormal, or unacceptable. In fact, I nurtured my own desire and savored these powerful sexual feelings. My memory of desire enabled me to resist the psychological literature that suggests there is something amiss about girls who feel desire. However, in listening to these girls speak both unconsciously and frankly about the interplay of desire with danger, I have learned not only about adolescent girls' experiences of sexual desire but also about my own. Frightening memories of sexual assault and disappointment punctuated my idealization of my adolescent sexuality as purely about pleasure, power, and connection. Thus, I could no longer look back (longingly) on my adolescent experiences of sexuality as entirely positive and instead was forced to see the connection between the complexities of sexuality for girls and the contradictory experiences of desire I have had as an adult.[1]

FINDING NEW WAYS TO THINK
ABOUT SEXUAL DESIRE

As Amber Hollibaugh has said, "it is always dangerous to refuse the knowledge of your own acts and wishes, to create a sexual amnesia, to deny how and who you desire, allowing others the power to name it, be its engine or its brake. As long as I lived afraid of what I would discover about my own sexuality and my fantasies, I had always to wait for another person to discover and give me the material of my own desires" (1984, p. 406).

The notion that the institution of heterosexuality can be dismantled is met with disillusionment from many feminist quarters. While the sexual revolution of the 1960s and 1970s dismantled some of the barriers to female sexual subjectivity, what remained in place is the notion that boys and men cannot control themselves and that girls and women are responsible for controlling male sexuality, an absurd expectation when power differences remain so potent in heterosexual relationships (Amaro, 1995). Although sexual violence is now more recognized, it is still tolerated and blamed on men's inability to control their sexuality. In some places, limits on girls' and women's entitlement to sexual pleasure have been at best muted but not removed. Girls and women continue to take heat for sexual encounters that occur outside the condoned space of one particular form of relationship (as do homosexual and bisexual men). Ros Gill and Rebecca Walker spoke to the power of heterosexuality in their lives as feminists when they articulated the contradictions between their beliefs about their sexuality and what they actually feel and desire: "we live [our] desires through the discourse of patriarchal romances, not feminism. And the irony is *that we know it,* but that does not make the desires go away" (1993, p. 69). The dilemma of desire is not going to be easily eliminated. What is required is that we make our schools, neighborhoods, and other public and private spaces safer for girls and women. As a society, we need to commit to eradicating sexual violence and its roots in the oppression of girls and women, as well as dismantling sexual hierarchies among girls and women and creating equitable access to reliable methods of contraception and disease protection.

Although adolescents would like to have honest conversations with their parents about sexuality, few feel able to (Satcher, 2001). As Sophie intimated, they end up feeling they are supposed to learn this information through osmosis rather than direct talk. Whether out of fear for their children or their own discomfort with sexuality, the ways in which adults do speak to adolescents about sexuality are impoverished. School is an institution in which most adolescents spend a lot of time. As Michelle Fine (1988) observed, underlying sex education in school is the assumption that girls have to learn to protect themselves from boys, to say no. Girls are taught to talk about sexuality only in terms of learning how to say no to sexual behavior rather than in terms of communicating about what both partners do and do not want as part of their relationship.

Sex education is an obvious arena where changes can and should be made. The surgeon general recommended comprehensive sexuality education that is both developmentally and culturally appropriate (Satcher, 2001). Yet little of what teachers are able to say or do is grounded in research, and policy about sex education is fueled by politics and polemic rather than what the science tells us about girls' or boys' sexual health (Darroch, Landry, & Singh, 2000). The current federal regulations demanding the teaching of "abstinence only" or "abstinence only until marriage" are a case in point. Sexuality education does not "cause" adolescents to have sexual intercourse, and abstinence-only "education" does not prevent it. For those who do have sexual intercourse, comprehensive sexuality education is associated with an increased use of contraception and condoms, whereas students who have had abstinence education, many of whom subsequently have sex after the short-term effect of the abstinence-only message wanes, are much less likely to take these precautions (Kirby, 1997, 2001). A recent study found that in any given community where virginity pledges were made by either very few or by a majority of adolescents, there were no associated delays in initiating sexual intercourse (Bearman & Bruckner, 2001). Noting that pledging is embedded in an adolescent identity, the researchers observed that it is somewhat effective only when it is relatively non-normative; moreover, it is fragile. Disturbingly, promise breakers are less likely to use contraception when they do have intercourse for the first time.

Consider how "abstinence" is a truly insidious cover story that puts girls at risk. Abstinence implies an absence of (girls') sexuality, which denies the fact that we are all sexual beings. To deny adolescents their sexuality and information about it, rather than to educate them about the intricacies and complexities and nuances of their feelings, choices, and behaviors, is to deny them a part of their humanity. What "choice" do girls have when their own sexual feelings are not supposed to exist? This study underscores the importance of comprehensive sexuality education that actually informs adolescents about their *sexuality*. As Sophie suggests, "the way that you can help girls is if you let them know that everything they feel and think is normal."

A web site for adolescent girls called "Pink Slip" recently published an article suggesting that "what we should really be talking about here, when people say abstinence, is celibacy, which is the choice not to have a sexual partner for any period of time" (Corinna, 2000). The author notes that not telling adolescents "what to do" may lead to risky sexual behavior. In a society where the surgeon general was fired for mentioning masturbation (meaning, in fact, girls' masturbation, since it is assumed in most quarters that virtually all adolescent boys masturbate) and was as recently as April 2001 called "nuts" by the Reverend Jerry Falwell on national television (CNN, 2001), the political constraints on such straight talk are profound. If we really care about adolescents' sexual safety and health, then adults—parents, teachers, social workers, physicians, youth workers, therapists—need to speak to adolescents about the realities of sexuality: that girls as well as boys have sexual desire, which should be acknowledged and respected by both partners; that boys can be responsible for their sexual behavior; that sexual intercourse is not the only "adult" form of sexual expression; that sex is not a commodity or thing to get but a way to express one's feelings for another person; that masturbation and phone sex are safe sex.

Encouraging girls to "just say no" is what yields the cover story of "it just happened." As Megan astutely asked, why is it the girl who has to say no? And to what and whom is she saying no? This mantra does not help girls figure out what they do and do not wish to do, nor the conditions under which some choices are acceptable to them and others are not. Until girls can say yes and not be punished or suffer negative consequences, until girls have access to alternatives to the romance narrative—which offers them one line only, "no"—girls will continue to have their "no" mistaken for "token resistance" (Tolman & Higgins, 1996; Muehlenhard & Rodgers, 1998). Sharon Thompson (1990) offers the slogan "Just Say Not until I Know I Want To" as a much needed corrective to the kinds of advice we give girls. Michelle Fine has explained that "a genuine discourse of desire would invite adolescents to explore what feels good and bad, desirable and undesirable, grounded in experience, needs, and limits . . . would enable an analysis of the dialectics of victimization and pleasure, and would pose female adolescents as subjects of sexuality" (1988, p. 33).

Just as mothers cannot do this work alone, tinkering with sex education and conducting discussions with girls will not solve the problem. This is a social problem that demands change at a societal level, in how we think and talk as a society about adolescent sexuality, both girls' and boys'. Boys also face limited social constructions of their sexuality. We need to know more about boys' sexuality, in particular, how boys deal with our society's conviction that their desire is monstrous and uncontrollable. We need to learn about boys' wishes to be authentic with themselves and in relationships, given the pressures they are under to commodify sex, objectify girls and women, and not be vulnerable or out of control (Pollack, 1998; Tolman et al., 2002; Tolman et al., in press). We need to examine how different discourses about male sexuality that demonize some boys (for instance, black boys, Latino boys, homosexual boys) may constrain them and enable others. We cannot underestimate the importance of offering and nurturing a critical perspective on how current gender arrangements and the institution of heterosexuality are unfair and diminish the humanity of boys and girls. As bell hooks has said, "subversion of dominant cultural forms happens much more easily in the realm of 'texts' than in the world of human interaction . . . in which such moves challenge, disrupt, threaten, where repression is real" (1990, p. 22).

Sexuality is about emotions, intersubjectivity, and feeling close to another person, as well as feeling alive in your body. The girls who told me their stories included their embodied sexual feelings but also connected their powerful physical feelings to intense emotional feelings. In speaking about sexual desire, some of them told stories that revealed their urge to resist the split of intimacy and sexuality that pervades our society. The particulars of these girls' narratives—Inez's avoidance of the dancing that she loves, Rochelle's brilliant but lonely solution of feeling desire only when by herself, Trisha's use of alcohol to cover her desire, Melissa's pretense that her physical expressions of affection are not sexual, Barbara's sadness in denying her desire and also her insistence on having sexual pleasure in her life, Amber's reworking of her sexual object status into a powerful position—provide compelling empirical evidence for why girls' sexual desire matters and underscore girls' ongoing need for the validation of their embodied experiences, as well as a critical perspective on how society constructs adolescent sexuality. Amber's agency and confidence remind us that we have to engage in both overt and subversive transformative work to challenge, dismantle, and remake society's notions of gendered sexuality to make it possible for all girls, no matter where they live, to get beyond "it just happened." We have to demand, ensure, and protect girls' right to feel and act upon their own sexual feelings without having to be encumbered by unfair and unnecessary dilemmas of desire.

ON METHODOLOGY / NOTES / REFERENCES / INDEX

The "standard practice" of the Listening Guide method typically involves proceeding four separate times through an interview, listening for four distinct voices. This process enables the listener to develop multiple perspectives on a single narrative, producing a complex, multilayered interpretation, while retaining the structure of the narrative (Miller, 1991). Each time the researcher reads through the interview she underlines with a different color the parts of the narrative that express a particular voice. Then the relevant parts of the narrative are transferred onto worksheets, creating a "trail of evidence" (Brown et al., 1989) for the interpretation of the narrative. Using worksheets that separate the words of the interviewee and the listener's interpretation of those words, the listener supports her interpretation with specific words from the text, providing a good or credible interpretation.

The first time through the narrative the listener attends to the story told and to her own responses to this story. The second time through she attends to the interviewee as the narrator of the story. The purpose of this reading is to identify the "self story" in the narrative, the ways the person speaks about and knows herself in and through the narrative. This reading is done by underlining all statements that refer to the self: "I," "my," "me." Listening for self efficiently reveals where the narrator places herself in relation to her experience. Of particular interest to me was whether and how these girls experienced and knew themselves as agents in relation to their desire. The reading for self makes agency and absence of agency, as well as a girl's experience of herself as an object, readily audible.

In the standard practice of this method, the third and fourth readings draw the listener's attention to relational voices, specifically articulated in the original version of this method as the moral voices of care and justice. The relationship between self and these relational voices is then assessed. Given my focus, the relational voice I conceptualized was a voice of desire. But when I began listening for such a voice, I discovered *two* desire voices in these narratives, which I call for the purposes of this analysis (1) an erotic voice and (2) a response voice. While I have highlighted the erotic voice in this book, the portraits are developed as well from the girls' response to their desire. In addition to these two voices of desire I was interested in a fifth voice in these narratives: a voice of the body. Because I wanted to know what girls did and did not say about their bodies, and in what relationship they placed their bodies to their experiences of themselves and their desire, I followed how they did and did not give voice to their bodies in these narratives. I found that a voice of the body is almost always subsumed in the erotic voice, and I concluded that it is virtually always an embodied voice, so I do not discuss the voice of the body separately in these portraits (for an exception, see Tolman, 2000).

Although it was these voices of desire that I identified at this point in my analysis of the narratives, I strongly suspect that there are other voices or features of girls' experiences of desire that are not captured by listening in these ways; that is, these voices are not necessarily the only way to understand girls' experiences of desire. But they are one way into these desire narratives, and they highlight important aspects of the girls' experiences. For instance, another approach would be to read for Hollway's (1989) "have/hold discourse," in which women are the subjects in that "it is women who want and need commitment" (p. 64). Hollway's distinction between discursive analyses and psychoanalytic interpretations would also be an important avenue to explore in developing further the Listening Guide technique I outline here.

The technique I used enabled me to braid together the two perspectives or interpretive lenses that anchor these analyses: (1) the individual developmental theory that girls' experiences with their desire are highly contextualized by their individual circumstances and (2) Adrienne Rich's feminist theory of how female sexuality is organized by the institution of heterosexuality. These perspectives led me to identify specific voices expressing how each participant speaks about herself (by listening for the self) and how she speaks about her desire (by listening for two desire voices and a voice of the body). I am among the first researchers to have used this method, about which I have already written extensively (Tolman, 1994a, b, 1996, 1999, 2000, 2001; Tolman & Szalacha, 1999), and I am actively involved in broadening its use for a larger range of research questions about personal experience.

Listening for these voices was fruitful for most of the narratives told by these girls. Most narratives contained erotic and response voices that were not difficult to discern; and when these voices were absent from a narrative in which a girl is describing an experience of sexual desire, what was missing proved informative. The prevalence of these voices across different stories suggests to me that they reveal aspects of the experience of desire that are viable for these girls. The descriptions of the voices that I offer are far from complete or all-inclusive, however.

The matter of reliability of "coding" voices is a complex one for this kind of qualitative analysis. Calculating "agreement," such as the relative percentage of words that two analysts underlined separately, is neither feasible nor sensible given the epistemology of this approach to research. Such precise quantification assumes a single, objective, replicable truth that can be identified in precisely the same manner by any two individuals. In qualitative research, the concept of reliability differs somewhat. The practice of interpretation is premised on the understanding that different individuals will react to and make sense of the same material in various ways. Thus, calculating correlations between two coders' identifications of precisely the same words is not a meaningful way to determine reliability. Instead, an interpretive process is considered reliable if a second person can follow rather than reproduce what the original coder claims she did in making the interpretation, and then find those claims credible, even if the second coder disagrees with the ultimate interpretation (Maxwell, 1996). To establish this form of reliability, another woman listened to a random sample of these narratives using the same criteria that I did. Following my criteria, she was able to identify the presence of each of the four voices in all of these narratives. We were in solid agreement about which parts of the text could be underlined for each of the voices for which I was listening. Most important, she found my claims about what I heard in listening to each of these four voices credible, that is, she concurred that the claims I made were supported by the evidence I offered for them.

I underlined for the erotic voice when I heard girls describing or signifying (by laughing, breathing sharply, or taking long pauses) strong feelings or representations of strong feelings, such as "I was really sweaty." I underlined any descriptions of the process of wanting, any instances in which a girl described or revealed an understanding of her own wanting, whether she specifically labeled it as sexual or not. I counted as examples of the erotic voice any time a girl voiced her knowledge of desire, from her own experience or from other sources, such as observations of others. When I say "knowledge," I include both conscious and subconscious knowing, that is, I underlined metaphors for the erotic that a girl did not necessarily state was her experience of desire but suggests some kind of knowing about it that she carries in her psyche or body, including any descriptions of her knowledge of how sexual desire operates in herself and others. I also made note of when a girl described knowing the wanting of others as another contour of knowledge of desire. Another aspect of reading for the erotic voice was to focus on the explicitly anti-erotic, the vociferous denial of sexual feelings, which I conceptualize as a part of the erotic voice.

The response voice captured how girls responded or reacted to the desire they felt, what their thoughts, feelings, reactions, and behaviors were in the wake of feeling desire. The response voice expresses girls' resolutions to the dilemma of desire, and often their perception of it as a dilemma. This voice embeds both conscious and unconscious responses to desire, at the point of the body (the embodied response), as well as responses that include conscious decision making. In listening for the response voice, I underlined thoughts, feelings, or behaviors that a girl described having in response to her identified experience of desire. I included anything that she identified as contributing to her response to these feelings, such as the presence of others or her fear or concern about the reactions or potential actions of others or herself. For example, I underlined for response Trisha's explanation of what she does when she sees someone for whom she feels sexual desire: "I'll just have a few drinks, I mean, to the point where I get flirty, 'cause I won't do it if I'm straight [laughs]. I have to wait 'til I get flirty and then I'll just say let's go." While I did not distinguish whether a girl's response to her felt desire was conscious or seemed to "just happen" in the narrative, in the actual reading for the

response voice I did note this aspect of her response in the interpretations I made on the worksheets.

After reading each narrative for these voices and transferring the
relevant data to the worksheets, I began to construct interpretations of each voice as I had heard it. I engaged in a common qualitative data analysis practice, looking for patterns in the data by
displaying the information gathered in matrices (Miles & Huberman, 1984). I created two separate matrices: one that organized the
data according to each psychological response and one in which I
compared the urban girls with the suburban girls. Using these
matrices, I identified the patterns I describe and illustrate in the
three chapters devoted to the findings of the study (Chapters 3, 4,
and 5) and in the discussion of the differences between the urban
and the suburban girls (Chapter 6).

In performing this analysis I began to notice a parallel process
occurring in myself. This method demands that the listener be sensitive to how her own responses may contain information about
what is occurring in these research relationships, information that
can help a researcher understand what is and is not being said to
her. This parallel process can be thought of and has been called a
method of analysis (Berg & Smith, 1988). As I heard enactments of
real events and took in images of violence, I tracked my own
excitement, disappointment, frustration, fear, and loss of pleasure.
This strategy often helped me consider an interpretation of girls'
erotic or response voices that otherwise may not have occurred to
me. Knowing my own responses also increased my ability to know
my own feelings and to consider whether they were providing
additional information about a girl's words or getting in the way of
my ability to hear what she was saying to me; by staying attuned to
my own feelings, I increased the possibility of hearing what the
girls were telling me about their experience and not having my
own experience supplant their words.

As a white, middle-class woman listening to girls who were poor, working class, black, and Latina, I tried to embrace what Ruth Frankenberg has called a "white anti-racist standpoint" (1993, p. 265), acknowledging the obvious limits on my ability to do so. I strove to be actively conscious of the ways in which these girls' sexuality has been framed within their particular cultural contexts as well as particularly maligned by the dominant white, middle-class culture, and I consulted adult women from their racial and ethnic groups about my questions and experiences in interviews, as well as my interpretations of these girls' narratives. In the same vein, I worked to resist turning "white" and "middle class" into monolithic experiences (Fine, Powell, & Wong, 1997). The first pass through the narrative, the listener's response, provides a venue for attending to these concerns.

NOTES

1 GETTING BEYOND "IT JUST HAPPENED"

1. This estimate is based on information from 1997; in the previous few years, the rate of girls' sexual activity (defined as ever having had sex, as if they had been sexually "activated") had dipped slightly, to below 50 percent. What is on the rise is protected sex (Singh & Darroch, 1999), though there is considerable debate about how to account for substantially lower rates of pregnancy.

2. Tolman, 1994a. One group at the Population Research Center at the University of North Carolina has done research to determine whether differentials in hormonal levels are associated with or even cause girls' sexual activity and motivations (Smith & Udry, 1985; Udry, 1993; Halpern, Udry, & Suchindran, 1997; see also Finkelstein et al., 1998). To do so, they utilized a scale of "sexual 'turn on'" to assess frequency of arousal. The complexities that have recently surfaced about female reports of desire and arousal (i.e., Basson, 2000; Rosen et al., 2000) indicate that such measures may not capture female sexuality especially effectively.

3. According to Tijaden & Thoennes, 1998, of women disclosing rape, 22 percent were under age twelve when they were first raped, and 32 percent were between twelve and seventeen years of age.

4. In the last few years more studies on boys' sexual activity have been conducted in response to concern about boys' risk of contracting HIV (i.e., Gates & Sonenstein, 2000). The work of Joseph Pleck and

colleagues is also an important addition (i.e., Pleck, Sonenstein, & Ku, 1994a, 1994b). My group has recently begun to include boys in our research program, in which we conceptualize adolescent sexuality more broadly than frequency and prevalence of intercourse (i.e., Tolman et al., 2002; Tolman et al., in press).

5. In a similar vein, Wendy Hollway (1989) has identified "male sexual drive discourse" as constitutive of adult male sexuality. The question of the relative strength of male and female sexual desire, a question that dominates much sex research, is partially responsible. The study of whether or not, or to what extent, girls and women have biologically driven sexual desire has a long history. This debate has played out in feminist scholarship (i.e., Vance, 1984; Tiefer, 1995) and among sex researchers (i.e., Wallen, 1990; Andersen & Cyranowski, 1995). The measurement of levels of testosterone as the only relevant hormone underpinning female sexual desire is challenged by recent research on the possible importance of the adrenal hormone oxytocin (Carmichael et al., 1994) and of estrogen (Stanislaw & Rice, 1988), as well as of adrenal androgens in initial sexual interest in adolescence (McClintock & Herdt, 1996). In the case of adolescent sexuality, we find slippage from an argument about whose libido is strongest to the obfuscation of girls' embodied desire altogether.

6. This perspective has its roots in evolutionary biology. However, recent work suggests that this is only one theory of the role of sexuality in human evolution, and that there is another way of viewing primate behavior and imagining early human behavior that positions females as having active sexuality (i.e., Hrdy, 1981; Rabinowitz & Vallian, 1999).

7. The importance of the denial of homosexuality in men, and the ways in which violence against girls and women serves this denial, have been recently articulated in Tolman et al., 2002.

8. I am not referring to the process of repression, that is, unconscious processes of "exiling" desire; rather, I refer to dissociation (see Chapter 3).

9. Karin Martin (1996) has criticized this research for not including boys. However, the goal was not to compare male and female adolescent sexual experiences but to develop a deep understanding of girls' sexuality.

2   VOICES OF DESIRE

1. The range in age is due to the relatively older age of some of the urban girls, who had been held back one or more grades for various reasons, and to the inclusion of two sophomore girls from a support group for sexual minority youth. These data were collected in 1991. Well aware that many years have passed since I collected these desire narratives, I have continued doing research on female adolescent sexuality over the last decade, including interviews with girls the same age about their relationships and sexuality, supported by the Ford Foundation, the Spencer Foundation, and the National Institute of Child Health and Development. There is a remarkable consistency between the way the girls in this study talked about their sexual experiences and the way the girls who are participants in my current research program do. The greatest difference is that current participants are more likely to acknowledge their concern about risk of HIV when asked, although they do not identify this possibility spontaneously (Tolman, 1999). The consistency I have observed reflects that found in large-scale sexual behavior surveys, such as the General Social Survey, over the same time period (Michael, 2001).

2. In addition, random selection provided an opportunity to conduct quantitative analyses at a later time (see Tolman & Szalacha, 1999; see also Chapter 6). Another option would have been to use a purposive sampling technique.

3. I used a clustered sampling technique in the suburban sample; race and ethnicity were identified by school personnel on rosters of the entire class of junior girls.

4. This strategy was designed to provide girls both the opportunity and the motivation to engage with their parents about participation in the study, to create space for "interruptions" in silences that girls may have been dealing with at home.

5. Interestingly, the one study in which girls' desire had been touched upon (Fine, 1988) had included only urban girls.

6. In fact, thirty-one girls were interviewed for this study; unfortunately, technical difficulties with the audiotape of one of the suburban girls, Julia, made it impossible to include her in the analyses across the girls

in the study. I was still able to discern some of the themes and qualities in her desire narratives.

7. This rate is precisely what would be expected, on the basis of national statistics which indicate that a quarter to a third of all women experience sexual abuse by the time they are eighteen years old (Benson, 1990; Finkelhor & Dziuba-Leatherman, 1994).

8. Muehlenhard & Rogers (1998), in a study of token resistance to sex, found that participants' written narratives reflected a chasm between what the researchers meant by token resistance and how the participants interpreted it, thus raising doubts about years of survey research on this topic. The interview provides an opportunity to clarify what the researcher means and how the participant is making sense of the questions, and how well each is understanding the other.

9. Billig, 1997. A recent innovation of this method is to videotape girls, to incorporate their body language into the interpretive process (Brown, 2001). However, given the sensitive topic and the overall design of this study, which entailed one interview with each girl, this option was not viable.

10. To preserve the girls' confidentiality, I have changed most recognizable characteristics and any specific details that could reveal their identities. I did not change their racial or ethnic identities, or their sexual orientation. In some cases, specific physical qualities or specific circumstances were crucial for understanding the girls' narratives; in such cases, I changed everything I could to disguise the girls, such as what they were wearing during the interview, what their families did for a living, or what activities they pursued.

11. I have focused on this difference in my other publications derived from these data (see Tolman, 1994a, b, 1996; Tolman & Higgins, 1996; Tolman & Szalacha, 1999).

12. One could also frame these ways of talking about desire as discourses of sexual subjectivity (see Phillips, 2000).

3 SOUNDS OF SILENCE

1. It is common for women not to remember experiences of childhood sexual abuse until they are in their thirties or forties.

2. Kelly, 1991. It has also been observed that the threat of danger can be experienced as exciting in a culture that eroticizes danger (Griffin, 1981; Phillips, 2000), and there has been a great deal of dissent within the feminist community about how to deal with the role of violence in female sexuality (see Vance, 1984). Some feminists have argued that controlled violence in the context of sadomasochistic relationships offers a kind of antidote to feeling out of control in society at large (Califa, 1989), while others believe that such desires of women are a result of false consciousness, a profound internalization of patriarchy that produces "unfemale" desires (MacKinnon, 1989). This argument about the nature of female sexual desire and how it relates to patriarchy has divided the feminist community, producing "the sex wars" of the 1980s, premised on different conceptions of female desire as "naturally" not aggressive or dominant and thus corrupted by patriarchy or as whatever women desire (Snitow, Stansell, & Thompson, 1983; Sawicki, 1988).

3. This feeling of a constant threat of violence is experienced by gay men, transvestites, and transgendered people, who violate the norms of compulsory heterosexuality and thereby often are threatened with violence or actually attacked (Herek et al., 1997).

4. I am referring here to dominant cultural (white, middle-class) conventions of femininity, and so too are most of the other feminist theorists whose work I cite at this point: Gilligan, 1982; Jordan, 1987; Bartky, 1990; Gilligan, Rogers, & Tolman, 1991; Brown & Gilligan, 1992; Taylor, Gilligan, & Sullivan, 1995; Brown, 1999. Although it is not only important but crucial to understand how culturally specific femininities construct female (and male) sexuality and relationships, and how girls and women negotiate and transform these norms (i.e., Spillers, 1984; Parker et al., 1995; Fine, Roberts, & Weis, 2000; Nichter, 2000), all girls must in some way deal with this particular form of femininity through public institutions such as school (Brown, 1999; Tolman & Porche, 2000).

5. For instance, Freud's patient Elizabeth von R. suffered paralysis of one of her legs (Breuer & Freud, 1895/1982).

6. This ability soon became lost to him as he elaborated his theories of repression and other psychodynamic processes, as is evidenced in his

later work. It has been recently argued that this shift was at least in part due to his refusal to accept his female patients' reports of sexual abuse by well-respected male relatives (Masson, 1984).

4 DANGERS OF DESIRE

1. See the edited volumes *Pleasure and Danger* (Vance, 1984) and *Powers of Desire* (Snitow, Stansell, and Thompson, 1983), as well as the work of Susie Bright, Pat Califa, Andrea Dworkin, Susan Griffin, and Catherine MacKinnon for discussions of the "true" nature of women's sexual desire, whether some forms of desire are the product of false consciousness and thus anathema to women, and the right of women to have and act on any sexual feelings.

2. Tolman & Debold, 1993, p. 301. Recent research suggests that African American girls are less vulnerable to some of these concerns, likely because of a cultural emphasis on internal as opposed to external beauty and a greater acceptance of a fuller, more nourished female body. Constructions of beauty may also be greatly influenced by socioeconomic or other social circumstances; the value of thinness may be pervasive among middle-class African American girls.

5 PARAMETERS OF PLEASURE

1. Zines are small-scale magazines often put out by girls themselves as a kind of underground alternative to mainstream media.

2. Controlling discourses, narratives, and "command" performances, such as those that produce the practices and limited range of feelings that femininity requires, including sexual passivity, are obviously powerful and woven virtually seamlessly into Western culture. However, resistance to them through critique and the generation of alternative discourses and narratives is possible and crucial in defining and then defying oppression (Freire, 1970; Bordo, 1993a; Martin-Baro, 1994). That is, we are not simply automatons subjected to these ways of being; we have the potential for agency and subjectivity on different terms (Hudson, 1984). Such resistance is often made possible or buoyed by alternative paradigms. As Ramazanoglu and Holland explained, "femi-

nism . . . has offered women very forceful analyses of sexuality and the body which identify 'normal' heterosexual practices and relationships not just as social rather than natural, but as constructed in men's interests to control women's bodies and subordinate women" (1993, pp. 240–241). Such potential resistance is equally applicable to the lived experiences of the body. Judith Butler suggested that while "the body is a legacy of sedimented acts" (1997, p. 406), it "is not passively scripted with cultural codes, as if it were a lifeless recipient of wholly pregiven cultural relations. But neither do embodied selves preexist the cultural conventions which essentially signify bodies" (p. 410). The sexual revolution was one such form of resistance. In the realm of sexuality, various forms of feminism have provided perspectives or standpoints "on the margins" (Hooks, 1984) of mainstream culture. These alternatives are grounded in women's experience, which is not fully held or explained by the available discourses or narratives in mainstream society.

3. In part, this is because the sexual revolution was not grounded in women's desire (Jeffreys, 1990) but "allowed" women to take on a male model of sexuality, in which sex is commodified and feelings of intimacy are split off from physical desire. In addition, the social expectation that men do not want monogamous, committed relationships (Hunter, 1993) was not challenged.

4. This statement reflects the notion that it is a girl's responsibility to identify a male who will not take advantage of his various privileges within the institution of heterosexuality, including being able to besmirch a girl without challenge (see Phillips, 2000).

5. It is likely that Barbara's experience of abuse makes her particularly vulnerable to feeling ashamed of her own sexual responses (Kaplan, 1991).

6. While she is part of the youth group, she is among the youngest and least experienced; like Megan, she feels somewhat intimidated even in this context, which is meant to offer her a sense of freedom to say and be who she is.

7. Lisa Diamond (1998, 2000) has demonstrated that in adolescence girls' sexual identities or feelings may indeed fluctuate.

8. As with several girls in this study, when their own question about their sexual desire surfaces, the question of "how much I'm really like attracted to her personally" becomes the central question of our interview.

6 GEOGRAPHIES OF DESIRE

1. Constance Nathanson, Deborah Rhodes, and others have observed that this portrait was highly exaggerated (Nathanson, 1991; Lawson & Rhodes, 1993), leading to a moral panic about out-of-wedlock adolescent pregnancy.

2. In addition to the theoretical justification for this analysis, there was a practical one as well. Owing to the size of the sample, there were insufficient numbers of girls within any of these gross groupings ("white," "black," "Latina") to examine differences within or between the girls when divided in this way. For example, there was only one girl of color in the suburban sample. I also did not conduct analyses to compare these girls on other meaningful differences in the arena of sexuality, such as their religions or family histories. Nevertheless, I believe that such analyses are important and ultimately requisite for developing a sufficiently complex understanding of female adolescent sexuality.

3. Although I was careful to take into account an understanding of how female sexuality is constructed within the specific cultures of each of the girls, I did not give priority to this perspective in analyzing the girls' narratives. This choice has produced one particular take on the stories; others are possible, in fact likely, but I felt that I could not do justice to the important nuances within these groups. For instance, some of the black girls in the study come from Haiti and other parts of the Caribbean, some are from families who have been in this country for centuries, and others are of mixed heritage. There are also contradictory perspectives in the feminist community about white women's ability to "hear" girls of color.

4. Collins, 1990; see also Spillers, 1984. These dehumanizing images render the problems of desire and sexual subjectivity for all black adolescent girls, regardless of their socioeconomic status, especially com-

plex. And there are also significant differences within the black community in how female sexuality is constructed. Evelynn M. Hammonds (1997) describes a "politics of silence" around sexuality among middle-class black women, which she traces back to the efforts of nineteenth-century black women reformers to gain entrée into the desexualized but morally superior, and exclusively white, "cult of true womanhood" (Cott, 1978; see also Carby, 1987; Brown, 1994; Wyatt, 1997). Noting the invisibility of black women's sexual subjectivity, Hortense Spillers has identified the complicated "interstices," or missing words, of sexuality for black women, including not only the negative but also the positive aspects of sexuality—for instance, through "the singer who celebrates, chides, embraces, inquires into, controls her womanhood . . . she is in the moment of performance the primary subject of her own being. Her sexuality is precisely the physical expression of the highest self-regard and, often, the sheer pleasure she takes in her own powers" (1984, pp. 87–88; see also Omolade, 1983). Mimi Nichter, Sheila Parker, and their colleagues (1995) have found that black girls feel more comfortable about their bodies and seem less vulnerable to disengaging from or monitoring their bodies in the ways that their white counterparts do. Hammonds (1997) and other women of color (i.e., Anzaldua, 1981, 1990; Espin, 1999) note the added layer of complexity for lesbians of color, who must negotiate what is often an especially taboo form of female sexual expression within communities that are already marginalized, as well as the doubled oppression from dominant society.

5. In Latinas' cultures of origin, female sexuality is framed consistently as entirely passive and submissive; marianismo, the notion that women's sexuality is a male possession and that it is women's duty (only in marriage) to provide for and "suffer" men's sexual needs, renders the possibility of sexual subjectivity in adolescence even more complex (Espin, 1984; Comas-Diaz, 1987; Hurtado, 1996; Vasquez & des las Fuentes, 1999), especially in the context of varying levels of acculturation among family and community members (Espin, 1999; Fine, Roberts, & Weis 2000). Having to consider the impact of their adolescent sexual

choices on the desires of potential husbands and other men and women in their families means that their sexuality is culturally constructed as a matter not of their own desire but of family honor (Espin, 1984).

6. This disembodiment is evident in relation to food as well (Tolman & Debold, 1993; Nichter, 2000).

7. Cott, 1978. See Hammonds, 1997, for a discussion of comparable efforts made by black middle-class women.

8. I set aside the very wealthy urban dwellers, who carve out a separate society of expensive stores and private schools, from which many who live in the community are explicitly excluded.

9. Consistent with my experience with narratives from other girls attending urban schools, the urban girls in this study often told their stories with an economy of words. Some of them were remarkable storytellers, seeming to revel in the act of narrating their experience to an interested listener. But they were able to communicate a surprising amount in relatively few words. In contrast, many of the suburban girls told dense narratives. More of the suburban girls tended to tell longer stories and to demonstrate obvious comfort with "having the floor" in the interview (Tolman & Szalacha, 1999).

10. While it may be argued that the girls did not mention HIV or AIDS more frequently because the study was done in the early 1990s, it is significant that this school did have comprehensive sexuality education that addressed these risks specifically.

11. See Tolman & Szalacha, 1999, for detailed information about the coding and quantitative analyses of these data, as well as the supplementary qualitative analysis.

12. We were aware that "collapsing" such very different experiences of violence is highly problematic, and that there are often different outcomes associated with the intensity and type of violent experience, as well as with the duration of and age at which it occurred (i.e., Terr, 1990; Herman, 1992). This variable is thus meant only as a gross proxy to capture what we found to be a significant difference in these girls'

experiences of sexuality and relationships. Further study of specific types and characteristics of sexual and relationship violence are warranted by this finding.

13. See Terr, 1990, for elaboration of the notion of "psychic priming" due to previous experiences of trauma producing varying vulnerabilities for subsequent trauma.

14. The qualitative similarity in how desire was described by the majority of the urban girls, regardless of their sexual violation status, explains the weakness in the statistical interaction between geography and sexual violation.

7 SPEAKING OF DESIRE

1. The connection between adolescent and adult experiences is suggested by a recent study of adult sexual dysfunction. Based on a nationally representative study of adult sexuality published in the *Journal of the American Medical Association,* Edward Laumann and his colleagues (1999) declared that the high prevalence of adult sexual dysfunction constitutes a public health crisis. While the majority of men in the study reported problems of premature ejaculation or impotence, over a third of the women reported problems with arousal or desire, in comparison with a tiny percentage of the men. Those with low educational achievement and minority status had higher risk of sexual dysfunction, echoing the urban girls in this study. The stories of these girls suggest that the roots of adult women's "disorders of desire" (Irvine, 1990) may be adolescent dilemmas of desire. With the current rush to render women's sexual dysfunction a physiological problem that can be cured with a "magic bullet" boost in testosterone, Ellyn Kaschak and Leonore Tiefer (2002, which includes the collectively authored "New View on Women's Sexual Problems") urge us to (re)consider the sociopolitical, relational, and individual histories of women's lives to understand why their sexual desire may be diminished, rather than assume a physical root and antidote to difficulties with sexuality (see also Basson, 2000). These findings highlight as well

the crucial role of the selection of questions in research. For instance, there has been little research on sexually assertive women (Anderson & Struckman-Johnson, 1998), leaving us to wonder what new dimension of women's sexuality might be revealed when we ask about this issue.

Abma, J., & Sonenstein, F. L. (2001). *Sexual Activity and Contraceptive Practices among Teenagers in the United States, 1988 and 1995* (Vital Health Statistics, ser. 23, no. 21). Washington, D.C.: National Center for Health Statistics.

Abma, J., Driscoll, A., & Moore, K. (1998). "Young Women's Degree of Control over First Intercourse: An Exploratory Analysis." *Family Planning Perspectives,* 30(1), 12–18.

Aguilera, C. (1999). "What a Girl Wants." On *Christina Aguilera.* Los Angeles, BMG/RCA, August 24.

Alan Guttmacher Institute. (1976). *Eleven Million Teenagers: What We Can Do about the Epidemic of Adolescent Pregnancy in the United States.* New York and Washington, D.C.

Alan Guttmacher Institute. (1998). *Issues in Brief: Support for Family Planning Improves Women's Lives.* New York and Washington, D.C.

Alan Guttmacher Institute. (1999). *Facts in Brief: Teenage Sex and Pregnancy.* New York and Washington, D.C.

Amaro, H. (1995). "Love, Sex, and Power: Considering Women's Realities in HIV Prevention." *American Psychologist,* 50 (6) (June), 443–447.

Amaro, H., Russo, N. F., & Pares-Avila, J. A. (1987). "Contemporary Research on Hispanic Women: A Selected Bibliography of the Social Science Literature." *Psychology of Women Quarterly,* 11, 523–532.

American Association of University Women. (2001). *Hostile Hallways: Bullying, Teasing, and Sexual Harassment in School.* Washington, D.C.

Andersen, B. L., & Cyranowski, J. M. (1995). "Women's Sexuality: Behaviors, Responses, and Individual Differences." *Journal of Consulting and Clinical Psychology,* 63(6), 891–906.

Anderson, P. B., & Struckman-Johnson, C. (Eds.). (1998). *Sexually Aggressive Women: Current Perspectives and Controversies.* New York: Guilford Press.

Anzaldua, G. (1981). "La prieta." In C. Moraga & G. Anzaldua (eds.), *This Bridge Called My Back: Writings by Radical Women of Color.* Watertown, Mass.: Persephone Press.

Anzaldua, G. (Ed.). (1990). *Making Face, Making Soul—Haciendo Caras: Creative and Critical Perspectives by Women of Color.* San Francisco: Spinsters/Aunt Lute.

Articles (2000) found at the web site <http://missclick.chickclick.com/articles/315690p1.html>.

Asch, A., & Fine, M. (1992). "Beyond Pedestals: Revisiting the Lives of Women with Disabilities." In M. Fine, *Disruptive Voices.* Albany: State University of New York Press.

Bartky, S. L. (1990). *Femininity and Domination: Studies in the Phenomenology of Oppression.* New York: Routledge.

Basson, R. (2000). "The Female Sexual Response: A Different Model." *Journal of Sex and Marital Therapy,* 26, 51–65.

Bearman, P. S., & Bruckner, H. (2001). "Promising the Future: Virginity Pledges and First Intercourse." *American Journal of Sociology,* 106(4), 859–913.

Benson, P. (1990). *The Troubled Journey.* Minneapolis: Search Institute.

Berg, D., & Smith, K. (1988). "The Clinical Demands of Research Methods." In D. Berg & K. Smith (eds.), *The Self in Social Inquiry: Researching Methods.* Newbury Park, Calif.: Sage Publications.

Bernardez, T. (1988). "Women and Anger: Cultural Prohibitions and the Feminine Ideal." Wellesley, Mass.: Stone Center Working Papers, no. 31.

Billig, M. (1997). "The Dialogic Unconscious: Psychoanalysis, Discursive Psychology, and the Nature of Repression." *British Journal of Social Psychology,* 36, 139–159.

Bochenek, M., & Brown, A. W. (2001). *Hatred in the Hallways: Violence and Discrimination against Lesbian, Gay, Bisexual, and Transgender Students in U.S. Schools.* New York: Human Rights Watch.

Bordo, S. (1993a). "Feminism, Foucault, and the Politics of the Body." In C. Ramazanoglu (ed.), *Up against Foucault* (pp. 179–202). New York: Routledge.

Bordo, S. (1993b). *Unbearable Weight: Feminism, Western Culture, and the Body.* Berkeley: University of California Press.

Breuer, J., & Freud, S. (1895/1982). "The Case of Elizabeth Van R." In J. Strachey (trans.), *Studies on Hysteria.* New York: Basic Books.

Brodkey, L., & Fine, M. (1998). "Presence of Body, Absence of Mind." *Journal of Education,* 170(3), 84–89.

Brooks-Gunn, J., & Furstenberg, F. F. J. (1989). "Adolescent Sexual Behavior." *American Psychologist,* 44(2), 249–257.

Brown, E. B. (1994). "Negotiating and Transforming the Public Sphere: African American Political Life in the Transition from Slavery to Freedom." *Public Culture,* 7(1), 107–146.

Brown, L. B. (2001). "White Working-Class Girls, Femininities, and the Paradox of Resistance." In D. L. Tolman & M. Brydon-Miller (eds.), *From Subjects to Subjectivities: A Handbook of Interpretive and Participatory Methods* (pp. 95–110). New York: New York University Press.

Brown, L. M. (1991). "Telling a Girl's Life: Self-Authorization as a Form of Resistance." In C. Gilligan, A. G. Rogers, & D. L. Tolman (eds.), *Women, Girls, and Psychotherapy: Reframing Resistance* (pp. 71–86). Binghamton, N.Y.: Haworth Press.

Brown, L. M. (1999). *Raising Their Voices: The Politics of Girls' Anger.* Cambridge, Mass.: Harvard University Press.

Brown, L. M., & Gilligan, C. (1990). "Listening for Self and Relational Voices: A Responsive/Resisting Reader's Guide." Paper presented at the American Psychological Association meeting, Boston, August.

Brown, L. M., & Gilligan, C. (1992). *Meeting at the Crossroads: Women's Psychology and Girls' Development.* Cambridge, Mass.: Harvard University Press.

Brown, L. M., Debold, E., Tappan, M., & Gilligan, C. (1991). "Reading Narratives of Conflict for Self and Moral Voice." In W. Kurtines & J. Gewirtz (eds.), *Handbook of Moral Behavior and Development* (pp. 25–61). Hillsdale, N.J.: Erlbaum.

Brown, L. M., Tappan, M. B., Gilligan, C., Miller, B. A., & Argyris, D. E. (1989). "Reading for Self and Moral Voice: A Method for Interpreting Narratives of Real-Life Moral Conflict and Choice." In M. J. Packer & R. B. Addison (eds.), *Entering the Circle: Hermeneutic Investigation in Psychology* (pp. 141–164). Albany: State University of New York Press.

Brumberg, J. J. (1997). *The Body Project: An Intimate History of American Girls.* New York: Random House.

Butler, J. (1997). "Performative Acts and Gender Constitution: An Essay in Phenomenology and Feminist Theory." Reprinted in K. Conboy, N. Medina, & S. Stanbury (eds.), *Writing on the Body: Female Embodiment and Feminist Theory* (pp. 401–417). New York: Columbia University Press

Califa, P. (1989). *Macho Sluts.* Boston: Alyson Publications.

Caraway, N. (1991). *Segregated Sisterhood: Racism and the Politics of American Feminism.* Knoxville: University of Tennessee Press.

Carby, H. (1987). *Reconstructing Womanhood: The Emergence of the Black Female Novelist.* New York: Oxford University Press.

Carlip, H. (1995). *Girl Power: Young Women Speak Out.* New York: Warner Books.

Carmichael, M., Warburton, V., Dixen, J., & Davidson, J. (1994). "Relationships among Cardiovascular, Muscular, and Oxytocin Responses during Human Sexual Activity." *Archives of Sexual Behavior,* 23, 59–79.

Carpenter, L. M. (1998). "From Girls into Women: Scripts for Sexuality and Romance in *Seventeen* Magazine, 1974–1994." *Journal of Sex Research,* 35(2), 158–168.

Centers for Disease Control and Prevention. (2000). "CDC Surveillance Summaries." *Morbidity and Mortality Weekly Report 2000,* 49(SS-5).

Christian-Smith, L. K. (1990). *Becoming a Woman through Romance.* New York: Routledge.

Collins, P. H. (1990). *Black Feminist Thought: Knowledge, Consciousness, and the Politics of Empowerment* (vol. 2). Boston: Unwin Hyman.

Comas-Diaz, L. (1987). "Feminist Therapy with Mainland Puerto Rican Women." *Psychology of Women Quarterly,* 11, 461–474.

Corinna, H. (2000). "Does Abstinence Make the Heart Grow Fonder?" Retrieved May 18, 2000, from the web site <http://www.scarleteen.com/pink/abstinence.html>.

Cosgrove, L. (2001). "Materialist . . ." Paper presented at the Female Sexual Function forum, Boston, October.

Cott, N. (1978). "Passionlessness: An Interpretation of Victorian Sexual Ideology, 1790–1850." *Signs,* 4 (Winter), 219–236.

Darroch, J. E., Landry, D. J., & Singh, S. (2000). "Changing Emphases in Sexuality Education in U.S. Public Secondary Schools, 1998–1999." *Family Planning Perspectives,* 32(5), 204–211.

D'Augelli, A. R. (1992). "Lesbian and Gay Male Undergraduates' Experiences of Harassment and Fear on Campus." *Journal of Interpersonal Violence,* 7, 383–395.

De Beauvoir, S. (1961). *The Second Sex.* New York: Bantam Books.

Debold, E. (1996). "Knowing Bodies: Gender Identity, Cognitive Development, and Embodiment in Early Childhood and Early Adolescence." (Ed.D. diss., Harvard University Graduate School of Education.

Debold, E., Wilson, M., & Malave, I. (1993). *Mother Daughter Revolution: From Betrayal to Power.* Reading, Mass.: Addison-Wesley.

Degler, C. N. (1974). "What Ought to Be and What Was: Women's Sexuality in the Nineteenth Century." *American Historical Review,* 79, 1467–1490.

Diamond, L. M. (1998). "Development of Sexual Orientation among Adolescent and Young Adult Women." *Developmental Psychology,* 34(5), 1085–1095.

Diamond, L. M. (2000). "Sexual Identity, Attractions, and Behavior among Young Sexual-Minority Women over a Two-Year Period." *Developmental Psychology,* 36(2), 241–250.

DiClemente, R., Hansen, W., & Ponton, L. (Eds.). (1996). *Handbook of Adolescent Health Risk Behavior.* New York: Plenum Publishing.

Dodson, L. (1998). *Don't Call Us Out of Name: The Untold Lives of Women and Girls in Poor America.* Boston: Beacon Press.

Drill, E., McDonald, H., & Odes, R. (1999). *Deal with It! A Whole New Approach to Your Body, Brain, and Life as a gurl.* New York: Pocket Books.

Edut, O. (Ed.). (1998). *Adios, Barbie: Young Women Write about Body Image and Identity.* Seattle: Seal Press.

Espin, O. M. (1984). "Cultural and Historical Influences on Sexuality in Hispanic/Latin Women: Implications for Psychotherapy." In C. S. Vance (ed.), *Pleasure and Danger: Exploring Female Sexuality.* Boston: Routledge and Kegan Paul.

Espin, O. M. (1999). *Women Crossing Boundaries: A Psychology of Immigration and Transformations of Sexuality.* New York: Routledge.

Fausto-Sterling, A. (2000). *Sexing the Body: Gender Politics and the Construction of Sexuality.* New York: Basic Books.

Fine, M. (1984). "Coping with Rape: Critical Perspectives on Consciousness." *Imagination, Cognition, and Personality,* 3(3), 249–267.

Fine, M. (1986). "Why Urban Adolescents Drop into and out of High School." *Teachers College Record,* 87, 393–409.

Fine, M. (1988). "Sexuality, Schooling, and Adolescent Females: The Missing Discourse of Desire." *Harvard Educational Review,* 58(1), 29–53.

Fine, M. (1991). *Framing Dropouts: Notes on the Politics of an Urban High School.* Albany: State University of New York Press.

Fine, M., & Macpherson, P. (1992). "Over Dinner: Feminism and Adolescent Female Bodies." In M. Fine (ed.), *Disruptive Voices: The Possibilities of Feminist Research* (pp. 175–203). Albany: State University of New York Press.

Fine, M., & Macpherson, P. (1995). "Hungry for an Us." *Feminism and Psychology,* 5(2), 181–200.

Fine, M., & Weis, L. (2000). "Disappearing Acts: The State and Violence against Women in the Twentieth Century." *Signs,* 25(4), 1139–1146.

Fine, M., Powell, L., & Wong, M. (1997). *Off White: Readings on Race, Power, and Society.* New York: Routledge.

Fine, M., Roberts, R., & Weis, L. (2000). "Refusing the Betrayal: Latinas Redefining Gender, Sexuality, Culture, and Resistance." *Review of Education/Pedagogy/Cultural Studies,* 22(2), 87–119.

Fine, M., Weis, L., Weseen, S., & Wong, L. (2000). "For Whom? Qualitative Research, Representations and Social Responsibilities." In N. K. Denzin & Y. S. Lincoln (eds.), *Handbook of Qualitative Research,* 2d ed. Thousand Oaks, Calif.: Sage Publications.

Fine, M., Genovese, T., Ingersoll, S., Macpherson, P., & Roberts, R. (1996). "Insisting on Innocence: Accounts of Accountability by Abusive Men." In M. B. Lykes, A. Banuazizi, R. Liem, & M. Morris (eds.), *Myths about the Powerless: Contrasting the Social Inequalities* (pp. 128–158). Philadelphia: Temple University Press.

Fineman, H., Breslau, K., Isikoff, M., & Klaidman, D. (1998). "Sex, Lies, and the President." *Newsweek,* 20 (February 2).

Fineran, S. (2001). "Sexual Minority Students and Peer Sexual Harassment in High School." *Journal of Social Work,* 11.

Finkelhor, D., & Dziuba-Leatherman, J. (1994). "Victimization of Children." *American Psychologist,* 49(3), 173–183.

Finkelstein, J. W., Susman, E. J., Chinchilli, V. M., D'Arcanelo, M. R., Heiman, J., Schwab, J., Demers, L. M., Liben, L. S., & Kulin, H. E. (1998). "Effects of Estrogen or Testosterone on Self-Reported Sexual Responses and Behaviors in Hypogonadal Adolescents." *Journal of Clinical Endocrinology and Metabolism,* 83(7), 2281–2285.

Fordham, S. (1993). "'Those Loud Black Girls': (Black) Women, Silence, and Gender 'Passing' in the Academy." *Anthropology and Education Quarterly,* 24(1), 3–32.

Foucault, M. (1980). *The History of Sexuality* (vol. 1, *An Introduction*). New York: Vintage Books.

Frank, A. (1957/1989). *The Diary of Anne Frank: The Critical Edition.* New York: Doubleday.

Frankenberg, R. (1993). *White Women, Race Matters: The Social Construction of Whiteness.* Minneapolis: University of Minnesota Press.

Freire, P. (1970). *Pedagogy of the Oppressed.* New York: Continuum.

Gates, G. J., & Sonenstein, F. L. (2000). "Research Note—Heterosexual Genital Sexual Activity among Adolescent Males: 1988 and 1995." *Family Planning Perspectives,* 32(6), 295–298.

Gee, J. P. (1985). "The Narratization of Experience in Oral Style." *Journal of Education,* 4, 9–35.

Gergen, K. J. (1985). "The Social Constructionist Movement in Modern Psychology." *American Psychologist,* 40(3), 266–275.

Gibbs, J. T. (1985). "City Girls: Psychosocial Adjustment of Urban Black Adolescent Females." *Sage,* 2(2), 28–33.

Gil, R., & Walker, R. (1993). "Heterosexuality, Feminism, Contradiction: On Being Young, White, Heterosexual Feminists in the 1990s." In S. Wilkinson & C. Kitzinger (eds.), *Heterosexuality: A Feminism and Psychology Reader.* Newbury Park, Calif.: Sage Publications.

Gilligan, C. (1982). *In a Different Voice: Psychological Theory and Women's Development.* Cambridge, Mass.: Harvard University Press.

Gilligan, C. (1990). "Joining the Resistance: Psychology, Politics, Girls, and Women." *Michigan Quarterly Review,* 29(4), 501–536.

Gilligan, C. (1996). "The Centrality of Relationships in Human Development: A Puzzle, Some Evidence, and a Theory." In G. Noam & K. Fischer (eds.), *Development and Vulnerability in Close Relationships* (pp. 237–261). Mahweh, N.J.: Erlbaum.

Gilligan, C. (1997). "Remembering Iphigenia: Voice, Resonance, and the Talking Cure." In E. R. Shapiro (ed.), *The Inner World in the Outer World: Psychoanalytic Perspectives.* New Haven, Conn.: Yale University Press.

Gilligan, C., Brown, L. M., & Rogers, A. (1990). "Psyche Embedded: A Place for Body, Relationships, and Culture in Personality Theory." In A. I. Rabin, R. Zucker, R. Emmons, & S. Frank (eds.), *Studying Persons and Lives.* New York: Springer.

Gilligan, C., Rogers, A. G., & Tolman, D. L. (Eds.). (1991). *Women, Girls, and Psychotherapy: Reframing Resistance.* New York: The Haworth Press.

Gray, M. (2001). "Sexual Revolution." On *The Id.* Los Angeles, Sony/Epic.

Griffin, S. (1981). *Pornography and Silence: Culture's Revenge against Nature.* New York: Harper and Row.

Haag, P. (1999). *Voices of a Generation: Teenage Girls on Sex, School, and Self.* Washington, D.C.: American Association of University Women Educational Foundation.

Halpern, C. (In press). "Biological Influences on Adolescent Romantic and Sexual Behavior." In P. Florshein (ed.), *Adolescent Romantic Relations and Sexual Behavior: Theory, Research, and Practical Implications.* Mahweh, N.J.: Erlbaum.

Halpern, C. T., Udry, J. R., & Suchindran, C. (1997). "Testosterone Predicts Initiation of Coitus in Adolescent Females." *Psychosomatic Medicine,* 59, 161–171.

Hammonds, E. M. (1997). "Toward a Genealogy of Black Female Sexuality: The Problematic of Silence." In J. Alexander & C. T. Mohanty (eds.), *Feminist Genealogies, Colonial Legacies, Democratic Futures.* New York: Routledge.

Harlap, S., Kost, K., & Forest, J. D. (1991). *Preventing Pregnancy, Protecting Health: A New Look at Birth Control Choices in the United States.* New York: Alan Guttmacher Institute.

Heiman, J. (2001). "Sexual Desire in Human Relationships." In W. Everaerd, E. Laan, & S. Both (eds.), *Sexual Appetite, Desire, and Motivation: Energetics of the Sexual System* (pp. 117–134). Amsterdam: Royal Netherlands Academy of Arts and Sciences.

Herek, G. M., Gillis, J. R., Cogan, J. C., & Glunt, E. K. (1997). "Hate Crime Victimization among Lesbian, Gay, and Bisexual Adults." *Journal of Interpersonal Violence,* 12, 195–215.

Herman, J. L. (1992). *Trauma and Recovery: The Aftermath of Violence—From Domestic Abuse to Political Terror.* New York: Basic Books.

Hillier, L., Harrison, L., & Warr, D. (1998). "When You Carry Condoms All the Boys Think You Want It: Negotiating Comparing Discourses about Safe Sex." *Journal of Adolescence,* 21, 15–29.

Holland, J., Ramazanoglu, C., Sharpe, S., & Thomson, R. (1992). "Pleasure, Pressure, and Power: Some Contradictions of Gendered Sexuality." *Sociological Review,* 40(4), 645–674.

Holland, J., Ramazanoglu, C., Sharpe, S., & Thomson, R. (1994). "Power
and Desire: The Embodiment of Female Sexuality." *Feminist Review,*
46, 21–38.

Holland, J., Ramazanoglu, C., Sharpe, S., & Thomson, R. (1996). "Reputations: Journeying into Gendered Power Relations." In J. Weeks &
J. Holland (eds.), *Sexual Cultures: Communities, Values, and Intimacy* (pp. 239–260). New York: St. Martin's Press.

Holland, J., Ramazanoglu, C., Scott, S., Sharpe, S., & Thomson, R. (1992).
"Pressure, Resistance, Empowerment: Young Women and the Nego-
tiation of Safer Sex." In P. Aggleton, P. Davies, & G. Hart (eds.),
AIDS: Rights, Risk, and Reason (pp. 142–162). Washington, D.C.:
Falmer Press.

Hollibaugh, A. (1984). "Desire for the Future: Radical Hope in Passion
and Pleasure." In C. S. Vance (ed.), *Pleasure and Danger: Exploring
Female Sexuality.* Boston: Routledge and Kegan Paul.

Hollway, W. (1989). *Subjectivity and Method in Psychology.* Thousand
Oaks, Calif.: Sage Publications.

hooks, b. (1984). *Feminist Theory from Margin to Center.* Boston: South
End Press.

hooks, b. (1990). *Yearning: Race, Gender, and Cultural Politics.* Boston:
South End Press.

"How Far Should Sex Education Go?" (2001). On *Crossfire,* April, CNN.

Hrdy, S. (1981). *The Woman That Never Evolved.* Cambridge, Mass.: Harvard University Press.

Hudson, B. (1984). "Femininity and Adolescence." In A. McRobbie &
M. Nava (eds.), *Gender and Generation* (pp. 31–53). London:
Macmillan.

Hunter, A. (1993). "Same Door, Different Closet: A Heterosexual Sissy's
Coming Out Party." In S. Wilkinson & C. Kitzinger (eds.), *Heterosex-
uality: A Feminism and Psychology Reader* (pp. 150–168). London:
Sage Publications.

Hurtado, A. (1996). *The Color of Privilege: Three Blasphemies on Race and Feminism*. Ann Arbor: University of Michigan Press.

Hurtado, A. (1998). "Sitios Y Lenguas—Chicanas Theorize Feminisms." *Hypatia—A Journal of Feminist Philosophy*, 13(2), 151–161.

Irvine, J. (1990). *Disorders of Desire: Sex and Gender in Modern American Sexology*. Philadelphia: Temple University Press.

Jack, D. C. (1991). *Silencing the Self: Women and Depression*. Cambridge, Mass.: Harvard University Press.

James, W. (1890/1970). "Selections from *The Principles of Psychology*." In H. S. Thayer (ed.), *Pragmatism: The Classic Writings* (pp. 135–179). New York: New American Library.

Jeffreys, S. (1990). *Anticlimax: A Feminist Perspective on the Sexual Revolution*. London: Women's Press.

Jenkins, P. (2001). *Beyond Tolerance: Child Pornography on the Internet*. New York: New York University Press.

Jordan, J. (1987). "Clarity in Connection: Empathic Knowing, Desire, and Sexuality." Wellesley, Mass.: Stone Center Working Paper, no. 29.

Kahn, J. G., Brindis, C. D., & Glei, D. A. (1999). "Pregnancies Averted among U.S. Teenagers by the Use of Contraceptives." *Family Planning Perspectives*, 31(1), 29–34.

Kamen, P. (2000). *Her Way: Young Women Remake the Sexual Revolution*. New York: New York University.

Kaplan, L. (1991). *The Dynamics of Desire: Early Sexual Abuse and Adult Sexual Desire*. Dedham: Massachusetts School of Professional Psychology.

Kaschak, E., & Tiefer, L. (Eds.). (2002). *A New View of Women's Sexual Problems*. Binghamton, N.Y.: Haworth Press.

Kelly, L. (1991). *Surviving Sexual Violence*. Minneapolis: University of Minnesota Press.

Kirby, D. (1997). "No Easy Answers: Research Findings on Programs to Reduce Teen Pregnancy." Paper presented at the National Campaign to Prevent Teen Pregnancy, Washington, D.C.

Kirby, D. (2001). *Emerging Answers: Research Findings on Programs to*

Reduce Teen Pregnancy. Washington, D.C.: National Campaign to Prevent Teen Pregnancy.

Kirkman, M., Rosenthal, D., & Smith, A. M. A. (1998). "Adolescent Sex and the Romantic Narrative: Why Some Young Heterosexuals Use Condoms to Prevent Pregnancy but Not Disease." *Psychology, Health, and Medicine,* 3(4), 355–370.

Kitzinger, C., & Wilkinson, S. (1993). "Theorizing Heterosexuality." In S. Wilkinson & C. Kitzinger (eds.), *Heterosexuality: A Feminism and Psychology Reader* (pp. 1–32). London: Sage Publications.

Kitzinger, J. (1995). "'I'm Sexually Attractive but I'm Powerful': Young Women Negotiating Sexual Reputation." *Women's Studies International Forum,* 18(2), 187–196.

Laumann, E. O., Paik, A., & Rosen, R. C. (1999). "Sexual Dysfunction in the United States: Prevalence and Predictors." *Journal of the American Medical Association,* 281(6), 537–544.

Lawson, A., & Rhodes, D. L. (1993). *The Politics of Pregnancy: Adolescent Sexuality and Public Policy.* New Haven: Yale University Press.

Lees, S. (1986). "Language and Discourse." In S. Lees (ed.), *Losing Out: Sexuality and Adolescent Girls* (pp. 155–167). London: Hutchinson Education.

Lees, S. (1993). *Sugar and Spice: Sexuality and Adolescent Girls.* London: Penguin Books.

Levy, B. (1991). *Dating Violence: Young Women in Danger.* Seattle: Seal Press.

Lorde, A. (1984). *Sister Outsider: Essays and Speeches.* Trumansburg, N.Y.: Crossing Press.

Luttrell, W. (1997). *School-Smart and Mother-Wise.* New York: Routledge.

MacKinnon, C. (1989). *Towards a Feminist Theory of the State.* Cambridge, Mass.: Harvard University Press.

Martin, K. A. (1996). *Puberty, Sexuality, and the Self: Girls and Boys at Adolescence.* New York: Routledge.

Martin-Baro, I. (1994). *Writings for a Liberation Psychology: Ignacio Martin-Baro.* Cambridge, Mass.: Harvard University Press.

Masson, J. (1984). *The Assault on Truth: Freud's Suppression of the Seduction Theory.* New York: Farrar, Straus and Giroux.

Maxwell, J. A. (1996). *Qualitative Research Design: An Interactive Approach,* vol. 41. Thousand Oaks, Calif.: Sage Publications.

McClintock, M., & Herdt, G. (1996). "Rethinking Puberty: The Development of Sexual Attraction." *Current Directions in Psychological Science,* 5(6) (December), 178–183.

Michael, R. (2001). Personal communication, July 29.

Miles, M., & Huberman, A. M. (1984). *Qualitative Data Analysis: A Sourcebook of New Methods.* Beverly Hills, Calif.: Sage Publications.

Miller, B. (1991). "Adolescents' Relationships with Their Friends." Ph.D. diss., Harvard University.

Miller, J. B. (1976). *Toward a New Psychology of Women* (2d ed.). Boston: Beacon Press.

Miller, J. B., & Stiver, I. P. (1997). *The Healing Connection: How Women Form Relationships in Therapy and in Life.* Boston: Beacon Press.

Miller, P. Y., & Simon, W. (1980). "The Development of Sexuality in Adolescence." In J. Adelson (ed.), *Handbook of Adolescent Psychology* (pp. 383–407). New York: John Wiley and Sons.

Mishler, E. (1986). *Research Interviewing.* Cambridge, Mass.: Harvard University Press.

Moore, K. A., & Snyder, N. O. (1994). "Facts at a Glance." *Facts at a Glance,* January, 1–11.

Moore, K. A., Driscoll, A. K., & Lindberg, L. D. (1998). *A Statistical Portrait of Adolescent Sex, Contraception, and Childbearing.* Washington, D.C.: National Campaign to Prevent Teen Pregnancy.

Moore, S., & Rosenthal, D. (1993). *Sexuality in Adolescence.* New York: Routledge.

Muehlenhard, C. L., & Hollabaugh, L. C. (1988). "Do Women Sometimes Say No When They Mean Yes? The Prevalence and Correlates of Women's Token Resistance to Sex." *Journal of Personality and Social Psychology,* 54(5), 872–879.

Muehlenhard, C. L., & Rodgers, C. S. (1998). "Token Resistance to Sex: New Perspectives on an Old Stereotype." *Psychology of Women Quarterly,* 22, 443–463.

Nathanson, C. A. (1991). *Dangerous Passage: The Social Control of Sexuality in Women's Adolescence.* Philadelphia: Temple University Press.

Nichter, M. (2000). *Fat Talk: What Girls and Their Parents Say about Dieting*. Cambridge, Mass.: Harvard University Press.

Nichter, M., Ritenbaugh, C., Nichter, M., Vuckovic, N., et al. (1995). "Dieting and 'Watching' Behaviors among Adolescent Females: Report on a Multimethod Study." *Journal of Adolescent Health*, 17(3), 153–162.

Odem, M. E. (1997). "Delinquent Daughters: Protecting and Policing Adolescent Female Sexuality in the United States, 1885–1920." *Reviews in American History*, 25(2), 258–264.

Omolade, B. (1983). "Hearts of Darkness." In A. Snitow, C. Stansell, & S. Thompson (eds.), *Powers of Desire: The Politics of Sexuality*. New York: Monthly Review Press.

Orenstein, P. (1994). *Schoolgirls: Young Women, Self-Esteem, and the Confidence Gap*. New York: Doubleday.

Painter, N. (1992). "Hill, Thomas, and the Use of Racial Stereotypes." In T. Morrison (ed.), *Race-Ing Justice, En-Gendering Power: Essays on Anita Hill, Clarence Thomas, and the Construction of Social Reality*. New York: Pantheon.

Parker, R., & Gagnon, J. (Eds.). (1995). *Conceiving Sexuality: Approaches to Sex Research in a Post-Modern World*. New York: Routledge.

Parker, S., Nichter, M., Nichter, M., Vuckovic, N., Sims, C., & Ritenbaugh, C. (1995). "Body Image and Weight Concerns among African American and White Adolescent Females: Differences That Make a Difference." *Human Organization*, 54(2), 103–114.

Peiss, K. (1983). "'Charity Girls' and City Pleasures: Historical Notes on Working-Class Sexuality, 1880–1920." In A. Snitow, C. Stansell, & S. Thompson (eds.), *Powers of Desire: The Politics of Sexuality*. New York: Monthly Review Press.

Petchesky, R. P. (1984). "Abortion and Heterosexual Culture: The Teenage Question." In R. P. Petchesky (ed.), *Abortion and Women's Choice: The State, Sexuality, and Reproductive Freedom* (pp. 205–238). New York: Congman.

Petersen, A. C., Leffert, N., & Graham, B. L. (1995). "Adolescent Development and the Emergence of Sexuality." *Suicide and Life-Threatening Behavior*, 25 (supp.), 4–17.

Phillips, L. M. (2000). *Flirting with Danger: Young Women's Reflections on Sexuality and Domination.* New York: New York University Press.

Pleck, J. H., Sonenstein, F. L., & Ku, L. C. (1994a). "Attitudes toward Male Roles among Adolescent Males: A Discriminant Validity Analysis." *Sex Roles,* 30(7/8), 481–501.

Pleck, J. H., Sonenstein, F. L., & Ku, L. C. (1994b). "Problem Behaviors and Masculinity Ideology in Adolescent Males." In R. Ketterlinus & M. E. Lamb (eds.), *Adolescent Problem Behaviors* (pp. 165–186). Hillsdale, N.J.: Lawrence Erlbaum.

Plummer, K. (1995). *Telling Sexual Stories.* London: Routledge.

Pollack, W. (1998). *Real Boys: Rescuing Our Sons from the Myths of Boyhood.* New York: Random House.

Rabinowitz, V. C., & Vallian, V. (1999). "Sex, Sex Differences, and Social Behavior." *Annals of the New York Academy of Sciences,* 196–207.

Rabinowitz, V. C., & Weseen, S. (2001). "Power, Politics, and the Qualitative/Quantitative Debates in Psychology." In D. L. Tolman & M. Brydon-Miller (eds.), *From Subjects to Subjectivities: A Handbook of Interpretive and Participatory Methods* (pp. 12–28). New York: New York University Press.

Ramazanoglu, C., & Holland, J. (1993). "Women's Sexuality and Men's Appropriation of Desire." In C. Ramazanoglu (ed.), *Up against Foucault* (pp. 239–264). New York: Routledge.

Raymond, D. (1994). "Homophobia, Identity, and the Meanings of Desire: Reflections on the Cultural Construction of Gay and Lesbian Adolescent Sexuality." In J. Irvine (ed.), *Sexual Cultures and the Construction of Adolescent Identities* (pp. 115–150). Philadelphia: Temple University Press.

Reinharz, S. (1992). *Feminist Methods in Social Research.* New York: Oxford University Press.

Religious Institute on Sexual Morality, Justice, and Healing. (2001). "The Religious Declaration on Sexual Morality, Justice, and Healing." Declaration posted at <http://www.religionproject.org/declaration.html>.

Rich, A. (1983). "Compulsory Heterosexuality and Lesbian Existence." In

A. Snitow, C. Stansell, & S. Thompson (eds.), *Powers of Desire: The Politics of Sexuality* (pp. 177–205). New York: Monthly Review Press.

Rosen, R., Brown, C., Heiman, J., Leiblum, S., Meston, C., Shabsigh, R., Ferguson, D., & D'Agostino, R. (2000). "The Female Sexual Function Index (FSFI): A Multidimensional Self-Report Instrument for the Assessment of Female Sexual Function." *Journal of Sex and Marital Therapy, 26,* 191–208.

Rubin, G. (1984). "Thinking Sex: Notes for a Radical Theory of the Politics of Sexuality." In C. S. Vance (ed.), *Pleasure and Danger: Exploring Female Sexuality.* Boston: Routledge and Kegan Paul.

Ruddick, S. (1989). *Maternal Thinking: Toward a Politics of Peace.* Boston: Beacon Press.

Satcher, D. (2001). *The Surgeon General's Call to Action to Promote Sexual Health and Responsible Sexual Behavior.* Washington, D.C.: U.S. Department of Health and Human Services.

Savin-Williams, R. C. (1998). "Lesbian, Gay, and Bisexual Youths' Relationships with Their Parents." In C. Patterson & A. R. D'Augelli (eds.), *Lesbian, Gay, and Bisexual Identities in Families* (pp. 75–98). New York: Oxford University Press.

Savin-Williams, R. C. (2001). *Mom, Dad, I'm Gay: How Families Negotiate Coming Out.* Washington, D.C.: American Psychological Association.

Sawicki, J. (1988). "Identity Politics and Sexual Freedom: Foucault and Feminism." In I. Diamond & L. Quinby (eds.), *Feminism and Foucault: Reflections on Resistance* (pp. 177–191). Boston: Northeastern University Press.

Schillinger, L. (1999). "Exile in Guyville: Is a Film about Girls and Sex Too Hot to Handle?" *New York Magazine,* June 21, 15.

Sexuality Information and Education Council of the United States. (1995). *National Commission on Adolescent Sexual Health.* New York.

Shalit, W. (1999). *A Return to Modesty: Discovering the Lost Virtue.* New York: Simon and Schuster.

Silverman, J. G., Raj, A., Mucci, L., & Hathaway, J. E. (2001). "Dating Violence against Adolescent Girls and Associated Substance Use, Unhealthy Weight Control, Sexual Risk Behavior, Pregnancy, and

Suicidality." *Journal of the American Medical Association,* 286(5), 572–579.

Singh, S., & Darroch, J. E. (1999). "Trends in Sexual Activity among Adolescent American Women: 1982–1995." *Family Planning Perspectives,* 31(5), 212–219.

Smith, E. A., & Udry, J. R. (1985). "Coital and Non-coital Sexual Behaviors of White and Black Adolescents." *American Journal of Public Health,* 75(10), 1200–1203.

Smith-Rosenberg, C. (1985). *Disorderly Conduct: Visions of Gender in Victorian America.* New York: Knopf.

Snitow, A., Stansell, C., & Thompson, S. (eds.). (1983). *Powers of Desire: The Politics of Sexuality.* New York: Monthly Review Press.

Spillers, H. J. (1984). "Interstices: A Small Drama of Words." In C. S. Vance (ed.), *Pleasure and Danger: Exploring Female Sexuality.* Boston: Routledge and Kegan Paul.

Stanislaw, H., & Rice, F. J. (1988). "Correlation between Sexual Desire and Menstrual Cycle Characteristics." *Archives of Sexual Behavior,* 17, 499–508.

Stern, P. L. (1994). *Sexuality, Poverty, and the Inner City.* Menlo Park, Calif.: Henry J. Kaiser Family Foundation.

Tanenbaum, L. (1999). *Slut! Growing Up Female with a Bad Reputation.* New York: Seven Stories Press.

Taylor, J. M., Gilligan, C., & Sullivan, A. M. (1995). *Between Voice and Silence: Women and Girls, Race and Relationship.* Cambridge, Mass.: Harvard University Press.

Terr, L. (1990). *Too Scared to Cry: Psychic Trauma and Childhood.* New York: Harper and Row.

Thompson, S. (1990). "Putting a Big Thing into a Little Hole: Teenage Girls' Accounts of Sexual Initiation." *Journal of Sex Research,* 27(3), 341–361.

Thompson, S. (1995). *Going All the Way: Teenage Girls' Tales of Sex, Romance, and Pregnancy.* New York: Hill and Wang.

Thorne, B. (1993). *Gender Play: Girls and Boys in School.* New Brunswick, N.J.: Rutgers University Press.

Tiefer, L. (1987). "Social Constructionism and the Study of Human Sexuality." In P. Shaver & C. Hendrick (eds.), *Sex and Gender* (pp. 70–94). Beverly Hills, Calif.: Sage Publications.

Tiefer, L. (1995). *Sex Is Not a Natural Act and Other Essays.* Boulder: Westview Press.

Tijaden, P., & Thoennes, N. (1998). *National Violence against Women Survey.* Washington, D.C.: U.S. Department of Justice, National Institute of Justice, Centers for Disease Control and Prevention.

Tolman, D. L. (1991). "Adolescent Girls, Women, and Sexuality: Discerning Dilemmas of Desire." *Women and Therapy,* 11(3/4), 55–70.

Tolman, D. L. (1994a). "Daring to Desire: Culture and Bodies of Adolescent Girls." In J. Irvine (ed.), *Sexual Cultures: Adolescents, Communities, and the Construction of Identity* (pp. 250–284). Philadelphia: Temple University Press.

Tolman, D. L. (1994b). "Doing Desire: Adolescent Girls' Struggles for/with Sexuality." *Gender and Society,* 8(3), 324–342.

Tolman, D. L. (1996). "Adolescent Girls' Sexuality: Debunking the Myth of the Urban Girl." In B. J. R. Leadbeater & N. Way (eds.), *Urban Girls: Resisting Stereotypes, Creating Identities* (pp. 255–271). New York: New York University Press.

Tolman, D. L. (1999). "Femininity as a Barrier to Positive Sexual Health for Adolescent Girls." *Journal of the American Medical Women's Association,* 54(3), 133–138.

Tolman, D. L. (2000). "Object Lessons: Romance, Violation, and Female Adolescent Sexual Desire." *Journal of Sex Education and Therapy,* 25, part 1, 70–79.

Tolman, D. L. (2001). "Echoes of Sexual Objectification: Listening for One Girl's Erotic Voice." In D. L. Tolman & M. Brydon-Miller (eds.), *From Subjects to Subjectivities: A Handbook of Interpretive and Participatory Methods* (pp. 130–144). New York: New York University Press.

Tolman, D. (2002). "Female Adolescent Sexuality: An Argument for a Developmental Perspective on the New View of Women's Sexual Problems." In E. Kaschak & L. Tiefer (eds.), *A New View of Women's Sexual Problems* (pp. 195–210). Binghamton, N.Y.: Haworth Press.

Tolman, D. L., & Debold, E. (1993). "Conflicts of Body and Image: Female Adolescents, Desire, and the No-Body Body." In P. Fallon, M. Katzman, & S. Wooley (eds.), *Feminist Perspectives on Eating Disorders* (pp. 301–317). New York: Guilford Press.

Tolman, D. L., & Higgins, T. (1996). "How Being a Good Girl Can Be Bad for Girls." In N. B. Maglin & D. Perry (eds.), *Bad Girls/Good Girls: Women, Sex, and Power in the Nineties* (pp. 205–225). New Brunswick, N.J.: Rutgers University Press.

Tolman, D. L., & Porche, M. V. (2000). "The Adolescent Femininity Ideology Scale: Development and Validation of a New Measure for Girls." *Psychology of Women Quarterly,* 24(4), 365–376.

Tolman, D. L., & Szalacha, L. A. (1999). "Dimensions of Desire: Bridging Qualitative and Quantitative Methods in a Study of Female Adolescent Sexuality." *Psychology of Women Quarterly,* 23(2), 7–39.

Tolman, D. L., Spencer, R., Rosen-Reynoso, M., & Porche, M. V. (2002). "Sowing the Seeds of Violence in Heterosexual Relationships: Early Adolescents Narrate Compulsory Heterosexuality." *Journal of Social Issues.*

Tolman, D. L., Spencer, R., Harmon, T., Rosen-Reynoso, M., & Striepe, M. (In press). "The Trouble with Boys: Early Adolescent Boys' Experiences with Romantic Relationships." In N. Way & J. Chu (eds.), *Adolescent Boys in Context.* New York: New York University Press.

Udry, R. (1993). "The Politics of Sex Research." *Journal of Sex Research,* 30(2), 103–110.

Udry, J. R., Talbert, L. M., & Morris, N. M. (1986). "Biosocial Foundations for Adolescent Female Sexuality." *Demography,* 23 (2), 217–228.

Ussher, J. M. (1997). *Fantasies of Femininity: Reframing the Boundaries of Sex.* New Brunswick, N.J.: Rutgers University Press.

Vance, C. S. (1984). "Pleasure and Danger: Toward a Politics of Sexuality." In C. S. Vance (ed.), *Pleasure and Danger: Exploring Female Sexuality.* Boston: Routledge and Kegan Paul.

Vasquez, M. J. T., & des las Fuentes, C. (1999). "Immigrant Adolescent Girls of Color: Facing American Challenges." In N. G. Johnson, M. C. Roberts, & J. Worell (eds.), *Beyond Appearance: A New Look at Adolescent Girls.* Washington, D.C.: American Psychological Association.

Walker, A. (1992). *Possessing the Secret of Joy*. New York: Harcourt Brace Jovanovich.

Walkerdine, V. (1997). *Daddy's Girl: Young Girls and Popular Culture*. Cambridge, Mass.: Harvard University Press.

Walkowitz, J. (1980). *Prostitution and Victorian Society: Women, Class, and the State*. Cambridge: Cambridge University Press.

Wallen, K. (1990). "Desire and Ability: Hormones and the Regulation of Female Sexual Behavior." *Neuroscience and Biobehavioral Reviews*, 14, 233–241.

Ward, J. (2001). *The Skin We're In: Teaching Our Children to Be Socially Smart, Emotionally Strong, Spiritually Connected*. New York: Free Press.

Ward, J. V., & Taylor, J. M. (1992). "Sexuality Education for Immigrant and Minority Students: Developing a Culturally Appropriate Program." In J. T. Sears (ed.), *Sexuality and the Curriculum: The Politics and Practices of Sexuality Education* (pp. 183–202). New York: Teachers College Press.

Way, N. (1994). Personal communication via e-mail, March 15.

Way, N. (1998). *Everyday Courage: The Lives and Stories of Urban Teenagers*. New York: New York University Press.

Way, N. (2001). "Using Feminist Research Methods to Explore Boys' Relationships." In D. L. Tolman & M. Brydon-Miller (eds.), *From Subjects to Subjectivities: A Handbook of Interpretive and Participatory Methods* (pp. 111–129). New York: New York University Press.

"Why I Hate Monica Lewinsky" (2000). Message posted at <http://www.smileandactnice.com/news/lovehate/monicalewinsky/hate/index.html>.

Wolf, N. (1997). *Promiscuities: The Secret Struggle for Womanhood*. New York: Random House.

Wyatt, G. E. (1994). "The Sociocultural Relevance of Sex Research: Challenges for the 1990s and Beyond." *American Psychologist*, 49(8), 748–754.

Wyatt, G. E. (1997). *Stolen Women: Reclaiming Our Sexuality, Taking Back Our Lives*. New York: John Wiley and Sons.

Yoffe, E., Marszalek, D., & Selix, C. (1991). "Girls Who Go Too Far." *Newsweek,* July 22, 58–59.

Young, L. (1992). "Sexual Abuse and the Problem of Embodiment." *Child Abuse and Neglect,* 16, 89–100.

Geographic context (*cont.*)
176–180; differences and
similarities, 172–173; and self-
protection, 172, 173–176, 178;
urban girls, 173–176; of violence,
174, 177, 180; of vulnerability,
181–182; of sexual abuse, 182–184;
mind-body interplay, 183–184;
sexual minority girls, 184–185

Gill, Ros, 201–202

Gilligan, Carol, 38–39, 54, 134–135,
200

Good girl/bad girl dichotomy, 8–12,
45–46, 81–82, 105–106, 131;
political consciousness of,
118–119, 140–141; entitlement
and, 119–121, 129; geographic
context, 170–171, 179; trust
and, 195–196. *See also* Double
standard

Gray, Macy, 187

Guilt, 128–129

Hammonds, Evelynn, 225n4

Handbook of Adolescent Development
(Miller and Simon), 3

Have/hold discourse, 211

Heterosexuality, institution of,
17–18, 38, 164, 188, 211;
compulsory heterosexuality,
16–17, 46, 111–114; threat of
sexual violence, 52–53; critique
of, by girls, 100–101, 107–111;
resistance to, 118–119, 131–134,
189, 222–223n2; entitlement and,
122–123; geographic context, 179,
184–185. *See also* Danger; Double

standard; Femininity; Good
girl/bad girl dichotomy; Rich,
Adrienne; Romance narrative;
Sexual minority girls

HIV/AIDS, 10, 53, 90–91, 103, 162,
166–167, 174, 176, 217n4, 219n1,
226n10

Holland, Janet, 14, 222–223n2

Hollibaugh, Amber, 201

Hollway, Wendy, 211, 218n5

Homosexuality, 218n7. *See also*
Sexual minority girls

Honore, 29, 36–37

hooks, bell, 205

Hormones, 13–15, 217n2, 218n5

Hypotheses, 43

Industrial Revolution, 171

Inez, 1–2, 21–22, 29, 42,
94–100, 115–117, 175,
183, 192

Interviews, 1–2, 31–37, 66–67,
195–197; groups, 31–33, 195

"It just happened" stories, 1–2,
21–22, 60–64, 67, 89–90, 95

Jack, Dana, 128

James, William, 20

Jane, 29, 42, 45

Janine, 29, 55–60, 175

Jenny, 29, 60–65, 78, 179, 181,
192

Jordan, Judith, 29, 36

Julia, 29, 45

Kim, 29, 45, 71–77, 78, 181

Kitzinger, Celia, 199